Kitchen Culture

FIFTY YEARS OF FOOD FADS

Kitchen Culture

FIFTY YEARS OF FOOD FADS

Gerry Schremp

PHAROS BOOKS
A SCRIPPS HOWARD COMPANY
NEW YORK

Copyright © 1991 by Gerry Schremp
All rights reserved. No part of this book may be reproduced in any form or by any means without permission in writing from the publisher.

First published in 1991.

Printed in United States of America

SPAM is a registered trademark of Geo. A. Hormel & Company for luncheon meat.

Cover design: Suzanne Reisel
Interior design: Laura Hough
Cover illustration: Jenny Oppenheimer

Pharos Books
A Scripps Howard Company
200 Park Avenue
New York, New York 10166

10 9 8 7 6 5 4 3 2 1

Library of Congress Cataloging-in-Publication Data

Schremp, Geraldine.
Kitchen culture : fifty years of food fads / Gerry Schremp
p. cm.
Includes bibliographical references and index.
ISBN 0-88687-523-4 : $14.95
1. Cookery—United States—History—20th century. 2. Food habits—United States—History—20th century. 3. Fads—United States--History—20th century. I. Title.
TX645.S36 1991
394.1'2'097309045—dc20   91-4102

Contents

Prologue
xi

The Forties: War and Peace
1

The Fifties: America the Bountiful
35

The Sixties: An Age of Contrasts
67

The Seventies: Turbulent Years
97

The Eighties: Health and Wealth
131

Epilogue
179

Bibliography
185

Index
191

Acknowledgments

This book would never have been written if Jim Beard hadn't taught me about cooking when I was a reporter at *Life* magazine and he was the consultant for food articles.

Jim became a friend as well as an adviser, and I have been lucky enough since then to work with countless other congenial cooks, chefs, and food writers. The list starts with Elsa Harrington, who prepared many of the foods pictured in *Life*, and includes Louis Diat, Florence Brobeck, Poppy Cannon, Rudy Stanish, Fred Bridge, Rose Kerr, Paula Peck, Craig Claiborne, and Pierre Franey.

The chief consultant to Time-Life Books *Foods of the World*—where I was a writer and text editor—was the unforgettable Michael Field, the chief cook was John Clancy. Other consultants and writers included M.F.K. Fisher, Julia Child, George Lang, Florence Lin, Grace Chu, Irma Rhode, José Wilson, Nika Hazelton, Devika Teja, and Shirley Sarvis.

When I edited *The Good Cook* series for Time-Life Books, I was lucky enough to work with brilliant food experts: chief consultants Carol Cutler and Richard Olney were aided and abetted by Francois Dionot, Jeremiah Tower, Jolene Worthington, Judith Olney, Julia Dannenbaum, Albert Kumin, Tina Ujlaki, Ann Ready, and Richard Sax.

Many of these people have helped me sort out names and dates for this book. So have Carolyn Stallworth, Nancy Shuker, Sandra Streepey, Arthur Schwartz, Paula Wolfert, Alice Waters, Pat Baysinger, Jeannette Miller, Polly Fink, Jane and Tom Alexander, Betsy Frankel, and Aileen Claire. Booksellers Jan Longone and Marilyn Einhorn sped my search for out-of-print books.

Don Kirschnick kindly supplied many of the vintage 1940 and 1950 photographs.

I am also indebted to scores of helpful individuals representing corporations, restaurants, and trade associations: Mary Kreps, Alto Shaam, Inc., Menomenee Falls,

WI; Ann Humbert, Amana Refrigeration Inc, Amana, IA; Anchor Brewing Co., San Francisco; C. Eugene Moore, Armstrong World Industries, Inc., Lancaster, PA; Jeffrey Mendel, Association of Brewers, Boulder, CO; Baskin-Robbins USA, Co., Glendale, CA; William P. Roenigk, National Broiler Council, Washington, D.C.; W. Atlee Burpee Company, Warminster, PA; Campbell Soup Company, Camden, NJ; The Catfish Institute, Belzoni, MS; Karen Rutkiewicz, The Chef's Catalog, Northbrook, IL; Citicorp Diners Club, Inc.; Jerry E. Wright, Corning Incorporated, Corning, NY; Michael Kinane, Culinary Institute of America, New Hyde Park, NY; Mayburn Koss and Carl Sontheimer for Cuisinart history; Roy Larsen, American Cyanamid Company, Wayne, NJ; American Dairy Association, Rosemont, IL; Michael Jenkins, Domino's Pizza, Inc, Ann Arbor, MI; Dow Brands, Indianapolis, IN; American Egg Board, Park Ridge, IL; Lloyd Singer, Epoch 5 Marketing, Inc., Huntington, NY; Food Institute Information Center, NJ; Henry Ford Museum, Dearborn, MI; Jill Sandin, Frieda's Finest, Los Angeles, CA; Laura A. Kinkle, United Fresh Fruit and Vegetable Association, Alexandria, VA; Friday Associates Incorporated, Louisville, KY; National Frozen Food Association, Hershey, PA; Hall of History Foundation, General Electric Company, Schenectady, NY; Katie McElroy, General Mills, Inc., Minneapolis, MN; Pam Madden, *Gourmet*, 560 Lexington Avenue, New York City; Hamilton Beach Inc., Washington, NC; American Home Appliance Manufacturers, Chicago; V. Allan Krejci, Geo. A. Hormel & Co., Austin, MN; Barbara Hunter and Grace Thompson, Hunter MacKenzie Cooper, New York City; KraftMaid Cabinetry, Inc., Middlefield, OH; King Kullen Grocery Co. Inc., Westbury, NY; Joy Barrett Sabol, Knapp Communications Corporation, Los Angeles; Elizabeth Adkins, Kraft General Foods, Inc., Morton Grove, IL; Nancy Pollard, La Cuisine, Alexandria, VA; Anita Fial, Lewis & Neal, Inc., New York City; Thomas McDermott, National Livestock and Meat Board, Chicago; Brad Trask, McDonald's Corporation, Oak Brook, IL; Maytag Dairy Farms, Newton, IA; American Meat Institute, Washington, DC; Milk Industry Foundation, Washington, DC; Myers Communicounsel, Inc., New York City; NCR Corporation, Dayton, OH; Nestle Foods Corporation, Purchase, NY; Jula Kinnaird, National Pasta Association, Arlington, VA; Madeline Strasser, Perrier Company, Greenwich, CT; Ed Matthews, Piggly Wiggly, Jacksonville, FL; Marlene Johnson, The Pillsbury Company, Minneapolis, MN; National Pork Producers Council, Des Moines, IA; Edward M. Rider, The Procter & Gamble Company, Cincinnati, OH; Rainbow Room, 30 Rockefeller Plaza, New York City; Raytheon, Lexington, MA; Robin Cruise, Rancho La Puerta, Escondido, CA; National Restaurant Association, Washington, DC; Restaurant Associates Industries, Inc., New York City; George Meredith, Association of Retail Marketing Services, Red Bank, NJ; Anne F. Waring, Reynolds Metals Company, Richmond, VA; Elizabeth Whelan, Sc.D., M.P.H., American Council on Science and Health, New York City; Eric Wildermuth, Shakey's, South San Francisco, CA; Kim Kimmy, Space Needle Corporation, Seattle, WA; The Sugar Association, Inc., Washington, DC; Lawrie Pitcher Platt, Tupperware Home Parties, Orlando, FL; National Turkey Federation, Reston, VA; Whirlpool Corporation, Benton Harbor, MI; Williams-

Sonoma, San Francisco; Weber-Stephen Products Company, Palatine, IL; Weight Watchers, Jericho, NY; and the Wisconsin Milk Marketing Board, Madison, WI.

Special thanks to librarians and researchers who repeatedly and kindly gave me help: Willie Scott, James Fox, and Walter Stubbs, Southern Illinois University-Carbondale, Carbondale, IL; Carbondale Public Library, Carbondale, IL; Barbara Lazewski, Steenbock Memorial Library, University of Wisconsin-Madison, Madison, WI; M. Earthaline Harried, USDA, Washington, DC; the Library of Congress, Washington, DC; and the National Archives, Washington, DC.

The two most patient people in the country probably are my husband, Bill Schremp, and my editor, Hana Lane. Without their encouragement, I could not have faced the word processor day after day after day. Thank you.

Prologue

There's been a revolution in the kitchen during the past fifty years. The changes in what and how and where Americans cook and eat have been so vast that hardly an ingredient or appliance—or attitude—remains as it was in 1940.

The supermarket that Americans take for granted didn't exist back then. Most of the foods it now carries weren't even a gleam in a scientist's eye. Some staples like baking powder might be the same, but yeast isn't, and salt and peppercorns come in a slew of forms these days. White sugar and butter taste like they used to, but their place in American life is profoundly different.

New fruit and vegetable hybrids and imports fill produce counters. Meats have been re-graded; birds don't hang from tied feet behind the butcher anymore, but are packaged cut-up, even boned and skinned. Processed foods—fresh, canned, frozen, dehydrated, irradiated—vary endlessly. Wherever a shopper looks are foodstuffs Grandmother never dreamed of. Methods for totting up the grocery bill have been modernized.

Today's cookware and appliances, both large and small, are often close to downright miraculous in the ways they take work out of housework. Using them, the contemporary American cook can handle—with aplomb—both simple and complicated recipes, some borrowed as always from the neighbors, but others borrowed from cuisines an ocean away. Attitudes toward diets and nutrition have shifted with the decades. Even mealtimes got shuffled.

For most Americans, eating out was once a treat, or a sandwich and thermos of soup in a lunchbox. No more. Restaurants, plain and fancy, play significant roles in American lives and culinary sophistication today. These establishments bear little resemblance to their counterparts of 1940. The proverbial blue-plate special belongs in the Smithsonian; modern menus would baffle the chefs as well as customers of yesterday's cafeterias and cathedrals of *grande cuisine.*

This book traces the revolution in kitchen culture with words underscored by numbers and illustrated, wherever possible, by photographs. A sampling of recipes demonstrates how a cooking style reflects the fashions of the decade, both in its approach to just-discovered ingredients and in its "up-to-date ways" of handling old-fashioned ones.

The Forties: War and Peace

Reminiscences about feasts of days gone by, of holiday dinners when a dozen smiling family members crowded around the table, make the food of the past sound so special. Roast turkey burnished to amber. Whole hams studded with cloves and glistening with sugary glaze. Crusty prime ribs all rosy pink inside. Piles of just-boiled shrimp or blue crabs. Bowls of steaming-hot fresh-picked corn, buttery new peas mixed with tiny white onions, baked sweet yams, potatoes scalloped in cream. And the cakes! And the pies and ice cream....

That was fine eating. Or perhaps nostalgia gives it more savor. Fifty years ago, some cooks were indeed geniuses—as they are remembered. They had a gift for creating excellent dishes, and they seemed to enjoy doing whatever work was required. Most grandmothers and grandfathers, though, were not culinary wizards. Happy occasions might inspire them to outdo themselves, but the best ingredient on the menu they served was love.

POULTRY FOR EVERY POT Fresh-killed birds like these were part of every butcher's window display in a day when roast chicken was a treat. For cooks who planned to fry them, the butcher would cut the birds into the required pieces free of charge.

Furthermore, cooking was a hard job that took a lot of time. Iceboxes and wood-burning stoves look more appealing to us now than they did to the cooks who relied on them then. And in 1940 more than one-third of America's 35 million families counted emptying the drip-pan under the ice and stoking the firebox with kindling as daily chores. Odds are, most of these families were among the quarter of the American population that census takers classed as rural dwellers. Urban housewives tended to be luckier, with more modern kitchens. They usually had a gas or electric stove (8 to 1, it was gas) and a refrigerator—often a Monitor Top with a huge coil above a box that had a capacity of only 5 to 7 cubic feet (today 18 feet is common) and freezing space for nothing more than two or three trays of ice cubes.

In any early 1940s kitchen, cooking "three square meals" a day would take four or five hours. Breakfast was a sit-down affair for the whole family, with cooked cereal or bacon and eggs or both. The noonday meal on the farm was called dinner and it was substantial enough to "stick-to-your-ribs," while in the city lunch generally meant sandwiches or leftovers. Whereas farm families ate together at noon, city families were dispersed to factories, offices, and schools with only mother remaining at home. The evening meal on the farm was a supper composed mostly of what remained from noontime; in the city, the family ate a dinner specially prepared for that hour.

Just about every part of every meal was made *from scratch*—a term not invented until the 1950s. The cook's "convenience foods" were few—notably canned soups, baked beans, chili (Americanized in the 1920s), biscuit and pancake mixes, and the Jell-O that seemed ubiquitous in both salads and decorative desserts.

BAKE-OFF EXCITEMENT The Grand National Recipe and Baking Contest that Pillsbury sponsored in 1949 caught the imaginations of cooks across the country. Held in the Grand Ballroom of the Waldorf-Astoria Hotel in New York, it was the chance of a lifetime for 100 amateurs to show their skill at what the press called a "bake-off." Pillsbury liked that name, and it's a registered trademark now. By the time of the 1950 Bake-Off shown here, so many young cooks applied that there was a special contest for teenagers ages 12 to 19.

KITCHEN CULTURE

Can She Bake A Cherry Pie?

Winner of the national pie-baking contest held in Chicago in February 1942 was Mary Elizabeth Lush, 17, of Ames, Iowa. She defeated finalists from nine states with this recipe, which features honey as sweetener and lard as the pastry shortening.

FILLING:
3 cups sour cherries, pitted, with juice
1/4 cup cornstarch
1 1/4 cups honey
1 tablespoon butter

PASTRY:
1 1/2 cups bread flour
1/4 teaspoon salt
1/2 cup plus 2 tablespoons lard
1/3 cup ice water

For filling, combine 1/4 cup reserved cherry juice and cornstarch in pan. Add honey and cook over low heat until thick. Remove from heat. Add cherries and butter. Let cool. Preheat oven to 425°F.

For pastry, put flour and salt into a bowl and cut in 1/2 cup lard with pastry blender. Add ice water gradually. Halve dough and roll out each half to large circle. Spread each with 1 tablespoon of remaining lard, then fold and reroll to an 11-inch circle. Line 9-inch pie plate with one circle of dough. Add cherry mixture and cover with remaining dough. Crimp edges. Make decorative slits in pie. Bake for 10 minutes, then reduce heat to 350° and bake for 20 minutes longer or until pie crust is brown and crispy. Serves 6 to 8

GETTING FOOD FOR THE TABLE

Perishable foods could not be stored for long, so a housewife likely went to the grocery herself two or three times a week, and sent one of her own children or a neighbor's child to fetch small items she needed between shopping trips. In the city, milk and other dairy products could be delivered daily for a small extra price; so could bread and pastries, although most housewives baked their own cakes, cookies, and pies—and not a few, especially if they lived south of the Mason-Dixon line, prided themselves on serving fresh hot breads and biscuits.

Because even the biggest supermarkets of the time carried relatively few items (2,000 to 3,000 compared to 25,000 to 35,000 today), the same foods reappeared on a family's menu often enough to be predictable.

Sunday's roast with potatoes and carrots produced Monday's hash; the rest of the week usually followed a pattern—the family knew that "if it's Tuesday, we'll get meat loaf." Chops, ground meats, and stews predominated except in fishing and hunting seasons, when the catch of the day was often featured. Most families regularly ate innards—beef and veal tongue, liver, and kidneys, sweetbreads and chicken giblets. Even non-Catholics took advantage of the superior assortment of fish and seafood available at the shops on

Chocolate Chip Cookies

In 1930, Ruth Wakefield who ran the Toll House Inn at Whitman, Massachusetts, cut pieces off a bar of semisweet chocolate to give extra flavor to cookies she was making. To her delight, the pieces softened but kept their identity when she baked the dough. She notified Nestle Foods Corporation, which first put a recipe for "Toll House Cookies" on their semisweet bar chocolate, and then in 1939 introduced the already cut pieces known far and wide as chocolate chips.

1 cup butter, softened
1 cup granulated sugar
1/2 cup brown sugar
1 teaspoon vanilla extract
2 eggs
2 1/2 cups flour, sifted with
1 1/2 teaspoons baking powder
12 ounces semisweet chocolate chips

Beat butter, granulated and brown sugar, and vanilla together until creamy. Beat in eggs. Gradually add flour and baking powder mixture. Stir in chocolate chips. Drop by heaping teaspoonfuls onto baking sheets, spacing cookies about 2 inches apart. Bake at 375° for 7 or 8 minutes or until lightly browned and firm.
Makes about 8 dozen 2-inch cookies

Fridays. Saturday was busy, a good day for serving simple macaroni and cheese.

Grocers offered local produce in season; some farmers drove wagons along city streets and downalleys to hawk their wares, or they congregated at informal markets downtown. Most of the year, though, a housewife's choices were few: vegetables that kept well such as turnips, carrots, white and sweet potatoes, or cabbages, or easily stored fruits like apples. Fresh produce was costly out of season, and not likely to be found outside the metropolitan areas. In the North, oranges and bananas were expensive enough to be considered special treats.

Putting up fruits, vegetables, jams, and jellies was an essential part of every family's summer. But even with home-canned foods and home-baked breads, a

INSIDE A WELL-STOCKED PANTRY At a time when a housewife expected to put up fruits and vegetables every summer, pantry shelves were usually chockful of jellies and jams. Here fancy labels show the kinds of fruit in each of the dozens of neatly arrayed jars.

city family's food bill was close to one-third its income, averaging about $2.20 per person per week. Though the prosperous 1920s were dim memories for most Americans, the economy was slow to recover from the stock market crash of 1929 and the Depression that followed. But the start of World War II was to change all that.

THE START OF WAR

In 1939, two world's fairs opened in the United States: San Francisco's Golden Gate Exposition and New York's World of Tomorrow. Although both fairs projected a rosy future, most Americans realized that it was only a matter of time before they went to war with Germany, which had already taken over Austria and Czechoslovakia, and conquered Poland.

Denmark, Norway, the Netherlands, Belgium, and France fell to the Nazis in 1940, and the Battle of Britain began. The United States started its first peacetime draft that year. Franklin D. Roosevelt negotiated the loan of fifty over-age destroyers to Britain in exchange for use of half a dozen Caribbean air and naval bases, an arrangement later formalized and expanded under the 1941 Lend-Lease Act.

Contemporary newspapers termed the period from 1939 to 1941 the "Phony War." Years later, *New Yorker* essayist E.B. White compared those years to the "time you put in in a doctor's waiting room…the time of the moist palms and irresolution." Surprisingly, the impetus that thrust the U.S. into war came not from Europe but from Asia. On December 7, 1941, Japanese planes bombed Pearl Harbor. Within four days, the United States was at war with Japan and with its Axis partners, Germany and Italy.

HOME ON THE RANGE In December 1944, Senator Burton K. Wheeler did his part to alleviate wartime shortages by posing for this picture of him eating buffalo meat. Wheeler was from Montana where buffalo still roamed. Their meat was considered a possible substitute for the diminishing supply of beef.

Americans sprang into action. Both the Army and Navy were swamped by waves of volunteers. More than 12 million men and women went into the armed services during the first year; over the course of the war, 16 million served in either the European or Pacific theaters. Never before had the supply lines been so long, nor the diets so scientifically planned as the much-maligned A, B, C, D, and K rations that were presented to those troops.

Industry converted factories to manufacture armaments and went full blast supplying America and its allies. Out of production for the duration of the war went such civilian products as automobiles and electric appliances. Shoe manufacturers now

GOOD EATING GUIDANCE During the war, governmental agencies sponsored lectures to educate women's groups about nutrition. Rationing and food shortages had upset eating habits everywhere, and an alarming number of draftees were rejected for health reasons that could be traced to poor diet. In testimony before a congressional committee in 1944, the chief medical consultant for the National Association of Manufacturers, Victor Heiser, declared that in a population of about 130 million, 100 million were ill-fed, and that malnutrition was not a matter of dollars alone.

produced boots for the armed forces; silk (and later nylon) went into parachutes instead of stockings. Metals, rubber, gas, cigarettes—all were in short supply on the home front.

Foods and spirits that had been imported from Europe or Asia all but disappeared, not to be seen again until after the war. Liquor consumption increased from 140 milllion gallons prewar to 190 million gallons in 1942—and what the domestic distillers had considered a five-year stock was exhausted even before they could convert to industrial alcohol production for the war. Toward the end of the war, distillers were permitted to fill liquor orders during the single month of August. By then moonshiners were flourishing and importers bringing in wine and spirits from Mexico, Cuba, and other parts of Latin America.

SOCIAL PATTERNS CHANGE

At long last, there were jobs for everyone, skilled and unskilled. Unemployment virtually disappeared. Slowly at first, then with a rush, factories began to hire women to replace the men who had gone to war. Rosie the Riveter was the heroine of a song and of many a factory. Ultimately, 6 million women took wartime jobs, although most still had to run their households, and many had young children.

The social upheaval was tremendous. Experts calculate that no fewer than 40 million people out of a total national population of 130 million changed residence during the war. Because some people moved several times, exact counts are elusive; even so, the estimates indicate how astounding the population shift was. In addition to the servicemen themselves, almost 3 million wives moved, at least tem-

NUTRITION POSTER Feeding troops got first priority, but the government also worried about nutrition among civilians. This is the first (December 24, 1941) of a series of posters issued from Washington. Although modern-day nutritionists may not agree with all the recommendations, the poster presented the best dietary rules of that day.

porarily, to be with their husbands.

An estimated 15 million civilians moved across county lines—probably to take jobs. An additional 8 million moved to nearby states, while 4 million went to other parts of the country. Of these, almost 1.5 million people moved to California, and a like number migrated from southern to northern states.

Almost a million workers left the farm for better-paying work in the cities. Nevertheless, huge quantities of food were needed for the increasingly prosperous civilian population, the armed forces, and America's allies.

Planting and harvesting of crops often necessitated calling on volunteers such as the Women's Land Army or using conscripts from U.S. prisons or prisoner of war camps. But with the help of government subsidies, farmers were able to buy more fertilizer, use better feed for livestock and poultry, and mechanize more

---

Fashionable Farmhands

Like the first world war, the second created serious labor shortages on America's farms. In both emergencies, help for farmers came from a Women's Land Army, a volunteer organization that women could join for a year, a summer, or a few weeks at planting or harvest time.

Although most of the women wore their own slacks and shirts, uniforms were available. Here, models show off World War I and World War II outfits. In the "new" style, loose-fitting, full-length overalls were worn over a tailored shirt; in the old uniform, reminiscent of that worn by the troops, a woman wore knee britches and a smock that was belted at the waist.

fully. The number of farm tractors rose from about 1.5 million in 1940 to almost 2.5 million in 1945—helping farmers meet the tremendous demands for more food.

The production of U.S. farms increased 250 percent during the war. In the process, small farms consolidated and 100 acres or more became the norm.

SHORTAGES AND RATIONING

Double-digit inflation by the end of 1941 prompted the government to set price ceilings at both the wholesale and retail level on nearly 6,000 food items. And in April 1942, the Office of Price Administration announced sugar would be rationed: imports from the Philippines were cut off, while the ships that carried sugar from Cuba and Puerto Rico had been drafted for defense use.

Americans had known for months that sugar was in short supply, and many stored 100-pound bags. But hoarding did little good. When rationing started, families went to their local elementary schools to register, and were asked to declare how much sugar they had at home. Their stockpile was deducted from their allowance of ration coupons, good for a year's supply of 8 ounces of sugar per person per week. Later in the war, the ration was increased to 12 ounces per person. (Today those rations may seem high, but in the 1940s home

KETCHUP GOES TO WAR Like the shaving mugs in a nineteenth-century barbershop, bottles of ketchup photographed at this lunch counter in March 1944, carry their owners' names. The Office of Price Administration rationed ketchup during World War II, so regular customers brought their own bottles. The only alternative was to douse sandwiches with mustard or pickle relish, which unaccountably did not require ration points.

UNDERSTANDING COUPONS Ration stamps came in different colors and denominations—and they became usable on different dates. Keeping track of them was a major undertaking for an American housewife—and for all the stores, wholesalers, and manufacturers whose products she used.

PRICES AND POINTS During the war, a cook not only had to watch prices on rationed foods such as meats but also look for the number of coupon points those foods would require. Here, a price remains the same while the points are reduced—presumably because of an increase in the supply of that cut or kind of meat.

cooks needed sugar for the desserts they served daily and for preserving fruit whole or in jams as well as for coffee and tea.)

In November 1942, coffee was also rationed. In spring of 1943, canned meat and fish were rationed, then other canned foods were added to the list and—within weeks—so were fresh meats, fish, butter, and cheese.

Each individual was issued two ration books. One had blue coupons for canned foods and the other had red coupons for meat, fish, and dairy products. Each coupon carried a specific point value—1, 2, 5, or 8—and everyone was allowed 48 blue points and 64 red points per month, or about two pounds of canned fruit and vegetables and 28 ounces of meat plus 4 ounces of cheese. A housewife shopping for a family of four had eight books, and could spend 192 blue points and 256 red points every month.

Each month, on a date fixed by the Office of Price Administration, a housewife got a new set of ration books or new coupons in the old books became valid—and her unused books or coupons became worthless. At the same time, new point values were given to foods depending on their relative scarcity.

When shopping, the housewife paid with coupons showing the correct number of points as well as with money. What a juggling act! And what a nightmare for the retailers and wholesalers who had to account for tens of thousands of flimsy coupons the size of postage stamps.

Rationing was intended to distribute fairly whatever food was available to civilian markets, but it did not guarantee that every-

THE FORTIES: WAR AND PEACE 9

one could find the foods they had coupons to purchase. When there were shortages, the existing supply went to the military, not to civilian markets. Furthermore, points were figured on a geographical basis, and food supplies differed from one region to another, even within a state, so that—for example—while some cuts of meat might require 12 points per pound in Cleveland, they would require only 6 points in Cincinnati.

The black market, of course, could supply just about anything—for a price. How *black* the market was depended on how the term was defined. In its mildest form, it meant grocers or butchers who held foods "under the counter" for special customers; at the other extreme, it described rustlers who killed and butchered stolen cattle. While many communities

LEGALIZED HORSEMEAT During World War II, there were rumors that butchers were trying to pass off horsemeat as beef, thus sparing themselves the need to deal with ration coupons. After all, the French—those quintessential gourmets—were said to relish horsemeat. How bad could it be? In Oakland, California, enterprising butchers opened Scottie's Pony Markets and got government inspectors to approve their products. They did a land-office business in luncheon meats and Whinny Burgers. (The inspectors ruled that frankfurter applied to beef products only and could not be used.)

AXING THE AXIS? In January 1943, the Office of Price Administration decreed that bakeries should stop selling sliced bread. The bureaucrats' intention was to save wear and tear on machines that were probably irreplaceable in wartime. However, the public made such a fuss that the ruling was rescinded—but not before a photographer and model sent out this gag shot to the news services.

strove to eliminate unfairness, in metropolitan areas black marketeers often flourished as bootleggers had during Prohibition.

A legal way to best the system, at least in small measure, was for the housewife to save kitchen fat and exchange it at the butcher's for red points. (The fat contained glycerine, used in explosives.) She also saved tin cans, but feeling patriotic was the only reward; cans had to be washed, ends removed, and the cylinders stamped flat before they went to collection centers.

Even paper for grocery bags was in limited supply, and housewives were urged to reuse the bags; with care, it was said, a bag could survive ten trips to the market. A

"Fat to Fry the Axis"

Fighting words characterized the campaign that the American Meat Institute launched in 1942, asking housewives to bring used kitchen fats and oils to their butcher, who would in turn send them on to a central collection point. One pound of waste cooking fat was said to contain enough recoverable glycerine to manufacture more than a pound of gunpowder; two pounds of fat made enough to fire five antitank shells.

American kitchens, it was estimated, discarded up to 2 billion pounds of fat a year. Later in the war, the government allowed butchers and grocers to offer 4 cents and 2 ration points for one pound of fat.

---

sign in many Kroger stores indicated: FIVE POUNDS OF PAPER SAVED PACKS ANOTHER ARTILLERY SHELL TO FIRE AT THE JAPS OR NAZIS.

STRETCHING THE FOOD SUPPLY

Sending flour to the armed forces and to the Allies created a shortage in the domestic market. Some millers began to produce soy flour, or a combination wheat-and-soy flour. Toward the end of the war, in February 1946, to make existing wheat supplies go further the government imposed regulations requiring millers to extract 80 percent of the wheat kernel instead of the 68 percent to 72 percent normally extracted. Because the resulting flour contained more bran, it was relatively lower in protein and grayish in color. Proud millers created special names for the product so that their reputation would not be blemished. Happily, the regulations were lifted a year later and white flour became snowy again.

Innovation was the watchword. Poultry and fish consumption rose. Lacking sugar, cooks did less home baking and preserved less fruit. But the can-do American spirit inspired writers for newspapers and magazines to create a spate of recipes for sugarless or low-sugar cakes and cookies; few were satisfactory. On their own, housewives tried to substitute honey, molasses, sorghum, and maple syrup for sugar, but none worked just right and in any case these substitutes soon became scarce, too. Stealing beehives was such a problem that some apiarists put brands on them so they

JUST SAY CHEESE! By reducing the ration points required for certain products, the Office of Price Administration controlled inventories and avoided surpluses or shortages. Cheese sales got a boost at this butcher shop with posters as the display.

Butter Stretcher

During World War II, cooks tried many recipes for stretching butter with top milk. Because milk was not homogenized then, the part richest in butterfat rose to the top of the bottle, and could be poured off for separate use. Half-and-half is the closest modern equivalent to top milk.

2 teaspoons unflavored gelatin
2 cups top milk
1 pound butter, at room temperature
1 teaspoon salt
Yellow food coloring

Soften gelatin for 1 minute in 1/4 cup milk. Set cup in a pan of hot water and stir until gelatin dissolves. With rotary beater, mix gelatin into butter. Gradually beat in remaining milk. Add salt, then drops of food coloring until mixture is desired color. Refrigerate until firm. The butter will keep for about a week. Makes 4 cups

---

could identify them.

Margarine, which had been considered "poor man's butter" before the war, turned up on many tables. Resourceful cooks tried to stretch genuine butter by beating it with light cream or unsweetened custard. Cottage cheese was also often used as a meat substitute and its sales skyrocketed from about 110 million pounds in the 1930s to 500 million pounds in 1944.

General Mills' Betty Crocker urged the women of America to help preserve democracy "by saving food so the hungry may eat. If you American wives and mothers rise bravely to this new challenge—as you always have in the past—you will help protect yourselves and your own families for the future."

However bad it got, though, the American housewife could find some solace in knowing that the English housewife was making do with two-thirds—or less—of the meat, butter, sugar, and canned foods she had.

To assist in keeping spirits high, presumably, and as a time-saver for women working in wartime jobs, Gold Medal flour introduced the one-bowl cake—a harbinger of technician-driven foods of the future. In this streamlined mixing method, all dry ingredients were sifted together into a bowl, then shortening and liquid added. When baked, the cake was not as light in texture as if it had been made by conventional methods, but families appreciated its fresh, home-baked taste.

Housewives revived the casserole and stew recipes that had been developed in the Depression, stretching meat with potatoes, macaroni, rice, and dried beans. Or they made main dishes with cheese, which usually called for fewer ration points than did meats. Those families who could, hunted or trapped game for supper. Some butchers went so far as to sell horsemeat; rumors were that some of the "beef" came from horses.

Victory gardens sprouted everywhere, and brought a welcome change to the nation's menus. Three out of four families put up their home-grown vegetables, on average about 165 jars a year.

During the war, as a response to concern about the American diet, commercial bakers began enriching white bread with iron, niacin, riboflavin, and thiamin—all nutrients lost in the milling and bleaching processes. Decades later, when *Consumer Reports* did animal growth studies to compare various breads as an only food, they found: "As a

Tuna and Noodle Casserole

Quick and cheap, this was the bride's stand-by.

1 can (10 1/2 couances) concentrated cream of mushroom soup
1 soup-can of milk
1 can (7 ounces) tuna, broken into flakes with a fork
1 box (10 ounces) frozen peas or cut asparagus
2 cups cooked wide noodles
Salt and pepper
1/2 cup buttered bread crumbs or crushed potato chips

Preheat the oven to 350°F. Combine soup concentrate with milk. Stir in tuna, peas or asparagus, noodles, and salt and pepper to taste. Spoon into buttered 1-quart casserole or 4 individual casseroles. Top with crumbs. Bake for 15 minutes or until brown and bubbly. If necessary, brown top quickly under broiler.
Serves 4

Chile con Carne

Adding a lot of tomatoes and beans made a little meat go a long way in this bland wartime version of a spicy Tex-Mex dish.

2 onions, chopped
2 tablespoons vegetable oil
1 pound ground beef
2 cups crushed canned tomatoes, with liquid
1/2 cup tomato paste
1 teaspoon chili powder
Salt and pepper
4 cups canned red kidney beans, with liquid

Sauté onions in oil until golden. Add beef and stir until browned. Stir in tomatoes and tomato paste, and simmer 10 minutes. Add chili powder, and salt and pepper to taste. Stir in beans and heat through. Serve with boiled macaroni or rice.
Serves 8

---

group, white breads performed somewhat better than the wheats. If you eat salad, you get plenty of fiber."

BOOSTING TROOP MORALE

Bread was important to servicemen. It represented 10 percent of the food that troops consumed and normally was served three times a day. To supply the fresh-baked bread that boosted morale, no matter what else was on the menu, the Army Quartermaster Corps set up mobile bakery units as close to the front as they could. In some cases, the bread-baking equipment got ahead of the troops.

Doughnuts might have been a metaphor for the war: they were everywhere. Army camps, factories, and schools had doughnut-dispensing machines. Red Cross canteens also sold them. But the U.S.O. or United Service Organization, with 3,000 centers where soldiers or sailors could enjoy a clublike atmosphere and a Saturday-night dance, gave doughnuts away.

Secretary of the Navy James Forrestal gave distribution of ice cream to ships and bases the highest priority, after a report reached him that stated ice cream was more important to morale than beer. Starting in 1943, a dried ice cream mixture was distributed to troops, even in remote areas. Before then, according to Paul Dickson in *The Great American Ice Cream Book*, bomber crews placed their own concoctions in large cans in the rear gunners' compartments. The plane's vibrations and the freezing temperature in the sky were said to ensure the creation of a delicious ice cream.

Gardening for Victory

Patriots grew Liberty Gardens during World War I, so in 1942 it was only natural for Secretary of Agriculture Claude R. Wickard to encourage householders to plant Victory Gardens wherever they could find space.

Every scrap of land was used, though gardens might be only a few feet square or many acres. Flower beds were torn up; the strip of grass between sidewalk and street was transformed into a food supply; Boston's Copley Square and the land around Chicago's Cook County Jail held radishes and cabbages.

Although Wickard probably didn't realize it, the term VICTORY GARDEN dated to Elizabethan England. A book with that title, written in 1603 by the appropriately named Richard Gardner, argued "if any citie or towne should be besieged with the enemy, what better provision for the greatest number of people can be than every garden to be sufficiently planted with carrots?"

No enemy literally besieged American cities, but by 1945 there were said to be 20 million gardens producing about 40 percent of all American vegetables—1 million tons valued at $85 million. In 1944 and 1945, harvest festivals in New York City were held in Pershing Square, and the CHICAGO SUN sponsored festivals—complete with barn dancing—at Soldiers' Field.

Wilted Lettuce

One of the most rewarding Victory garden vegetables was leaf lettuce. It grew faster than weeds and could be harvested before summer began to dry out the other crops.

2 quarts bite-size pieces leaf lettuce
2 or 3 tablespoons finely cut chives
4 slices bacon
1/4 cup vinegar
2 teaspoons sugar
Salt and pepper

Place lettuce in serving bowl and sprinkle with chives. Fry bacon over medium heat; lift out slices and drain on paper towels. Stir vinegar and sugar into bacon fat remaining in pan. Add salt and pepper to taste. Pour this dressing over lettuce and toss well. Crumble, then add bacon slices. Serves 4 to 6

Spamville

Wherever they went, American troops took their sense of humor with them, as evidenced by the signs they erected spoofing their location—and their life. Thus an otherwise nameless part of a South Pacific island jungle was christened "Spamville" in 1942. Spam was not the first canned luncheon meat, but it became the best known—and most maligned—as mess cooks made it a staple of the GI diet in World War II. To get the men to eat it, cooks fried, baked, breaded, even creamed it. The recipe below is typical of the time.

In a 1966 letter to Geo. A. Hormel & Company, which produces the meat, President Dwight D. Eisenhower wrote "I ate my share of Spam along with millions of other soldiers. I will even confess to a few unkind words about it—uttered during the strain of battle, you understand."

From the other side of the world, Nikita Khrushchev, in his biography, states, "There were many jokes going around in the Army, some of them off-color, about American Spam; it tasted good nonetheless. Without Spam, we wouldn't have been able to feed our Army."

Spam Baked Like Ham

1 can Spam
2/3 cup brown sugar
1 teaspoon vinegar
2 teaspoons dry mustard
1 teaspoon Worcestershire sauce
1 to 2 teaspoons water
12 whole cloves

Preheat oven to 375°. Score Spam in a diamond pattern and place in baking pan. Mix brown sugar, vinegar, mustard, and Worcestershire. Add enough water to achieve consistency of prepared mustard. Spread mixture over loaf. Insert cloves at regular intervals in scored pattern. Bake for 30 minutes, basting two or three times.

Serves 4

THE END OF WAR AND THE START OF PROSPERITY

In May 1945, Germany surrendered; in August, Japan did too. The next year, price controls and rationing were ended, although shortages were still widespread. Under the Marshall Plan, the United States provided immediate food and shelter for war victims overseas, often creating temporary shortages at home as foods and other materials got stranded in warehouses or shipments were delayed.

When the United Nations Relief and Reconstruction Administration took over that job, America was a major contributor.

Relations with Russia soured as the war ended, and U.S. politicians revived the

Feeding the Troops

Servicemen were allocated 40 percent more food than civilians—theoretically, about 5 1/4 pounds daily, compared to 3 pounds—but the alphabet of rationing seldom meant eating high on the hog. In fact, unless troops were far enough from the front to get A-rations, or perishable food, they may not have got any part of that pig.

Both A- and B-rations came from their own unit's mess kitchen, but B menus were based on canned and dried foods, and made creamed chipped beef on toast famous as S.O.S. (…. on a shingle).

The original C-ration, providing three balanced meals, consisted of six 12-ounce cans: three M units containing meat dishes such as stew or pork and beans and three B, or bread, units holding C-square biscuits, or crackers. Canned heat was built into the meat containers so the food could be warmed. Besides being heavy and unwieldy, the cans required disposal. It is said that the litter of shiny empties guided enemy aircraft along routes of American convoys.

A lighter load designed by nutritionist Ansel Keyes was the K-ration, consisting of three boxes small enough to fit into the pockets of a paratrooper's uniform. Each box held a meal consisting of crackers, dextrose tablets, a canned meat or cheese mixture, soluble coffee, concentrated bouillon, fruit bars, lemon juice powder, sugar tablets, a stick of chewing gum, and four cigarettes. Not until 1944 did the army add halazone tablets to purify water, without which most of the ration was useless.

Both C- and K-rations were supplemented with D-rations: three 4-ounce 1,800-calorie "chocolate bars" said to taste worse than their mix of ingredients sounds: sucrose, skim milk, cocoa fat, and oat flour.

As time went on, the rations were improved in quality and variety. The C- and K-rations had been designed for moderate climates, not for the intense heat of North Africa where the foods dried and caked, or for the humidity of Pacific Islands, where they molded—not even for the Arctic where the food froze. Furthermore, C- and K-rations were intended for short term use. In practice, they became the only foods available for long periods of time. Men got sick gobbling rations because of stress, or threw them away because of their monotony and blandness.

Special diets were devised for airmen. Because they tended to eat sparingly before missions, meals served then consisted largely of high-calorie meat and dairy foods. Gas in the intestines expands two to three times at 20,000 feet and four times at 35,000 feet, so foods such as beans, cabbage, onions, and corn were omitted from the diet to avoid stomach problems. Ground crews, of course, rebelled and had to be fed similarly to preserve morale.

FRUIT AND COTTAGE CHEESE Cottage cheese gained popularity during World War II, when a favorite salad featured a scoop of cheese and fresh or canned fruit on a bed of salad greens. Here the greenery is chicory, but iceberg lettuce was more common in restaurants. These orange sections and grapes might be replaced with a canned pear or peach half beneath the cheese and a maraschino cherry standing on top.

"red scare" of the 1920s and 1930s. The "cold war" became part of the nation's worries and vocabulary. Nevertheless, after the war families were reunited and some servicemen brought home European and Asian war brides. As Americans adjusted to a hard-won peace, they found that the legacy of the war was prosperity.

Before the war, a college education had been beyond the reach of most Americans. The GI Bill of Rights (Servicemen's Readjustment Act), signed by President Roosevelt in June 1944, changed all that by entitling men and women who had served for ninety days or more to three years of higher education at $500 per year for tuition, plus $75 per month for living expenses. Millions of veterans took advantage of the opportunity for more education, and for a future with a higher standard of living as a result. College enrollments skyrocketed, jumping 1 million, or 80 percent. (As an alternative to education, the bill guaranteed $20 per week for up to fifty-two weeks for unemployed veterans—who soon dubbed the benefits the 52-20 club.)

A NATION OF HOMEOWNERS AND CAR OWNERS

The GI bill also enabled millions of families to realize their dream of owning a home. The government agreed to cover home, farm, or business loans up to $2,000, at an interest rate of 4 percent. During the war, housing construction had come to a halt, so the demand for new single-family houses and multiple-family units was now intense. Building began in earnest to end the housing shortage.

Most housing developments of the 1940s and 1950s owed their start to the GIs and to Detroit. Because land was cheap on the edge of town or just outside its limits, builders put new houses there—creating *suburbia*—not only a new word but a new life-style. The model for future developments was Levittown, New York, which contractor William Levitt opened in 1949, on what had been Long Island potato fields. Using mass-production techniques that he borrowed from factories, Levitt was able to build identical houses fast and sell them at low prices; the first models cost $6,990.

Getting to work from the suburbs and home again, even going to the supermarket, now often required a family car. October 26, 1945, was V-8 Day, when Ford brought out the first postwar model. No matter how exciting the ads had said it would be, the car was no more than a prettified 1942 model. Drivers would have to wait a while longer for revolutionary developments.

But the coupes and "tudor" models were priced modestly at less than $1,200. In 1949, the Volkswagen, or "people's car," came to America where it sold for $1,280. With low prices and pent-up demand, sales were high for both American and imported cars. Automobile registrations went from 26 million in 1945 to 40 million by 1950.

THE CHANGING ROLE OF WOMEN

Some women were reluctant to leave their wartime jobs and give up the extra income. But as the economy shifted from manufacturing to service, there were more jobs for which women were felt to be the most appropriate candidates: teachers, nurses, typists, store clerks, waitresses and the like. Besides such traditional employment, women entered professions at increasing rates and established a range of careers in business, communications, science, and government.

Most women, however, happily left war work behind them to resume housework. Couples who had postponed having families of their own now created the "baby boom." Individual incomes were double that of prewar years, with median family income going from $1,231 in 1939 to $2,854 in 1947, so growing families could afford to have mother stay at home with the children.

HOME COOKING

Traditional family values were extolled as women baked cookies and crocheted afghans. Nonetheless, women also were quick to take advantage of time-saving

CANDY FROM CEREAL Youngsters could start to cook at an early age by whipping up treats like these. The boxed bars and pale-colored balls consist of rice breakfast cereal and melted marshmallows; the dark-colored balls combine breakfast cereal flakes with melted chocolate and peanuts.

Beef Stroganoff

2 pounds lean, boneless beef, cut into thin strips
Flour
4 tablespoons butter
2 onions, chopped
1/2 pound fresh mushrooms, sliced
Salt and pepper
1 1/2 cups beef stock or water
1 cup sour cream
1 teaspoon dried dill

Dredge beef in flour. Melt 2 tablespoons butter in a skillet and brown meat; remove beef from skillet and set aside. Add remaining butter to skillet along with onions and mushrooms. Sauté 5 minutes, then return beef to skillet; season to taste. Stir in stock or water, cover, and simmer 20 to 30 minutes until beef is tender. Over low heat, stir in sour cream and dill. Correct seasoning, then heat through without boiling. Serve with noodles.
Serves 4

The Mystery Ingredient

In 1927, a California insurance salesman named Harry Baker invented a new type of cake. What he called "chiffon cake" was as light as angel food, yet as rich as pound cake. During the next twenty years he became famous in Hollywood, making the cake for restaurants and movie-industry parties. But Baker kept his recipe a secret until 1947. Then he sold the recipe to General Mills, and its home economists learned the mystery ingredient was salad oil.

Before introducing the recipe to the world, the home economists developed flavor variations to appeal to more cooks. They did, and sales of General Mills' cake flour increased 20 percent the next year. Now chiffon cake is sold as a mix, but only in lemon flavor. All a cook adds is water.

---

foods like French's Instant Potatoes and General Foods' Minute Rice when the products were introduced in 1946, or the frozen orange juice concentrate that Minute Maid started producing in 1947. Imagine their delight when General Foods and Pillsbury introduced cake mixes in 1947 and 1948.

Americans also resumed their love affair with meat. In 1946 per capita consumption of meat reached 154 pounds, 85 pounds of which were beef. Steak was the most popular cut, although ground meat was growing rapidly in popularity because of its convenience and relatively low cost. Vegetables came from the store, not the garden. Butter was more popular than margarine again; sugar sales rose as dessert once more concluded every lunch and dinner.

When families entertained, those who could afford the money and time gave formal dinners, with a damask tablecloth, bone china, sterling flatware—and a maid to cook and serve the food. Others with "champagne tastes and beer budgets" happily set-

---

A Regal Cook

Dione Lucas debuted her television cooking classes called "To a Queen's Taste" in New York on October 9, 1947. At first the program originated from Lucas's own Cordon Bleu restaurant, but on May 3, 1948, CBS took over. The network moved the classes to its studio and broadcast them nationally until December, 1949. Later classes were resumed for local broadcasts titled "The Dione Lucas Show." Lucas was a graduate of The Cordon Bleu Cooking School in Paris and an authority on international cuisine. Besides running her much-admired restaurant, she conducted a cooking school called Cordon Bleu and wrote many cookbooks.

Tamale Pie

A favorite casserole for potluck suppers.

1 1/2 cups cornmeal
1 1/2 cups cold water
3 1/2 cups boiling salted water
3/4 pound ground beef
3/4 pound ground pork
3/4 cup finely chopped onion
1 garlic clove, finely chopped
2 cups cooked or canned tomatoes
1 tablespoon finely chopped fresh parsley
1 tablespoon chili powder
1 teaspoon salt
1/2 teaspoon pepper
1/2 cup pitted ripe olives (optional)

Stir cornmeal into cold water; add slowly to boiling salted water and cook over very low heat until thickened.

Meanwhile, brown beef and pork in a skillet. Stir in onion and garlic. Add tomatoes, parsley, chili powder, salt, and pepper. Simmer for 20 minutes.

Preheat oven to 350° F. Line bottom and sides of a 2-quart casserole with about half the cornmeal. Add ripe olives to meat mixture, if using. Spoon mixture into casserole and cover with remaining cornmeal. Bake for 30 minutes or until done.

Serves 6

Crab Louis

This turn-of-the-century San Francisco combination of cold crab and pink mayonnaise was popular party fare for many generations. In some versions the topping is sweet; in other—like this—it's tangy.

1/2 cup mayonnaise
1/4 cup heavy cream, whipped
1/4 cup chili sauce
1 tablespoon prepared horseradish
1 tablespoon chopped scallion
1 tablespoon chopped fresh parsley
1 tablespoon lemon juice
Hot red pepper sauce
1 head iceberg lettuce, shredded
1 pound lump crab meat, flaked
Lemon wedges

For topping, combine mayonnaise, cream, chili sauce, horseradish, scallion, parsley, lemon juice, and 3 or 4 drops of hot pepper sauce. Taste and correct seasonings. Arrange lettuce on salad plates. Mound crab meat on it and spoon on topping. Garnish with lemon wedges.

Serves 4

---

tled for potluck suppers, at which each guest contributed a casserole and the hostess supplied the breads, salad, and dessert.

ADVENTURES IN COOKING

The war gave millions of Americans new eating experiences in countries where food and drink were treated as serious subjects. European and Asian war brides brought new tastes and kitchen methods to the United States as well. Still, most Americans wanted foods like "mom" cooked—after all, they had fought a war for her and apple pie.

"Foreign" foods were handled cautiously. While cooks experimented with French and Italian recipes, they seasoned them lightly to avoid offending families and friends not sophisticated about spices and herbs.

Nonetheless some foreign foods found their way into the American diet. Yogurt, for example, was sold chiefly in markets catering to Middle Eastern and Indian customers until 1947, when Dannon put strawberries in the bottom of the yogurt packed in a returnable glass jar. Fruit-flavored yogurt caught on, sales soared, and the company expanded to eventually become a national brand.

Experimental cooks got a helping hand during the spring of 1946, when NBC

French Dressing

1 cup sugar
1 tablespoon paprika
1 tablespoon dry mustard
1 1/2 teaspoon salt
1 cup vegetable oil
1 cup vinegar
3 tablespoons cold water
1 tablespoon grated onion

Combine ingredients in a 1-quart jar and shake to mix. Shake again before each use.
Makes about 2 1/2 cups

---

television put together a show called "Elsie Presents," sponsored by Borden Company, and starring Elsie the Cow in its advertisements. The show ran once a week for two years, and among its features were cooking lessons by James Beard, already a well-known food authority and cookbook author.

On October 9, 1947, the gifted cook and author Dione Lucas started bringing weekly cooking lessons to CBS television in a show called "To the Queen's Taste." The Lucas show started as a local New York program but became a network series seven months later. It ran for more than a year, and was repeated locally afterward.

COOKING BY THE BOOK

Women got out their cookbooks, but the favorite recipes were simple ones. Except for the batches of fudge they had learned how to make at long-ago slumber parties, many of them were complete novices in the kitchen. Even scrambling eggs and boiling macaroni were unfamiliar chores and they needed the guidance supplied by a basic book such as the *Settlement Cook Book*, Fannie Farmer's the *Boston Cooking-School Cook Book*, or Irma Rombauer's *Joy of Cooking*. *Better Homes & Gardens* boasted that its cookbook was outsold only by the Bible.

Although newspapers paid scant attention to food, ladies' magazines such as the *Woman's Home Companion* and *Ladies Home Journal* had regular features, as did so-called shelter magazines like

The Art of Fine Food

When Earle R. MacAusland launched GOURMET magazine in January 1941, he wrote, "The art of being a gourmet has nothing to do with age, money, fame or country. It can be found in a thrifty French housewife with her POT-AU-FEU or in a white-capped chef in a skyscraper hotel. Because he anticipated that Americans would be making more pleasure trips abroad in the years ahead, he set his writers and editors to demystifying exotic cuisines. Until the late 1950s, all GOURMET covers were painted by Henry Stahlhut, who produced the romantic scene left for the July 1946 issue. The first photographed cover appeared in 1957.

FREEZER LOCKERS Although individual freezers were not considered practical for family use, lockers in shared freezers were popular during the 1940s. This model designed for an apartment house could accommodate the food of five families.

AUTOMATIC FROZEN FOOD DISPENSER Self-service supermarkets and groceries found this frozen food dispenser helpful in 1947. The variety of products soon outnumbered the compartments available, and markets found the dispenser expendable.

American Home and *House Beautiful*. Food advertising in both newspapers and magazines regularly featured coupons offering recipe pamphlets free or available with a self-addressed and stamped envelope.

Gourmet was the only magazine devoted entirely to excellence in food and drink. Founder Earle R. MacAusland thought of *Gourmet* as a man's magazine, directing it at an upper-class audience. Besides articles on travel, restaurants, and wine, *Gourmet* published elegant recipes with a noticeable tilt toward French cooking.

SHOPPING PATTERNS SHIFT

Housewives still might patronize specialty stores selling only produce, meat, fish, or staple groceries. Milk companies and bakeries still delivered on some routes. But home delivery and neighborhood stores were losing ground. Only the richest and poorest customers needed them. The rich enjoyed telephoning in an order and having it brought to the door; the poor needed to buy on credit, where they were known by management.

A new kind of outlet came into existence after the war: the frozen food locker, which not only sold frozen foods but also rented lockers of different sizes where families could keep frozen the food they bought elsewhere—or their game birds and animals, and sports fish. Refrigerators of the time had freezer space for little more than ice cubes, yet Birds Eye was selling more than sixty kinds of "frosted foods,"

Brown 'n Serve

What a happy accident! The partly cooked bread loaves and rolls sold by many bakers owe their existence to Joseph Gregor, a baker in Avon Park, Florida, who was also a member of the local volunteer fire department. One day, while a batch of Parker House rolls was still only partly baked, the fire siren sounded. Gregor pulled the rolls out of the oven before leaving his bakery. When he returned hours later, he saw that the rolls had held their shape. On impulse, he put them in the oven for the remainder of their baking time.

The result was so delicious he soon began selling what he called Pop-n-Oven rolls. A salesman from General Mills, James Taggart, heard about the rolls and sent word of them to his headquarters. There, the kitchens perfected the process. Although General Mills patented the Brown 'n Serve technique, they passed it along free to the baking industry on the theory that "What is good for the baking industry is good for the milling industry."

---

including meat, poultry, fish, shellfish, fruit, and vegetables. (The term "frosted" was used for several decades because of concern that "frozen" might mean foods that had been kept in cold storage.)

Clarence Birdseye had perfected and patented a process for quick-freezing foods in 1923, but it wasn't until the 1930s, when General Foods Corporation took over, that his products began to enjoy commercial success. By 1939, Birds Eye brand foods were carried in almost 6,000 stores all across the United States.

Frozen foods wrought great and good changes in the American diet. With quick-freezing, vegetables that had never been widely known—brussels sprouts, for example—could be found everywhere; spinach and strawberries, which changed taste and color so radically in canning and therefore were seasonal treats, would still have their fresh characteristics after freezing. Fish and shellfish crossed the country unscathed if frozen.

Many food lockers also offered meat at reduced prices to customers who bought a half (a side) or a quarter of a carcass of beef, pork, or lamb. The locker's butcher cut the meat into steaks and roasts to the housewife's specifications.

Gradually, lockers disappeared as families bought refrigerators with ample freezer space or purchased home freezers. The first of these freezers were usually chests that looked like coffins because the lids lifted up; they took more floor space than early uprights, but these freezers held much more food.

THE RISE OF SUPERMARKETS

After the war, many cooks patronized supermarkets that had big parking lots so customers could drive to them from miles around. What was lost in personal service was amply repaid, customers felt, in savings and convenience.

The trend toward supermarkets had started a century before when food-trading companies, which could get discounts by buying in large quantities, started chains of cash-and-carry grocery stores. The Great Atlantic and Pacific Tea Company, or A & P, led the way. Next came self-service stores invented by Clarence Saunders. His first store opened in 1916 in Memphis, Tennessee, with 605 items. Unlike other stores, Saunders's Piggly Wiggly used tags to clearly identify the prices of foods. Customers entered the store, passing through a turnstile, where they were loaned a wicker basket. They walked up and down four aisles at their leisure to find items they wanted, and then left the store past a cashier; the average transaction was 96 cents. (In 1937, Sylvan Goldman of Standard Food Stores, a self-service chain in Oklahoma City, introduced the prototype shopping cart.) Saunders not only created the concept of self-service but also designed the shelves, racks, and refrigerated cases needed to display the merchandise. The only place customers got individual service was at the meat counter.

Because of self-service, products such as pickles and flour that previously had been sold from barrels or bins now needed to be packaged. The packaging had to answer questions about size and ingredients that clerks would have dealt with in a full-service store. Also, the packaging had to make the product look more appealing than others like it. Thus Saunders was responsible, indirectly, for the development of today's huge packaging industry.

About the origins of the name Piggly Wiggly, Clarence Saunders offered various explanations; the most likely is that it comes from the nursery rhyme line "This little piggie went to market." But there was nothing ambiguous about the success of the store. Saunders was soon franchising the name to other independent grocers across the country.

On August 4, 1930, Michael Cullen opened the first supermarket in Jamaica, Long Island, in what had been an automobile garage. By eliminating all the decora-

The Supermarket King

Self-styled as "King Kullen," Michael Cullen started a new kind of self-service grocery store with his Jamaica, New York, super markets. (The two words were put together by a supermarketeer who remains anonymous.) By refusing to dress up the premises, Cullen was able to keep food prices below those of other grocers. In the early 1930s photograph above left, his hard-sell slogan—Why Pay More?— is up front as part of the exterior sign. Above right, a clerk leans on the dairy cabinet in a June 24, 1940, picture of the interior of a typical King Kullen market.

24 KITCHEN CULTURE

tive frills, Cullen was able to set prices at King Kullen lower than those of any other self-service store. He advertised himself as the World's Greatest Price Wrecker, and claimed "This store will save every family from $2 to $5 every week in the year." Cullen reduced the price on a box of Shredded Wheat from 15 cents to 9 1/2 cents and sold a 25-cent can of Crisco for 21 cents.

During the 1930s, Cullen opened twenty more Long Island supermarkets of from 5,000 to 10,000 square feet, each originally carrying about 1,100 items. The low prices at these markets threatened small grocery chains and independents, who went so far as to try to get newspapers to refuse King Kullen advertising. But the supermarkets were such a success that chain grocers soon copied Cullen, closing down some outlets and enlarging the rest.

The war was responsible for an increase of nonfood items in these supermarkets. Shortages and rationing left empty shelves, so store owners began to sell periodicals, health and beauty aids, and a wide array of housewares to keep shelves filled. After the war, supermarkets prospered because their great buying power allowed them to pass their quantity savings along to customers.

A NEW LOOK FOR KITCHENS

Automobiles weren't the only consumer products coming off the assembly lines after the war. Refrigerators got high priority. So did new stoves that looked built in. These labor-savers quickly passed from being luxuries to being necessities.

In the 1920s, furniture companies built kitchen cabinets that could be fitted together to form a wall full of cupboards. At first the cabinets were wood, but easily cleaned enamelled steel cabinets, shiny and white as befitted a "food laboratory," seemed more modern and quickly became the bestsellers.

During the 1930s, porcelain sinks were designed to fit into the top of cabinets rather than stand on their own legs. Stoves, though, were leggy until the late 1930s, when designers finally put the oven under the burners instead of beside them. In the postwar period, the occasional stove got two side-by-side ovens.

On the work counters and underfoot was easy-to-care-for linoleum. Countertops generally were monochromatic with a

SIDE-BY-SIDE OVENS Eliminating the stove's tall legs and moving the oven from beside the burners to beneath them gave the appliance that streamlined look prized by housewives of the 1930s and 1940s. Stoves had a storage drawer beside the oven until 1948, when Westinghouse Electric introduced this double-oven model.

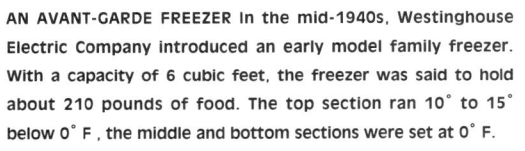

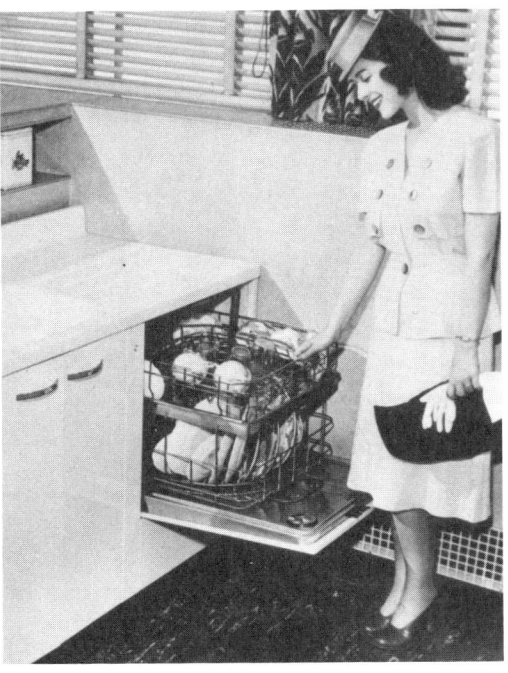

AN AVANT-GARDE FREEZER In the mid-1940s, Westinghouse Electric Company introduced an early model family freezer. With a capacity of 6 cubic feet, the freezer was said to hold about 210 pounds of food. The top section ran 10° to 15° below 0° F, the middle and bottom sections were set at 0° F.

FOR DISHES ONLY In 1946, Hotpoint introduced its first postwar dishwasher, produced by a plant that had just converted from the manufacture of .50 caliber armor-piercing bullets. The price was high, the capacity limited, and the dishwasher could not clean pans, but housewives envied anyone who had one.

stone or fabric texture, but the floors often had as many colors as Joseph's coat. At the top of the line was inlaid linoleum—perhaps inset with a custom pattern such as a monogram—extending from wall to wall. Less costly were linoleum rugs, available in a wide range of sizes to cover almost all of the floor.

APPLIANCES LARGE AND SMALL

Just before the war, manufacturers had introduced kitchen garbage disposers, familiarly known as "kitchen pigs" because they devoured everything. After the war, the "pigs" were put into mass production and became status symbols.

The dishwasher got off to a slow start because the first models were round, like the washing machines of the day. But by the late 1940s, designers had squared off the dishwasher to fit it into the wall of cabinets.

Other kitchen helpers returned, too: Toasters, coffee percolators, food mixers, and—joy of joys!—blenders. Cocktail parties were in vogue, and no such gathering was complete without frozen daiquiris made in a Waring Blendor.

Fred Waring was not an inventor, but the leader of The Pennsylvanians, one of the most popular bands of the era. The first blender had been patented in 1922 by Stephen J. Poplawski, who lived in Racine, Wisconsin, where the Horlick Corporation was located. Horlick had invented malted milk powder in 1887, and Poplawski designed his blender for soda fountain use. It went through several versions before 1936, when Waring invested in it, renaming the appliance a blendor—always spelled with an *o* to distinguish it from the competitors. The war brought production to a halt. By the time the Blendor was back on the market Waring had sold his interest in the company. Only his name remained .

POTS AND PANS

The most glamorous cookware, and a "must" gift for brides, was copper-bottomed, stainless-steel Revere Ware. Although the copper required frequent polishing, the pans were proudly displayed on the walls of kitchens everywhere. First put on the market in 1938, Revere Ware had been a casualty of the war, reintroduced after the war was over.

Another 1930s creation—the pressure cooker—came off the production line by the tens of thousands every month of the war, but exclusively for military use. Afterward, housewives rushed to buy this time-saver that could turn out pot roasts and baked beans in minutes instead of hours, and was perfect for canning foods as well. Unfortunately, dozens of manufacturers entered the market with unsafe cookers that gave the utensil a poor reputation. Even the best pressure cookers were suspect; sales plummeted, and only a few factories continued to make them.

THE AGE OF PLASTIC BEGINS

For many families, the most exciting new products were plastics. Polystyrene and melamine were developed in the late 1930s, but during the war polystyrene materials and facilities were needed for making synthetic rubber. Melamine was so wear resistant that it was all snapped up by the Quartermaster Corps to be molded into dinnerware for the armed services. After V-J Day, clear or colored polystyrene proved a low-cost material for measuring cups and egg trays. American Cyanamid's

---

Lobster Newburg

A chafing-dish party food, Lobster Newburg is said to have been concocted around the turn of the century by a chef at New York's Delmonico's restaurant, and named for a patron called Wenburg. After a now-forgotten altercation, Mr. Wenburg found another favorite restaurant—and Delmonico's turned "wen" into "new" to change the name of the dish.

4 tablespoons butter
2 cups cut-up cooked lobster meat (about 1 pound)
2 tablespoons brandy
1/4 teaspoon cayenne papper
1/4 teaspoon salt
1 cup heavy cream
3 egg yolks, lightly beaten with 2 tablespoons sherry
4 patty shells or toast points

Melt butter in a large shallow pan and saute lobster gently for 3 or 4 minutes until heated through. Add brandy, touch it with a match, and spoon brandy over lobster until flames subside. Stir in seasonings. Transfer lobster to top of a large double boiler—or deep top pan of chafing dish—set over simmering water. Stir in cream. Add a spoonful of hot cream to egg yolk-sherry mixture to warm it, then pour egg yolk mixture over lobster. Stir for 2 or 3 minutes until sauce is thick. Taste for seasoning. Spoon into patty shells.
Serves 4

AIRPLANE FOOD: AN OMEN On June 16, 1947, a Pan American World Airways stewardess proudly displays the type of meal that was to be served on the first around-the-world flight. Although china was still used for meals of first-class passengers, this flight was to introduce "modern" precooked and pre-portioned meals in plastic containers similar to those still common today.

melamine went into dishes; in the late 1940s, they hired such noted designers as Russel Wright to create colorful dinnerware from their Melmac.

Flexible yet durable polyethylene, invented in 1942 and introduced after the war, was suitable for products like bowls and cannisters. High-density polyethylene, introduced later, lent itself to large items like garbage cans.

Sadly, many of the plastic fabricators immediately after the war were inexperienced, while some were opportunistic. Plastics got a bad name from products that were not designed or manufactured properly, leading Dow Chemical to launch a quality control program in 1947 to oversee its Styron brand polystyrene.

EATING OUT IN STYLE

Before the war, elegant restaurants mostly were French, and rarely were located outside of big cities. In New York diners found Voisin and Cafe Chambord; in Chicago they went to L'Aiglon; in San Francisco, they patronized Ernie's; and in Los Angeles, Perino's. There was a maitre d'hotel to show guests to white linen-covered tables; a snap of the maitre d's fingers brought waiters and busboys. There was a sommelier with the traditional gold key to the wine cellar hanging from a chain around his neck. And there was food prepared to order that made dinner an evening's entertainment.

The notable exception to the big-city rule was New Orleans, where Creole and Cajun traditions had created a mecca for diners. Antoine's, Arnaud's, Brennan's, Gallatoire's, and Commander's Palace were perhaps best known, but every restaurant held fine food in high regard.

For travelers, railroad dining cars prided themselves on carefully cooked food served with finesse. The excellent airplane food came on china plates. Hotel restaurants offered some of the finest dining of the time: among them were the Ritz-Carlton and Plaza in New York, the Drake in Chicago, and the Palace Court in San Francisco. The Pump Room in the Ambassador East Hotel in Chicago was the dream child of Ernie Byfield. Here, every food that could be set afire was served on a flaming sword. Byfield's famous explanation was that "It doesn't seem to hurt the food, and the guests love it."

With the German invasion of France

and Belgium imminent, managers of the restaurants in those exhibits at the 1939 New York World's Fair elected to stay on in New York. In 1941, Henri Soule opened Le Pavillon; Andre Pagani opened the Brussels restaurant. Both were fortunate in that members of their staffs from the Fair remained with them so they did not have to hire all new maitre d's, sommeliers, chefs, and waiters.

During the war, these dining palaces suffered the same rationing, price fixing, and food shortages that turned home cooking into a battle of wits. The Waldorf-Astoria had its Victory Recipes. In Nebraska, the Carter Hotel served a 10-cent defense stamp on a clean dessert plate, instead of presenting the cake or pie of pre-war days.

A cup of coffee was just that: no refills. Sugar bowls were kept half-empty to discourage anyone from indulging his or her sweet tooth. Surprisingly, the most honest diners were sometimes tempted to slip sugar cubes into their pockets and purses.

Restaurateurs celebrated V-J Day as enthusiastically as did other citizens. After the war, Americans resumed their pattern of family travel and tourists soon flocked to see the sights the metropolises had to offer.

RESTAURANTS FOR EVERY DAY

Historically, restaurants were the domain of men; when women patronized them, male escorts were required. Some restaurants went so far as to have separate entrances for women.

Around the turn of the century, when women began to work in offices and shops, they needed somewhere to lunch. So did women shoppers. Tearooms opened independently and in department stores to serve these women, and women's

FLAMING FEASTS Rolling carts and blazing swords replaced pedestrian food trays at the Pump Room of the Ambassador East Hotel in Chicago. Here one waiter guides a cart of desserts while another prepares to ignite tidbits already skewered on a sword.

TOMATO TULIPS When the ladies of the 1940s lunched at tearooms or gave bridge parties, the opened tomato "tulip" was thought the epitome of elegance. Inside the tomato would be some sort of mayonnaise-moistened salad—shrimp salad is shown, but tuna and chicken salad were also popular. Fancy sandwiches (left) often accompanied the tulips, especially during the summer.

Turkey Croquettes

2 tablespoons (1/4 stick) butter
2 tablespoons flour
1 cup turkey or chicken stock
1 egg, plus 1 egg beaten with 2 teaspoons water
2 cups chopped turkey
1/2 cup finely chopped celery
2 tablespoons chopped fresh parsley
2 teaspoons grated onion
Salt and pepper
Hot red pepper sauce
1 cup seasoned dry bread crumbs
Oil for deep-frying
Heated mushroom or tomato sauce, or leftover turkey gravy

In a small skillet, melt butter. With a whisk, stir in flour and cook over low heat for 1 minute. Whisk in stock, bring to a boil, and cook until thick. Remove from heat to cool.

Stir in egg, then add turkey, celery, parsley, onion, and seasonings to taste. When mixture is cool enough to handle, divide into 8 portions and shape each into a short cylindrical croquette. Roll croquettes in egg beaten with water, then in crumbs. Stand on a rack to dry for at least 30 minutes.

Meanwhile, pour oil into a pan to a depth of 2 or 3 inches; heat oil to 350° F. Place 2 or 3 croquettes in a wire basket and immerse in oil for 3 or 4 minutes, or until they are evenly browned and crisp. Drain on paper towels. Serve accompanied by sauce or gravy.
Serves 4

Tomato Aspic Ring

Typically, the center of an aspic ring held chicken or seafood salad, or a mound of cottage cheese decorated with slices of stuffed olives.

2 envelopes unflavored gelatin
1/3 cup cold water
3 cups tomato juice
3 tablespoons vinegar
1 small onion, sliced
1 rib celery with leaves, cut up
2 bay leaves
3 whole cloves
6 black peppercorns
1 teaspoon salt
1 teaspoon Worcestershire sauce
Cayenne pepper
1 head iceberg lettuce, shredded

In a large bowl, sprinkle gelatin over cold water to soften. Combine tomato juice, vinegar, onion, celery, bay leaves, cloves, and peppercorns. Bring to a boil, then simmer 5 minutes. Strain and add to gelatin. Stir in salt, Worcestershire, and a dash of cayenne. Pour into an oiled 1-quart ring mold. Refrigerate until aspic is firm, then unmold onto lettuce to serve.
Serves 6 to 8

exchanges—organized for charity—raised money by serving chicken pot pies and weak tea. In big cities, the Young Women's Christian Association provided a respectable place for lunch.

When the war came, the problems of cooking with rationed foods, combined with the increased paychecks of defense work, encouraged more women—and families—to eat out. This was especially true near army or navy bases, where wives lived in rented rooms with no more than hotplates for cooking.

By the 1940s, moderate-priced restau-

LUNCH AT THE COUNTER It wasn't fancy, but the drugstore lunch counter provided such popular sandwiches as egg salad, tuna salad, or minced ham—on white bread, of course—for less than a quarter. And a dime bought a phosphate, made on the spot from seltzer water and the customer's choice of fruit-flavored syrup.

rants rarely aimed at culinary distinction; their goal was to provide wholesome foods quickly. Drugstores and dimestores served sandwiches at lunch counters; tearooms dispensed croquettes. But most shoppers as well as business men and women patronized lunchrooms, typically unpretentious places with tiny tables crowded into a small space on the ground floor of an office building. Their menus were composed of simple foods like meatloaf with green beans and fried chicken with mashed potatoes. Most lunchrooms were individually owned, although the more successful proprietors developed them into chains (Child's, Schrafft's, Waldorf).

Except for pizza parlors, ethnic restaurants usually stayed in foreign enclaves with neighbors as customers. The first pizza made in the U. S. was baked in Manhattan's Little Italy district in 1905. After that pizza went west with Italian cooks, and by the 1940s was well on its way to becoming Americanized. In fact, the deep-dish pizza was invented in Chicago at Pizzeria Uno in 1942 by Ric Riccardo and his Texan partner, Ike Sewell.

Caruso and Chef Boy-Ar-Dee

In 1910, the legendary operatic tenor Enrico Caruso helped a young waiter—Paul Boiardi—whom he had met in Italy to get a job at the Knickerbocker Hotel in New York City. Once in the United States, Paul saved and sent money to help his younger brothers Hector and Marco immigrate, too. Hector moved to Cleveland, where he opened a restaurant; as its reputation grew, he began packaging a spaghetti-and-meat-sauce dinner. He was unable to sell it to local grocers, however, until Paul—then maître d'hôtel at the Persian Room of the Plaza—gave a sample to John Hartford, son of the founder of the A & P. Soon that chain's customers were buying "Chef Boy-Ar-Dee" spaghetti—the name phoneticized to simplify pronunciation. And in 1941 the brothers reunited to establish a factory in Milton, Pennsylvania.

Self-service was as appealing to restaurateurs as to grocers, with the first cafeterias appearing during the 1890s, run by the Young Women's Christian Association and similar groups. In 1902, Joseph Horn and Frank Hardart carried the concept one step further with their Automat, offering a whole wall of self-service glass-fronted compartments each displaying a different food. Putting a coin (originally a nickel) into a slot beside a compartment released the lock on its door and allowed a customer then to help himself to the food. Compartments could be heated or chilled so all sorts of foods were available, from hot stew to ice cream. The first Automats were in Philadelphia, but the most famous was the one opened on July 2, 1912, in Times Square, New York City.

During the next decades, Automats were sprinkled through Midtown. An Automat was reckoned one of the sights for out-of-towners to see in New York, although the concept didn't succeed in other cities when Horn & Hardart and their imitators tried to extend them to Boston, Chicago, and Washington, D.C.

What caught on and spread farthest was a chain of hamburger stands called White Castle, which was started in Wichita, Kansas, in 1916 and grew to 115 outlets by the 1930s. The bun for the 1-ounce hamburger was heated over the

THE BUSY AUTOMAT Low price and high visibility for a precise portion of food gave the Automat customer control of his or her order. The "machine" operated simply: Put a coin in the slot beside the food to unlock the glass door in front it. Like a cafeteria, an Automat provided a tray to hold the customer's choices.

The Soda Jerk

During the 1940s, the place for teenagers to take a date, or look for one, was the soda fountain at the neighborhood drugstore or candy shop. The impresario of the fountain was the soda jerk, who worked his legerdemain—turning ice cream and milk into a shake or lining up three perfect spheres of ice cream between halves of a banana—from behind a long slab of marble. On one side of the marble counter were stools for customers and, on the other side, tubs of ice cream plus spigots dispensing syrups and soda water—and whipped cream. Behind him on a mirrored wall were shelves holding the malted milk blenders, toppings like nuts and cherries, and glistening glass containers for sodas, sundaes, malts, and soft drinks.

---

cooking meat to absorb some of its heat and flavor. The burger sold for a nickel and tasted better than it sounds. Many were the customers who followed the management's advice to "buy 'em by the sack."

Like its model, White Tower (1926) specialized in hamburgers. So did Richard and Maurice McDonald when they opened their first drive-in in 1937. After the war, the cost of labor increased. With money from the GI Bill paying for tuition, returning veterans went to school and the McDonalds had a hard time attracting reliable employees. In December, 1948, they converted their stand from a drive-in to self-service—for 15-cent hamburgers, 10-cent French fries and 20-cent milk shakes—to make history by initiating another trend in eating out.

Drive-ins, beginning in 1921 with the Dallas barbecue sandwich outlet, the Pig-Stand, suffered during the war, but then made up for lost time with a phenomenal boom afterward. The owner of one Texas chain was quoted as saying, "People with cars are so lazy they don't want to get out of them to eat."

He missed the point: eating in the privacy of a car instead of in public inside a restaurant was more relaxing, especially for a family with small children. And the parking lot was a sideshow with carhops (waiters or waitresses—often in costumes) rushing or roller-skating around a constantly changing scenery of automobiles.

The Fifties: America the Bountiful

What a life! Americans in the 1950s were pretty pleased with themselves. Despite ups and downs, those were vintage years. The legacy of World War II had been prosperity, and the U.S. population was the richest in the world in the 1950s. The middle class grew because employment was high, as were wages.

The United Nations' police action after North Korean Communists invaded South Korea brought the United States into a war in 1950, but the enemy seemed inconsequential compared to Germany and Japan. (Wrong. The war proved to be a major confrontation—the armistice wasn't signed until 1953.)

Our allies during World War II, the Soviet Union and China became *the enemies* afterward. Communism haunted the United States even when the histrionics of better-dead-than-red Senator Joseph McCarthy from Wisconsin ended; he accused the Army of being soft on communism, and was himself skewered by Army Counsel Joseph Welch in 1954.

The H-bomb was detonated at Eniwetok Atoll in the Pacific in 1952. The first Holiday Inn opened that year in Memphis and George Stephen of Weber Bros. Metal Works of Palatine, Illinois, introduced a $49.95 portable barbecue kettle. Tupperware parties were the rage.

Elizabeth II was crowned Queen of England in 1953. The Supreme Court unanimously declared racial segregation in public schools unconstitutional in 1954. In 1955 Betty Crocker got a new hairdo.

Salk's polio vaccine and the first transatlantic telephone cable were introduced in 1956. The Soviets sent up *Sputnik* in 1957—the same year, incidentally, that Dick Clark's "American Bandstand" debuted. The first U.S. satellite, *Explorer*, went into orbit in 1958. Frank and Dan Carney opened the first Pizza Hut in Wichita. In 1959, Alaska became the 49th state and Hawaii the 50th.

The Weber Kettle

When George Stephen started cooking outdoors he met the same winds and rain that spoiled the day for other lovers of barbecues. In 1951, he decided to make his own grill—with a cover that would not only beat the weather but also reflect heat so food cooked more evenly. Although his first kettle (left) looked a little crude, it did the job. Within a few years, it became such a commercial success that Stephen bought the Weber Company where he worked and changed its name to Weber-Stephen Products Co. His firm is the number one manufacturer of barbecue grills, which now are stylishly streamlined and conveniently wheeled (right).

HOMES AND FAMILIES

Men had steady jobs so families could buy their own homes; home ownership went from 23 million in 1950 to 33 million in 1960. Although only one American in six still lived on farms, agricultural production reached record levels.

During the 1950s, the men earned the money and the women stayed home raising families. An unkempt child or untidy house had represented poverty during the Depression, and memories of that time made it important for women to be model homemakers, keeping their sons and daughters in "Rinso white, Rinso bright" clothes.

If being the parents of one child was wonderful, having two was at least twice as nice. Large families of six or more children, rare for decades, became fashionable again. The baby boom that started in 1945 went on until 1960: 4 million babies were born in each of the first four years of the 1950s. The U.S. population increased almost 30 million during the decade, from 150 to 178 million. Many home builders followed Levitt's example of putting an unfinished attic above the main floor of their development tract houses; as a family grew in number, the attic provided space for two or more bedrooms. The do-it-yourself business got its start, too, helping fathers finish those rooms for their offspring.

Credit put spiffy new cars—mostly from Detroit—in the garages of 65 percent of Americans during the decade. In 1940, just 28 million cars were registered; in 1950, the number was 40 million and by 1960 it had leapt to 62 million. Houses were built with two-car garages, although for most families a second car was rare and that extra space

Duncan Hines, Adventurer

For three decades, any traveler in America knew that the place to eat, or to spend the night, was one with a sign saying "Recommended by Duncan Hines." That's Hines at right; his business partner, Roy Park, is shown below displaying the signs. Now, with nationwide chain restaurants and motels, it's hard to imagine a time when the only choices were locally owned establishments that ran the gamut from wonderful to terrible. How could the traveler tell which was which?

The guessing game ended in 1936 when traveling salesman Duncan Hines began publishing ADVENTURES IN GOOD EATING. The reliability of the volume earned it such prestige that it went through forty-six editions until it was discontinued in 1963—four years after Hines's death. LODGING FOR A NIGHT, a guide to hotels and inns, had thirty-five editions.

By 1938, Hines was working full time as a gourmet. He claimed to have traveled farther—2 million miles—by automobile, airplane, and train, and to have eaten in more restaurants than any man alive. Besides putting out the guide, he wrote a cookbook, magazine articles, and a column syndicated to 100 newspapers. Hundreds of restaurants and hotels leased a sign indicating they had his recommendation. Even travelers who did not buy his book could benefit from his research. (When owners or managers changed, he sometimes took back the sign.) In the 1950s Hines licensed select food packers to use his name on their products; Procter & Gamble still put it on some baking mixes in the 1990s.

Reckoned nationally as a food authority, Hines was also a prized lecturer and a guest on radio and television shows. As a jokester, he is credited with the line: "If the soup had been as warm as the wine; if the wine had been as old as the turkey; and if the turkey had had a breast like the maid, it would have been a swell dinner."

THE FIFTIES: AMERICA THE BOUNTIFUL

held bicycles and tricycles. With no real increase in the number of women with driver's licenses, carpooling became a necessity for many.

The ambitious interstate highway system begun by President Truman in 1951 was finished under President Eisenhower. By the mid-1950s more than 200,000 miles of super highways crisscrossed the country. Gasoline cost 15 or 16 cents a gallon. Motels opened up along the highways to provide lodging for motorists. For many men, vacation meant taking the family on a motor trip to see America.

WHERE'S THE DINING ROOM?

The most desirable new development houses were ranch styles with all the rooms on one floor, probably built upon a concrete slab; or they were split-levels with short flights of stairs going down to bedrooms on the lower floor and up to the living and dining rooms and kitchen (or vice versa).

With open planning—sometimes attributed to its renowned exponent, the architect Frank Lloyd Wright—walls around the entry of a house disappeared and the front door now opened into the living room. The living area flowed into the dining area, which often was separated from the kitchen by no more than a counter or cupboard. In smaller homes, there was no attempt to create even a dining area, as families ate at one end of the living room or in the kitchen. For them, the table was likely to be a dropleaf model that would be out of the family's way between meals.

In 1958 the Market Research Corporation of Chicago reported to the American Meat Institute that 70 percent of home meals were served in the kitchen, a room that builders and remodelers now made larger and more appealing than the cramped galley-style popular in the 1940s.

Women spent a good deal of time in the kitchen—not just feeding their fami-

COOKING ON THE GO When the 1950s family didn't want to go to the kitchen, the kitchen could be brought to them. Here, elements of a meal, appliances to cook it, and dishes for serving are all collected on a wheeled teacart.

TELEVISION AT THE TABLE When families planned a new kitchen or expanded an old one, most insisted on having a dining area. And somewhere in that space was a television set, placed so that the children could watch "Captain Kangaroo" during breakfast and "Kukla, Fran, and Ollie" at dinnertime.

lies but also telephoning, having coffee with neighbors (the stylish term *kaffee klatch* described this phenomenon), keeping household accounts, even sewing and doing laundry.

A window—preferably a newfangled picture window—above the kitchen sink seemed essential. A fireplace was a luxury until builders found they could open back-to-back hearths and let one chimney serve both living room and kitchen. Decorators talked of a "family kitchen" to describe a return to the multiuse room of earlier centuries. Pine or maple captain's chairs and braided rugs came back in fashion again.

The 1950s were television years. In 1946 a mere 8,000 families had a black-and-white television set. By 1950, almost 4 million homes had sets. By 1960, 46 million families—more than 70% of American families—could sit mesmerized in front of a television set. (Probably they watched a black-and-white picture; the first color television sets were sold by RCA in 1954 for $1,000.)

Television's influence was incalculable. TV trays, coffee tables and buffets superseded the dining table as members of the family began to eat their meals individually in front of the set. With television pictures that spoke louder than radio words had, commercials prompted families to change their menus to incorporate

DINNER WITH DINAH SHORE When television was new, nobody wanted to miss a minute of his or her favorite show. This heat-and-serve frozen dinner was an instant bestseller. Just in case the shopper didn't see "TV Dinner" on the package, the first cartons simulated television sets.

CORN PUPS In the days when mixes made news, an imaginative treat for a child's party was concocted from hot dog halves (pups) and corn-muffin mix. The hot dogs are encased by the mix, speared with wood lollipop sticks, then baked until the corn-muffin wrappers cooked through and browned lightly.

instant and "convenient" foods such as mixes and cold breakfast cereals.

In 1954 Swanson introduced its first TV dinner—turkey and cornbread dressing, peas, and whipped sweet potatoes. Just the thing to put on your TV tray and eat while watching Bert Parks in "Stop the Music." Competitors followed, and by the end of the decade TV dinners accounted for 10 percent of all frozen foods sold.

COOKING STYLES

Triumphantly flaunting shortcuts, the typical 1950s housewife had little use for old-fashioned skills. "You only need to spend an average of 90 minutes a day in the

Poppy Cannon

In 1952 Poppy Cannon made news with bestselling THE CAN-OPENER COOKBOOK. Using all manner of cans and mixes, Cannon showed how "the can opener is a magic wand" to be used without shame. Housewives embraced the book and its shortcuts through four printings, including THE NEW CAN-OPENER COOKBOOK and THE NEW NEW CAN-OPENER COOKBOOK.

Ms. Cannon was a columnist, radio and television lecturer, culinary adviser to restaurants and business, and finally food editor of the LADIES HOME JOURNAL.

Tomato Stuffed with Chicken Salad

The tomato "tulips" that were ubiquitous when ladies lunced in tearooms in the 1940s were still popular in the 1950s, often served as main dish salads.

4 tomatoes
Salt
1/2 cup mayonnaise
1 tablespoon lemon juice
1 teaspoon dry mustard
Freshly ground black pepper
Ground cayenne
2 cups diced, cooked chicken
1/2 cup diced celery
1/2 cup diced cucumber
Salad greens

Place each tomato stem-end down and carve it into 6 wedges—cutting to, but not through, the base. Turn the tomato over, gently spread the wedges apart and salt them lightly. Place base-side down to drain on paper towels. Combine mayonnaise with lemon juice, mustard, and season to taste with salt, black pepper and cayenne. Stir in chicken, celery, and cucumber. Spoon the chicken salad into the tomatoes. Arrange the tomatoes on serving plates.
Serves 4

Tomato Soup Cake

CAKE
2 cups flour
1 can (10 3/4 ounces) condensed tomato soup
4 teaspoons baking powder
1 teaspoon baking soda
1 1/2 teaspoons ground allspice
1 teaspoon ground cinnamon
1/2 teaspoon ground cloves
1 1/3 cups granulated sugar
1/2 cup shortening
2 eggs
1/4 cup water
CREAM CHEESE FROSTING
8 ounces cream cheese, at room temperature
2 tablespoons milk
1 teaspoon vanilla extract
1 box (16 ounces) confectioners' sugar

Preheat oven to 350° F. Grease and flour two 8-inch round cake pans. Combine all ingredients for cake in a large bowl. Stir until well mixed, then beat with rotary beater or whisk for about 5 minutes. (Or use electric mixer, beating at low speed until ingredients are blended, then at high speed for 4 or 5 minutes.) Pour batter into cake pans and bake for 35 to 40 minutes, or until a toothpick inserted in center comes out clean. Cool in pans on wire racks for 10 minutes. Remove cakes from pans and cool completely before frosting.
For frosting, beat cream cheese until smooth with rotary beater or electric mixer at medium speed. When cheese is fluffy, beat in milk and vanilla. Gradually add enough confectioners' sugar to bring frosting to spreading consistency.
Serves 8 to 10

---

kitchen as compared with the five hours your mother used," advised Campbell's in a book called *Easy Ways to Delicious Meals* aimed at "modern young-thinking cooks who enjoy using convenience foods."

Fine cooking did not have a high priority in most families. Menus were based on meat and potatoes—food that would "stick to your ribs." Mothers were more interested in getting children to Scout meetings or Little League practice than in baking cookies for them. With all the necessary sugar and flour and butter available again at last, pastry making lost its appeal.

One favored volume of those days was Poppy Cannon's *The Can-Opener Cookbook*, first published in 1952, then revised and reprinted three times. This bestseller "turned the use of convenience foods into an art." In most of its recipes, canned foods were spiked with herbs, spices, wines, lemon peel, and such. Modern Mornay Sauce mixed condensed cream of chicken soup, milk, and grated cheese; Brunswick Stew flavored cans of beef stew, chicken fricassee, tomatoes, succotash, and consomme with sherry and Tabasco. Where appropriate, the recipes also incorporated time-saving frozen and dried ingredients.

Such use of canned foods was widespread during the 1950s. Cooks generally considered canned soup an ingredient as well as a food. Soup of one flavor or another could be combined with cooked noodles and meat or fish for a last-minute one-dish meal. The word *casserole*, more often than not, suggested using leftovers. To put the kindest light on it, the results were uneven. Husbands by the score refused to even taste such creations.

Just in the nick of time for can-happy housewives, Udico Corporation introduced the first electric can opener in 1956. The next year seven other manufacturers had versions of electric can openers, plain and fancy, wall mounted or table models— one included a pencil sharpener.

Frozen raw and cooked foods proliferated, especially during the last half of the decade when refrigerators came with larger freezer sections and home freezers were powerful enough to be worthwhile investments.

Mixes for desserts increased in vari-

A New Classic: The Bundt Cake

Bundt cakes are so familiar it hardly seems possible that the prototype is only forty years old. In 1950, H. David Dalquist, owner of Nordic Ware and Northland Aluminum Products, was asked by the Minneapolis chapter of the Hadassah Society to make an aluminum version of a European cast-iron KUGELHOPF pan. He made a few for Hadassah members and some extras to sell in department stores.

Sales were slow, however, until the 1960 GOOD HOUSEKEEPING COOKBOOK showed a color picture of a pound cake baked in one. In 1966, sales rose again when the top prize in the Pillsbury Bake-Off went to a Tunnel of Fudge cake made in a Bundt pan.

By 1972, eleven of the top hundred winners in the Pillsbury contest called for a Bundt pan; the Grand Prize Winner was a Bundt Streusel Spice Cake. That year Pillsbury launched Bundt Cake Mixes, and sold $25 million worth. By now, more than 40 million pans have been made.

Popping from the Oven

Refrigerated dough became nationally available in the early 1950s. The technique for stacking unbaked biscuits, wrapping them in foil, and packing them in tubes for refrigeration was invented in the 1930s by a Louisville baker named Lively Willoughby. His kitchen was lively, too—a veritable shooting gallery with biscuits flying everywhere until he figured out how to keep them compressed. Willoughby sold his process to Ballard and Ballard Flour Company, which the Pillsbury Company bought in 1952. After refining the product, Pillsbury introduced refrigerated buttermilk biscuits in 1953.

Lemon Chiffon Pie

According to BETTER HOMES & GARDENS GOLDEN TREASURY OF COOKING, chiffon pie was invented by 16-year-old Monroe Strause, after he went into business with an uncle who made cream pies. Strause added beaten egg whites to cream filling until it was "so light that it nearly floated off the table."

1 envelope unflavored gelatin
1/4 cup water
1 1/4 cups sugar
3/4 cup strained lemon juice
1 teaspoon finely grated lemon peel
4 eggs, separated
9-inch pastry or crumb pie shell, fully baked and cooled

Soften gelatin in water for a few minutes in the top of a double boiler. Add 3/4 cup of the sugar, the lemon juice, and egg yolks. Stir until smooth. Then set over simmering water and stir constantly until this custard coats a spoon. Stir in lemon peel, then cover and refrigerate until custard is almost set.
Beat egg whites until frothy, add the remaining 1/2 cup sugar and continue beating until whites are stiff enough to stand in firm peaks. Fold whits into custard. Spoon mixture into pie shell. Cover and refrigerate until chiffon is set—about 3 hours.
Serves 6

---

ety. The frosting as well as the cake could be produced from a mix; so could brownies and cookies. Popover, muffin, and yeast-roll mixes sold well, although they did not spare the cook much time or effort, and they cost more than the ingredients for these breads would have.

BARBECUE

Families could now afford super steaks—not the 48-ounce Del Monico Specials of the Gay Nineties perhaps, but 2-inch thick sirloins and tenderloins. And the place they wanted to cook them was outdoors. Beef consumption rose from 63 pounds per capita in 1950 to 85 pounds in 1960. Sales of hot dogs as well as steaks reflected the rise in barbecue cookery—from 750 million pounds in 1950 to 1,050,000,000 in 1960.

Chicken was not as popular as beef, or even hot dogs, but its price became temptingly low. Poultrymen had learned how to grow the birds in cages indoors, cutting costs, because the chickens fattened up fast enough to be slaughtered earlier. The freshly killed poultry that had been widely available before World War II became a rarity (except in Kosher mar-

A TASTE FOR OUTDOORS Steaks were everyone's first choice for grilling, followed closely by spareribs and hot dogs. But with chickens selling for 29 cents a pound, the barbecue held more broiler halves than sirloins.

kets), as the supermarkets found sources for already packaged products.

Patios and backyard barbecues had once seemed peculiarly suited to California. Now they were in vogue nationwide. Home handymen and professional masons hurried to cement stones or bricks together for enormous monuments to the American barbecue.

Those who didn't want a concrete edifice could buy a rectangular grill on a heavy-duty aluminum cart, first made in 1951 by Big Boy Manufacturing Co. of Burbank, California; Sears Roebuck sold it for $79. In 1953, Big Boy added a motor-driven spit and a stainless-steel hood; this elegant rotisserie and smoker cost $300.

The most expensive grills were gas-fired Char-Glo Broilers put on the market in 1957 by Joseph Del Francia Company, Los Angeles. These spared the cook the trouble of lighting coals, but also failed to give the food a "charcoal grilled" taste—unless the cook spread Liquid Smoke flavoring over it. The cheapest grills were the Japanese hibachis: little cast-iron grills with shallow bases no more than 10 or 12 inches high or wide; these needed so few briquets they were considered safe for use on a fire escape or even a picnic table. By the end of the decade, there were a hundred or more manufacturers in the grill business. Charcoal briquets, sold at supermarkets and hardware stores, simplified fueling an outdoor fire. National brands of barbecue sauce were introduced to give foods the popular sweet-and-sour tang, and many cooks began to experiment with steeping foods in home-made marinades before grilling them.

The backyard became the center of entertainment and an extension of the living room, when swimming pools seemed affordable—particularly after the

Henry Ford's Briquets

Henry Ford sometimes gets credit for "inventing" charcoal briquets. Certainly he enjoyed camping and knew how to build a charcoal fire. Ford is shown here near Loon Lake in upstate New York, while on a camping trip with his friends who called themselves "The Vagabonds": at far left, Ford car dealer E.G. Kingsford; seated, John Burroughs, the naturalist; standing, Henry Ford, Harry Firestone, and their hosts.

In the early 1920s, the now-famous model Ts had wooden bow supports in their folding tops, and Ford needed a reliable source of timber. Kingsford had once been a forester, so he oversaw Ford's acquisition of about 400,000 acres of timber and iron land in Michigan's upper peninsula. Ford located a sawmill on the Menominee River to supply wood to his auto plants; in 1923 the area around the mill was incorporated as the village of Kingsford. Wood wastes from the mill were enormous, and Ford adapted existing technology to salvage hardwood chips by having them charred, ground, mixed with starch, and compressed into briquets. Soon the plant was producing nearly 100 tons of briquets daily. The first customers for the charcoal were industrial: meat and fish smokehouses, foundries, tobacco-curing plants. In 1932, plant engineer Walter Stoepple experimented with packing briquets in a cardboard box to create a kind of instant campfire. By 1935, a Ford Charcoal Picnic Kit was on sale at Ford showrooms across the United States. Soon Ford briquets were available by the bag at hardware stores. In 1951 investors bought the plant, set up the Kingsford Chemical Company (named for the village) and relabeled the briquets accordingly.

THE FIFTIES: AMERICA THE BOUNTIFUL

Chicken Tetrazzini

8 ounces spaghetti
4 tablespoons butter
1/4 cup flour
1 1/2 cups milk
1 cup chicken stock
Salt and black pepper
Ground red pepper
1/2 cup heavy cream
1 can (4 to 5 ounces) mushrooms, drained
4 tablespoons grated Parmesan cheese
2 cups cubed, cooked chicken
Parsley sprigs

Preheat oven to 425° F. Lightly grease a 9 by 12-inch baking dish. Cook spaghetti according to package directions. Drain. Meanwhile, melt butter in saucepan. Blend in flour. Stir in milk and stock. Cook, stirring frequently, until sauce thickens and boils. Stir in cream, mushrooms, and 2 tablespoons grated Parmesan. Season with salt, black and red pepper to taste. Combine with chicken and spaghetti. Spoon mixture into baking dish. Sprinkle with remaining cheese. Bake for 15 minutes, or until hot and delicately browned. Garnish with parsley.
Serves 4

Coquilles St. Jacques

Scallops were unusual in most of the country enough in the 1950s that cooks used this lavish French presentation to display them.

1 1/2 pounds scallops
1 1/2 cups dry white wine
1/2 cup water
1/4 cup chopped onion
1 teaspoon salt
6 black peppercorns
4 parsley sprigs
1/2 bay leaf
1/2 teaspoon dried thyme
1/2 pound fresh mushrooms, chopped
4 tablespoons butter
1/4 cup flour
3/4 cup milk
3 egg yolks, lightly beaten
1/2 cup heavy cream
1 teaspoon lemon juice
Ground red pepper
1/3 cup grated Swiss cheese

Preheat broiler. In a nonreactive pan, combine scallops, wine, water, onion, salt, peppercorns, parsley, bay leaf, and thyme. Bring to boil, cover, and simmer for 5 minutes. Strain off liquid and measure it; add more water to make 2 cups.
Rinse scallops; discard seasonings. Cut scallops into bite-size pieces.
Saute mushrooms in 2 tablespoons butter for about 10 minutes. Drain and reserve them.
Meanwhile, melt remaining butter in nonreactive pan and whisk in flour. Still whisking, add milk. When this sauce thickens, stir a spoonful into yolks to warm them, then whisk yolks into sauce. Whisk in cream, lemon juice, and a dash of red pepper. Stir in scallops and mushrooms.
Spoon mixture into six buttered scallop shells or individual casseroles. Sprinkle with cheese. Broil 6 inches from heat for 3 minutes, or until browned and bubbly.
Serves 6

Heavenly Hash Salad

The term "heavenly hash" is applied to various sweets. This spiced fruit salad accompanied ham.

SALAD
1/2 pound marshmallows
1 can (20 ounces) sliced or chunk pineapple, with juice
1/2 cup blanched almonds
2 cups seedless grapes
WHIPPED-CREAM DRESSING:
2 tablespoons lemon juice
1/2 teaspoon dry mustard
1 teaspoon flour
1 teaspoon sugar
1 teaspoon butter
1 egg yolk
1 cup heavy cream, whipped
Lettuce leaves

For salad, cut marshmallows into pieces and marinate overnight in juice drained from pineapple. Cut pineapple into small pieces, and add almonds and grapes. Combine with marshmallows. Refrigerate for at least 1 hour.

For dressing, combine lemon juice, mustard, flour, sugar, and butter in top of double boiler. When ingredients are dissolved, stir in egg yolk. Stirring constantly, cook over hot water until thick. Cool, then fold into whipped cream.

To serve, arrange lettuce leaves on individual plates. Spoon hash on top and coat with dressing.
Serves 4 to 6

Roast Rock Cornish Game Hens

This bantam bird created a commercial sensation in the 1950s. Pianist Victor Borge invested in, and promoted, a farm that raised ViBo brand game hens.

4 Rock Cornish game hens
Salt and pepper
4 small onions
Celery leaves
8 slices bacon

Preheat oven to 350° F. Wipe birds and season inside and out with salt and pepper to taste. Fill each cavity with an onion and a few celery leaves, and tie wings and feet. Set birds breast side up on a rack in an open roasting pan and drape 2 bacon slices over each one. Basting occasionally with pan drippings, roast for 45 minutes to 1 hour, or until the skin is well browned and the drumsticks can be moved easily.
Serves 4

---

development of the plastic-lined above-ground pool in the mid-fifties.

ENTERTAINING

Casual was the watchword. Instant foods were acceptable even when the boss brought his wife to dinner. The 1950s was a sociable time with a style of entertaining that was quick and easy.

Cookbooks suggested patio picnics, progressive dinners, and theme meals. In progressive dinners, each course was served at a different house or apartment; organizing transportation from one place to another could become a big job—and get more attention than the food. Theme parties might be planned around a place, a time in history, or a group of people. If the theme were Hawaii, for example, all the guests were expected to appear in tropical outfits and wear paper-flower leis; paper palm trees might ornament the walls, phonograph records (still likely 78 rpm) played ukelele music while somebody tried to hula. Rum drinks were served

FESTIVE MOLDS A pair of molded gelatin salads—one made with fruit segments, the other with grated cabbage and sliced olives—form the centerpiece of a New Year's party buffet. Gelatin and Jell-O were ubiquitous in the 1940s and 1950s, appearing both in salads like those above and in dozens of desserts resembling the tower of fruit at right.

along with food that was heavy on the pineapple chunks.

COCKTAIL PARTIES

After Prohibition had been repealed in 1933, the Depression and World War II kept Americans pretty sober until the 1950s. Then cocktail parties became *de rigueur*. Cocktails as a prelude to dinner, or sometimes lunch, had been familiar for decades. Now the cocktail party—with no meal to follow it—became the chic evening entertainment (usually from 5 to 7 P.M.).

The cocktail itself had been invented in America during the Revolutionary war, or so they say, and named by an unknown French soldier for the feather or "coq's tail" decorating a rum-and-fruit drink served in a New England tavern run by Miss Betsy Flanagan. However, mixed drinks probably date back to the earliest alcoholic beverages; the wines were sour and in need of sweetening, and the distilled spirits could be "improved" upon.

Martinis, Manhattans, old-fashioneds, and other popular cocktails of the decade were not new; being able to afford the makings was. Consumption of liquor rose from 190 million gallons in 1950 to 235 million gallons in 1960; sales of gin alone soared from 6 to 19 million gallons.

How to stir or shake cocktails, and what the proportions of ingredients should be, turned into the subject of serious debate. Martini drinkers were especially opinionated. Humorist Robert Benchley spoke for a large constituency when he said a martini should contain only enough dry vermouth to prevent the gin from looking watery.

With no dinner to serve, hostesses could concentrate attention on tidbits to

Grasshopper Pie

Liqueurs were stylish as drinks in the 1950s, and—when poured over ice cream—as desserts. More ambitious hosts combined liqueurs to make cocktails such as the "grasshopper" with green creme de menthe, white creme de cacao, and heavy cream. Adding melted marshmallows turned the cocktail into a rich filling for a cool, summery pie.

1 1/2 cups fine chocolate or vanilla wafer crumbs (about 1/2 pound)
1/2 cup sugar
6 tablespoons butter, melted
1/2 pound marshmallows
1/2 cup milk
1/4 cup green creme de menthe
1/4 cup white creme de cacao
1 cup heavy cream, whipped
Semisweet chocolate shavings

Preheat oven to 350° F. Combine crumbs and 1/4 cup sugar with butter, press mixture into 9-inch pie plate. Bake for 10 minutes to firm crust. Refrigerate at least 1 hour or until cold.

In top of double boiler, combine marshmallows and milk, and cook over simmering water—stirring often—until all marshmallows melt. Stir in creme de menthe and creme de cacao. Refrigerate for 30 minutes or until mixture begins to thicken. Fold marshmallow mixture gently into whipped cream. Spoon into pie crust. Cover. Refrigerate until firm, at least 2 hours. Before serving, garnish pie with chocolate shavings.

Serves 6 to 8

Cheese Fondue

One explanation for fondue's popularity may be that it's romantic. Each diner spears a chunk of bread on a fork (preferably a long fondue fork), twirls the bread in the hot cheese, then lifts the cheese-coated bread to his or her mouth. If a chunk falls into the fondue, the diner must forfeit a kiss.

1 garlic clove, halved
2 cups dry white wine
1 pound Swiss cheese, shredded (4 cups), and mixed with 2 tablespoons flour
2 tablespoons kirsch
Grated nutmeg
French bread, cut into bite-size chunks

Rub the inside of the fondue pot with cut sides of garlic. Pour in wine and bring to a simmer over low heat. Discard garlic. Use fork to stir a little cheese at a time into wine. When all cheese has melted, stir in kirsch and grate nutmeg over fondue. Serve at once.

Serves 4

---

accompany the cocktails. Since guests picked these up in their hands, the tidbits came to be called "finger food." The dips that revolutionized cocktail party foods in the 1950s owe their origin to the dried onion soup mix that Lipton brought out then. Some clever cook combined the mix with sour cream to create a tangy concoction just right for dipping in potato chips or raw vegetables. That creation, plus all the variations it spawned, made dips the tidbit of choice with cocktails.

Not a dip, but passing as one was the Swiss fondue that Americans adopted enthusiastically. The word *fondue* comes from the French verb *fondre*, meaning "to

Rumaki

Exotic certainly, Hawaiian possibly, but popular at cocktail parties anywhere.

1/2 cup soy sauce
1/4 cup dry sherry
1/2 teaspoon ground ginger
6 chicken livers, trimmed and quartered
12 water chestnuts, halved crosswise
12 bacon slices, halved crosswise

Blend soy sauce, sherry, and ginger in a shallow bowl. Add chicken livers and marinate 1 hour. Drape each chicken liver quarter around a chestnut half and wrap both in a bacon slice. Use a toothpick to skewer together. Broil 4 or 5 inches from heat, turning kabobs 2 or 3 times, for 5 minutes or until bacon crisps and browns. Serve hot.
Makes 24

Jan's Red Pepper Jelly

A sweet-hot garnish for fowl or pork, or a spread to put over cream cheese on crackers, this Southern invention appeared after the war. In SOUTHERN FOOD, John Egerton attributes the earliest recipe to the CHARLESTON RECEIPTS of 1950. Combine bell and chili peppers in whatever ratio you like—three cups sweet to one cup hot yields a sharp jelly.

5 pounds sugar (10 cups)
4 cups ground red bell and chili peppers
1 onion, ground with peppers
2 cups distilled white vinegar
1/2 teaspoon salt
3 packages (1 1/2 boxes) dry fruit pectin

Pour sugar into a large stainless steel or enameled pot. Add peppers and onion, vinegar, and salt. Stirring frequently, bring to slow boil and boil for 10 minutes. Add pectin, then bring to rapid boil for 1 minute. Skim foam, then pour into sterilized jars. Cover each jar with a sterilized lid or pour a 1/8-inch layer of paraffin over jelly. Fills about a dozen 1/2-pint jars

melt," and the dip was a pot of bubbling Swiss cheese into which guests plunged the cubes of bread they held on long forks. Rare, indeed, was the 1950s bride who did not get at least two fondue pots as wedding presents.

WINE AND BEER

Overseas assignments during World War II and travel abroad afterward introduced Americans to cultures where wine or beer was considered an important part of a meal. Beer consumption rose 50 percent from 12 gallons per capita per year to 17 gallons during the decade. Most of the beer was made in the United States, although European, Canadian, and Mexican beers began to find a market here.

Americans who drank wine were a small minority, most of whom preferred European vintages. Prohibition in 1919 had put just about all of America's wineries out of business. Getting started again during the Depression was difficult. After the war, a few vintners in California and New York produced simple table wine, sold in gallon bottles, that came to be called "jug wine." But more sophisticated American wines were rare until the 1970s.

MILK AND CHEESE

Homogenized milk, with its smooth and creamy taste, became standard in the 1950s. At the same time, consumers began to turn from whole milk to low-fat milk. In 1950, per capita consumption of whole milk was 134 quarts, of low-fat milk only 10 quarts. By 1975, annual whole-milk consumption was 91 quarts, low-fat milk

49 quarts. Additionally, dry milk, which was a low-fat product, rose in favor as Carnation introduced in 1954 its Magic Crystals, which dissolved in cold water.

Gradually, glass milk bottles gave way to paper containers. The original conical paper models were replaced by rectangular paper containers with gables at the top, which produced a spout for pouring when cut open. Sheffield Farms in New York had experimented with paper in 1929, but the Depression, then wartime restrictions slowed the container's development. By 1952, however, nearly 40 percent of all milk was being sold in paper containers.

Americans ate little cheese before World War II—about 6 pounds per capita in 1940. But after 1945 large-scale commercial production brought costs down and sales went up. Kraft introduced pre-sliced processed cheese nationwide in 1950, turning grilled cheese sandwiches into everybody's lunchtime favorite.

Two years later, Kraft brought out Cheese-Whiz spread, which was even easier to use in a sandwich. By 1960 annual cheese consumption was more than 8 pounds per capita, a figure inflated not only by grilled cheese sandwiches but also by increased acceptance of Italian foods, especially pizza. Cottage cheese consumption rose even faster, from 1.9 pounds per capita in 1940 to 4.7 in 1960.

Imports climbed as cheese specialty stores opened in metropolitan areas. Not only was more cheese available, but the choices increased far beyond Gruyère and Roquefort to include such hitherto unheard-of varieties as Danish Cream Havarti, French Reblochon, and Greek Feta. One enthusiastic entrepreneur started a mail-order "cheese of the month" club called Cheese Lovers International.

Meanwhile, European types of cheeses grew more common. Iowa State University patented a process for making blue cheese just before World War II, and the Maytag Dairy Farms in Newton, Iowa, began producing it then; after the war, cheese-making resumed for Maytag Blue's mail-order clientele. Wisconsin's diverse immigrants developed cheeses similar to those of their homelands—Switzerland, Italy, and Holland among them.

MARGARINE

In 1950, President Harry Truman's signature on the Margarine Act of 1950 ended the discriminatory federal taxes that the butter lobby had obtained. Until then butter outsold margarine by about two to one, but during the following decade the ratio would be reversed. (In states where dairies were an important part of the economy—and politics—state law made it illegal to sell yellow margarine. The consumer bought a package holding a capsule of food dye to knead into the white margarine before serving it.)

COOKING SCHOOLS

To counter all the kitsch in the kitchen, in 1955 cooking expert James Beard started a cooking school in New York City to teach the basics of fine cooking to interested adults. The school was an instant success, somewhat to the surprise of its innovator. At first, classes were held in borrowed kitchens, with Andre Surmain (who later opened Restaurant Lutece, in New York City) and Albert Stockli of Restaurant Associates as guest teachers. Finally, in

Epitome of the Epicures

Who knew more about food and drink than Jim Beard did? Certainly nobody enjoyed them more—as witnessed by the glee he took in drinking a toast with Regine of Regine's Restaurant in New York City. Beard was born in Oregon in 1903 and learned about the importance of cooking from his mother. He went to New York in the 1930s to pursue a career in music, but as early as 1932 he was giving private cooking lessons. From 1938 to 1940 he ran a catering business with his friends Irma and Bill Rhode; his first cookbook—in 1940—was about hors d'oeuvre. After World War II, he taught cookery on televison and in his Greenwich Village townhouse, while producing more than twenty cookbooks and working as a consultant to restaurants, wine dealers, and food suppliers. Beard traveled widely and frequently. Despite his expertise in international cuisines, he championed simple cookery, especially regional American fare. Beard died in 1985. (AP/Wide World Photo)

1960 Beard bought a building in Greenwich Village and had a kitchen designed for teaching as well as personal use.

Beard's were not the only classes for adults. Cookbook authors Dione Lucas and Helen Worth both conducted them. Dione Lucas ran the Cordon Bleu School and Helen Worth held classes for brides—and, at noon, "Learn Your Lunch" lessons for men. The China Institute in New York also started cooking classes in 1955; the renowned cook Grace Chu commuted from Washington, D.C., to teach. Her first class had ten students, eight of whom were home economics teachers in the New York City school system and were earning points toward salary raises by attending classes. An inspector from the education department visited the first class and ruled that the course contained enough cultural information to be worth two points.

Chu, Dorothy Lee, and Florence Lin alternated as instructors during the decade.

Cookbooks proliferated. James Beard himself produced half a dozen books on such subjects as barbecue and rotisserie cooking—Beard's mother had taught him the basics of outdoor cooking at family picnics on the Oregon coast years before—fish cooking, casserole cooking, cooking for entertaining, and mixing

Onion Sandwiches

When James Beard was in the catering business with Bill and Irma Rhode just before World War II, they invented these sandwiches using slices of brioche. Any kind of white or brown bread will serve, provided it is firm enough to be sliced very thin.

12 thin slices brioche
1 red onion, sliced paper thin
2 tablespoons butter, softened
1/4 cup mayonnaise
1/2 cup finely chopped fresh parsley

Butter bread lightly. With a cookie or biscuit cutter, cut two 2-inch rounds from each slice. Place onion slices on half of bread slices, and cover with remaining bread rounds. Spread edge of each sandwich with mayonnaise, then roll sandwich in parsley. Arrange sandwiches on serving plates, cover, and refrigerate for 1 hour or more.
Makes 12 sandwiches

ALL-AMERICAN PIZZA By 1956, when this photograph was taken, every ethnic group in the United States had adopted the pizza as "American," and home cooks were clamoring for recipes.

drinks. With his friend Sam Aaron, proprietor of Sherry Wine and Spirits in New York, he wrote *How to Eat Better for Less Money*, a volume that not only had recipes for dollar-stretching stews and chili dishes, but also discussed how to hold a cocktail or dinner party on a budget. *Betty Crocker's Cookbook* was first published in 1950. That same year *Gourmet* magazine published the first of two thick volumes of recipes; at $10 apiece these seemed outrageously expensive! Interest in regional American cooking spurred Clementine Paddleford of *This Week* magazine to produce a series of articles—later collected in a book—about *How America Eats*. Cookbooks by authors such as Myra Waldo, Florence Brobeck, Nika Hazelton, and the family team of Cora, Rose and Bob Brown took their readers further afield as they explored Latin American, European, and Asian cuisines.

CLEANING UP

Whatever the food, the leftovers needed wrapping—a job that had been simplified considerably when Reynolds Aluminum brought out its wrap in 1947. In 1952, Dow Chemical introduced Saran Wrap that not only covered the bowls and platters snugly, but was transparent and kept odors in so onions could sit next to milk.

The dreaded job of washing dishes after a meal got much easier in 1951 when Procter & Gamble introduced Joy liquid dishwashing detergent, which dealt with grease more effectively than soaps did. Lever brought out Lux Dishwashing Liquid in 1953.

SEE-THROUGH WRAPPING The first plastic food wrap to keep odor inside was the Saran Wrap that Dow introduced in 1953. A polyvinylidene chloride (PVDC) film, Saran was clear so food was visible through it. Later cooks would discover that the wrap would withstand the cold of a freezer.

buying, the markets were able to sell at prices 8 percent to 15 percent below the prices of traditional grocers, driving most competition out of business.

Markets grew in size to tens of thousands of square feet; even so, the battle for shelf space got increasingly competitive as markets added thousands of new convenience foods and non-foods. The total number of items in the average supermarket reached 5,600 by 1960. The newer markets located on the edge of town to ensure plenty of space for parking cars, and they stayed open for long hours (sometimes overnight).

STAMP-EDE Trading stamps lured the shoppers of the 1950s to supermarkets that carried them, because they seemed to represent something for nothing: one stamp for every dime the shopper would have spent anyway. Although stamps are still big business, supermarkets today usually rely on other customer incentives such as low prices or special services.

SHOPPING

In the 1950s, Americans turned into a nation of consumers, and retailers did everything they could to make shopping easier: The first shopping center was Northgate, built near Seattle in 1950 with a pedestrian mall linking stores that sold merchandise of every kind—including foods. The first "climate-controlled" (meaning enclosed) shopping center was Southdale Mall in Edina, Minnesota, near Minneapolis; designed by Victor Gruen Associates, it opened in October 1956.

Supermarkets accounted for 35 percent of food sales in 1950, but by 1960 the supermarket sold 70% of America's food for home consumption. With bulk

During the 1950s, part of the competition among supermarkets was waged with trading stamps. In 1896, Thomas A. Sperry and Shelly B. Hutchinson conceived and founded the cash-discount trading stamp business. (The company was acquired by the Beinecke family about 1916, went public in 1966, then was acquired by a holding company in 1984 but remains the S&H, or green stamp, Company.)

The shopper generally received one stamp for each dime spent, although some markets allowed stamps only on certain products and some gave out stamps only on request. The shopper saved stamps in a book to get any of about 1,500 items—mostly housewares and small appliances. Each book held 1,200 stamps. That's $120 worth of food—and other items if local service stations and drugstores also distributed stamps. The book had a buying value of about $3 only for merchandise from a stamp company's catalog or, in large cities, direct from a stamp redemption center.

In 1959, consumers got 275 billion trading stamps representing $32 billion in groceries. A reported 75 percent of families saved stamps; 50 percent saved more than one kind. S&H was the biggest stamp distributor; other major stamp companies were Gold Bond, Top Value, and Blue Chip. Some stores issued their own stamps, although most participated in a stamp-company plan.

The stamps cost markets 2 percent of their gross sales, so none of them was eager to dispense them, and did so only to stay competitive. Some supermarkets refused to carry stamps and advertised

MIXES IN HEADLINES During the 1950s, mixes made news as varieties of cakes and other baking products were perfected. This Devil's Food Cake requires fresh eggs although the manufacturer could have put dried eggs in the mix. Studies done by motivational researcher Ernst Dichter showed that women wanted some sense of participation in the making of the cake, and adding only water did not satisfy their need.

that they had lower prices as a result. By the end of the decade, neither stamps nor prices were strong enough factors to get and keep customers, however. Supermarkets began to differentiate in various other ways, stressing service or quality of merchandise, for example.

Supermarkets were a showcase for the American way of life: aisles of canned and packaged foods, already cut and trimmed meat and produce, freezers packed with foods that only needed heating—and all of it affordable. When Queen Elizabeth II visited in 1957, she wanted to tour a supermarket; so did Premier Nikita Khrushchev on his 1959 visit. At foreign expositions the supermarket became an American showpiece.

By 1958 *Life* magazine labeled the supermarket "a U.S. institution" and edito-

COOKING-SERVING-STORING WARE The glass-ceramic bowls and casserole dishes of the 1950s could withstand any temperature, hot or cold, and go from one to the other safely. Here beef stew is served from the dish in which it cooked—and in which leftovers will be refrigerated or frozen. A heavy wire stand acts as a trivet to hold the hot dish off the dining table.

Steak Diane

This recipe is designed for table cookery, in a chafing dish or electric skillet. For drama, you can flame each steak by pouring a dollop of brandy into the pan; let the fire die down before rolling the steaks.

4 slices boneless sirloin steak, cut 1/4 inch thick and pounded paper thin
8 tablespoons (1 stick) butter
4 tablespoons oil
Salt and black pepper
1 cup finely chopped scallions, white parts only
1 tablespoon Worcestershire sauce
1 teaspoon Dijon mustard
1/2 cup concentrated beef stock, made by boiling down 1 cup stock
2 tablespoons Madeira
1/4 cup chopped fresh parsley

For each steak, melt 2 tablespoons butter with 1 tablespoon oil in saute pan, chafing dish, or skillet. Sear steak quickly on both sides. Season with salt and pepper, and use 2 forks to roll the steak and transfer it to a heated platter. Saute the scallions for a few minutes in fat remaining in pan. Stir in Worcestershire and mustard, then concentrated stock. Add Madeira and parsley. Taste sauce for seasoning before pouring it over the steaks. Serve at once.
Serves 4

---

rialized, "Beyond their impact on consumers, supermarkets are having even more far-reaching effects. As their bright displays and mass-selling fill old demands at lower prices, they also create new demands, thereby creating new agriculture, new industry—and new living standards."

SMALL APPLIANCES

In 1911, Westinghouse introduced an electric skillet (or fry pan, as it was called). Turned upside down, it became a hot plate. Despite this duality, sales were poor and dropped out of the market.

Not until 1953 did another electric skillet appear—first a round one from National Presto Industries, then a square Automatic Frypan from the Sunbeam Corporation. Cooks could set the heat at predetermined temperatures, and know the skillet would not get hotter. Although the skillets couldn't be submerged in water for washing, women snapped them up. In 1954, H.K. Foster, an engineer for S.W. Farber Inc., solved the washing problem with what came to be called a "probe"— a removable heat control.

Skillets were followed by electric saucepans, deep-fat fryers, roaster ovens, and a table broiler that could hold a spit to turn it into a rotisserie. (The Rotissimat Corporation set up demonstrations in poultry stores to show off their appliance;

PORTABLE COOKING Breakfast seemed more convivial and easier to put together when a cook had an electric grill to set on the table or a counter where the family could eat.

an indirect result may be the chicken rotisseries now seen in many supermarkets.)

Over the years, manufacturers introduced such esoteric devices as electric chafing dishes, egg boilers, ice-cream freezers, bean pots, and corn poppers. Roasts were carved with electric knives and—a frightening thought—someone tried to sell an electric paring knife.

These new appliances, according to the *Complete Small Appliance Cookbook*, by John and Marie Roberson, were "the *social* way of preparing meals" because they went everywhere indoors or out to the porch or patio. The immovable kitchen stove looked pretty clunky, and the dining table seemed redundant, in what the Robersons called the "Golden Heydey of the Marvelous Mechanical Appliance."

MAJOR APPLIANCES

The 1950s were years of innovation in large kitchen equipment, too. In 1950 Westinghouse showed the first fully automatic defrosting refrigerator. The year 1955 saw the first side-by-side refrigerator-freezer, called a Foodarama, by Kelvinator. That same year General Electric displayed a wall model refrigerator-freezer that blended with a kitchen's top cabinets and had a storage capacity of more than 10 cubic feet. In 1958 Whirlpool had a frostless refrigerator.

The first freezers capable of freezing fresh food arrived in the 1950s. Makers of the 1952 Ben-Hur Farm and Home Freezer claimed the cook could end seasonal eating forever and save money in the bargain by buying fresh fruits and vegetables by the bushel, or beef or pork by the half or quarter, and freezing them at home. She could cook in advance for special occasions, freeze a week's supply of sandwiches for the family, and save leftovers for many weeks or months instead of mere days.

The year 1950 saw the introduction of the modular stove—wall ovens and separate burners to insert in countertops. The range with upper and lower ovens arrived later in the decade.

The garbage disposer was affordable, at last. Back in 1935 General Electric had introduced one, but it was so big and heavy it had to be mounted to the floor. The switch was on the side of the hopper, a fine arrangement when sinks hung on the wall with no cabinets below them. In 1941 General Electric brought out the Disposall that was suspended from the sink and had countertop controls, but it was 1947 before they made enough of them to show a profit.

Dishwashers became a status symbol. The earliest were so noisy that cooks left the house when they turned them on, but gradually insulation was added to quiet them. In 1952, a movable dishwasher appeared with its own four-gallon fiberglass water heater.

Soap makers had been working with detergent powders for over three decades. Dishwasher owners used either a light-duty type or a laundry powder until 1955, when Procter & Gamble brought out the first low-sudsing detergent designed for dishwashing called Cascade.

Until 1954 major appliances were white or wispy shades of yellow or green. That year General Electric made a splash in the marketplace by giving them assertive decorator colors: cadet blue, petal pink, canary yellow, turquoise green, and wood-tone brown.

Between 1945 and 1960, the remaining 15 percent of American homes were electrified. By 1960, almost all homes—98 percent—had refrigerators, 12 percent had freezers, and 6 percent had dishwashers.

UNBREAKABLE GLASS-CERAMIC

A Corning Glass Works scientist, Dr. Donald Stookey, created glass-ceramic in 1953. A unique product, it withstood heat and cold that no other glass or ceramic (and few metals) could tolerate. Its first use was as the nose cone of a space missile, where it was subject to hundreds of degrees of heat from air friction.

In April 1958, Corning developed cookware products from this glass-ceram-

ELECTRIFIED COOKING-SERVING WARE Just a year after Corning created a sensation with its all-temperature glass-ceramic bowls and casserole dishes, it went electric. Pyroceram was used in 1959 the electromatic percolators and skillets.

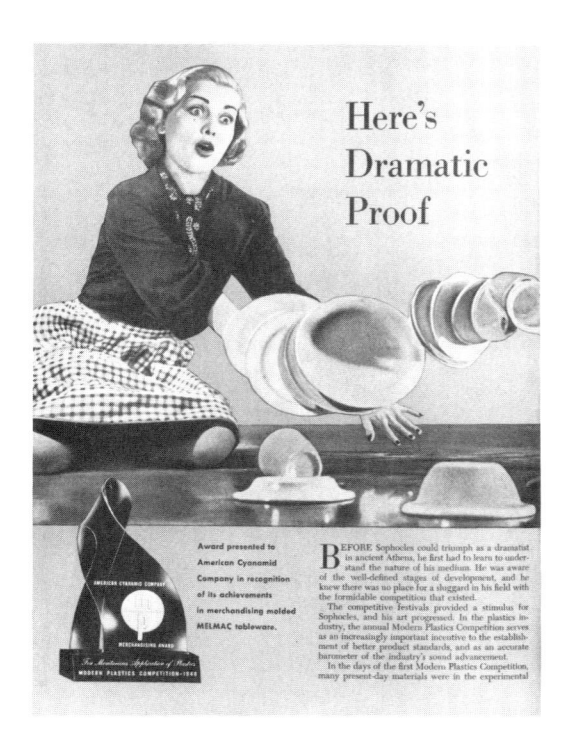

PLEASE DROP THE DISHES! In the 1950s, American Cyanamid's print and television advertising featured dropping the dishes—and watching them bounce. At a time when most consumers knew very little about the properties of plastics—and a lot about china breaking if dropped—the advertisements and demonstrations for Melmac dinnerware caused a sensation.

ELEGANCE IN PLASTIC Designed by Joan Luntz, these handsome and breakage-resistant melamine-plastic dishes reflected the nineteenth century American Victorian tradition of square serving plates as well as having a modern twentieth century European Bauhaus look. The twenty-piece starter set shown cost $17.95. The driftwood used as a centerpiece was as stylish in the 1950s as the plastic dinnerware.

ic. The snowy white skillets, saucepans, and casserole dishes with the brand name Pyroceram could go from freezer or refrigerator directly to a conventional or microwave oven, and were handsome enough to use as serving pieces. To demonstrate the material, Corning froze part of a piece of Pyroceram in a block of ice, then applied a blowtorch to the other part. The following year, Corning introduced electric percolators and skillets made of glass-ceramic. The blue cornflower design on everything is a registered symbol for Corning, recognized throughout the world.

PLASTICS

The 1950s were the years when plastics became respectable. American Cyanamid was promoting "Brookpark" dinnerware, made from Melmac, which resisted breaking, cracking, and chipping, and could be washed by hand or machine. The design was said to be inspired by Bauhaus modern architecture: the plates, saucers, and cups were square with rounded corners and came in stylish chartreuse, burgundy, emerald, and pearl.

For the cupboard and refrigerator, chemist and inventer Earl Tupper had introduced food-storage containers in 1945. But they languished on shelves of hardware and department stores until

Tupper Parties

The most famous plastics of the 1950s may have been those designed by Earl S. Tupper. When he first introduced his flexible polyethylene kitchenware in 1945, response was disappointing; so many earlier plastics had been brittle and easily broken that people distrusted the material. Although Tupper's food storage containers and bowls were flexible and unbreakable, those traits were not apparent while the products sat on store shelves. Furthermore, the unique Tupperware lid formed a virtually airtight, liquid-tight seal, but this feature needed demonstrating. In 1951, Tupper left retail stores and Brownie Wise invented the now famous Tupperware party plan, where a housewife sells to her friends, and friends of friends in ever-widening circles. By the 1980s, parties and demonstrations were held in offices as well as homes in more than forty countries. The Museum of Modern Art had fifteen Tupperware pieces in its permanent collection of "classic plastic designs."

Brownie Wise and Tom Damigella began showing them at home parties. The Tupper brand containers were flexible polyethylene and just about unbreakable. They were shaped for stacking and—because lids were a bit larger than the bases—containers were almost airtight so contents wouldn't spill. All this needed demonstrating. In 1951, Tupper took his products out of stores and hired Brownie Wise to create the unique direct selling system now known as Tupperware Home Parties.

EATING OUT

Elegant dining is always fashionable, whatever the cuisine, as Restaurant Associates proves. Organized in New York City in 1953, they opened there six restaurants by the end of the decade and served a breathtaking range of foods from Italian at Mama Leone's to Polynesian in the Hawaiian Room, from Latin American at La Fonda del Sol to Alsatian at the Brasserie, Roman at the Forum of the Twelve Caesars and continental at the Four Seasons.

To help make paying the tab for fine

Caesar Salad

The prototype of this salad was created on July 4, 1924, by Caesar Cardini, who owned restaurants in Tijuana, Mexico, across the border from San Diego. Originally, it was eaten with the fingers so the romaine leaves were kept whole, but you may prefer to tear them into pieces —as Cardini sometimes did. (He did not use anchovies.)

2 tablespoons plus 1/4 cup olive oil
1 garlic clove, sliced
1 cup cubed firm white bread
1 head romaine lettuce, separated into leaves, washed, dried, and chilled
6 oil-packed anchovy fillets, rinsed, patted dry, and minced (optional)
1 tablespoon lemon juice
Salt and black pepper
1 egg, coddled for 1 1/2 minutes
1/4 cup freshly grated Parmesan cheese

Heat 2 tablespoons oil in a skillet and sauté garlic until lightly colored. Add bread cubes and stir until brown. Drain croutons on paper towels and discard garlic. Place lettuce in a chilled bowl and moisten with remaining 1/4 cup oil. Stir in anchovies if you are using them, lemon juice, and salt and pepper to taste. Add egg, Parmesan, and croutons. Toss salad well.
Serves 4

Vichyssoise

In the 1950s almost every French restaurant celebrated the coming of summer by putting this soup on the menu. Although invented in America, its creator was French chef Louis Diat.

4 leeks, white part only, sliced
1 onion, sliced
4 tablespoons butter
4 potatoes, sliced
4 cups chicken stock
Salt
1 cup milk
1 to 2 cups heavy cream
Ground white pepper
Finely cut chives

In a heavy soup pot, sauté leeks and onion in butter for 20 minutes or until soft and golden. Add potatoes, stock, and 1 teaspoon salt. Bring to a boil, reduce heat, and simmer for 20 to 30 minutes or until potatoes are soft. Puree mixture in a food mill or push through a sieve, or process in small batches in a blender or processor. Return pureed mixture to pot, add milk, and 1 cup cream, and bring to a simmer. Let cool and add white pepper. Refrigerate. Before serving, taste for seasoning. Add more cream if needed for desired consistency. Garnish with chives.
Serves 6 to 8

food as painless as possible, Frank McNamara created charge cards for use in any restaurant anywhere: Diner's Club was initiated in February 1950.

In 1951 Franklin National Bank on Long Island, New York, issued a charge card accepted by local merchants, and nearly 100 other banks followed suit. But because the cards were usable only in the bank's local area, the profit was small and the cards disappeared. The first serious competition to Diners Club came in 1958 when American Express introduced its

Chicken Divan

Invented in the 1940s or 1950s—almost certainly at the Divan Parisien Restaurant in midtown Manhattan. This contemporary time-saving recipe has mayonnaise as the sauce base; other versions use mornay sauce.

4 stalks lightly cooked broccoli
4 thin slices chicken breast
1 cup mayonnaise
1 egg white, beaten until stiff
2 tablespoons grated Swiss cheese

Preheat oven to 325°F. Place 2 broccoli stalks on each of two heatproof dishes. Top them with chicken. Fold mayonnaise and egg white together and spoon over chicken. Sprinkle with cheese. Bake until sauce bubbles and browns slightly, about 15 minutes.
Serves 2

charge card, and Bank of America issued the BankAmericard that could be used anywhere in California.

Because restaurateurs paid a percentage of the total tab—albeit small—to the card operators, some owners would not accept the cards. But most felt the cards encouraged business and liked them as much as diners did.

During the 1950s, uptown coffee houses replaced tearooms as stylish places to have a pastry in the middle of the afternoon. With repertoires of a dozen or more brews—including exotic Viennese or Turkish coffees—they attracted crowds after the movies or theater. European newspapers were there for singles to read; classical music played in the background. Downtown and college area coffee houses, on the other hand, were casual gather-

Paradise for 25¢

What teenager could resist that glorious soda-fountain excess—the banana split? Glass companies even made special dishes for displaying this heavenly creation. All splits had banana halves on the sides of the dish, but every other element was custom designed. Typically, the split contained three scoops of ice cream, each a different flavor and topped by a different sauce—chocolate, marshmallow, and strawberry sauces were favorites. Nuts were sprinkled all around. Whipped cream was lavished over the sauces and a red or green maraschino cherry plunked on top.

KITCHEN CULTURE

Dinner on the Go

The dining car staffs on streamlined trains of the 1950s prided themselves on the excellence of their food and service, which were a match for any fine restaurant. Railroads became famous nationwide for particularly exceptional dishes: the Illinois Central, for example, was known for its French toast, the Gulf Mobile and Ohio for its chess pie. Breads and pastries were made on board, so were soups. Not only were the fruits and vegetables fresh, but cooks bought fish at stops along the way so they could serve it the day it was hooked. To finish the meal, the diner had a choice of coffee, Postum, or any one of four kinds of tea: Ceylon, Young Hyson, English Breakfast, and Orange Pekoe.

Steak was grilled to order on the Empire Builder that the Great Northern Railway ran between Chicago and Seattle-Portland.

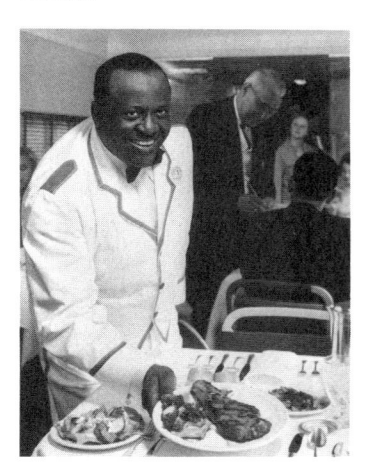

Two chefs work in the electric kitchen on the Santa Fe's El Capitan, where the dining car had two levels: kitchen beneath and seating room for eighty patrons above.

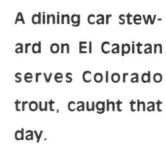

A dining car steward on El Capitan serves Colorado trout, caught that day.

Chefs check the groceries delivered in Chicago for the Santa Fe's Super Chief trip of 2,227 miles to Los Angeles.

THE FIFTIES: AMERICA THE BOUNTIFUL

ing places for freewheelers. An ornate *espresso-cappucino* machine, imported from Italy, dominated the room and an equally awesome American-made jukebox usually supplied music, although some of the more popular establishments hired folk singers.

By the end of the decade, medium-priced white-tablecloth restaurants serving simple American foods—Schraffts, Stouffers, White Turkey, and the like—began to disappear.

The trends were to informality and fast food. For many customers, a lunch counter in a drugstore spelled convenience and economy. A grilled cheese sandwich and a Coke cost only a quarter, but not everyone liked sitting on a stool. In the early 1950s, California lunch counters transformed themselves into coffee shops by putting padded stools with upholstered backs at their counters and supplementing the counters with Formica-topped tables, sometimes set in booths. (Unlike coffee houses, which sold only coffee and pastry, the coffee shops had full menus. They got their name from the promise to refill customers' coffee cups at no extra charge.) Googie's on Sunset Boulevard was a pioneer, followed shortly by Denny's, Bob's Big Boy, and Biff's. Gradually, motels and even hotels adopted the coffee shop as a supplement, or replacement, for the dining room.

At about the same time, Richard and Maurice McDonald's San Bernardino, California, restaurant was becoming recognized as the prototype for California self-service drive-ins. In 1954, Ray Kroc—a Chicago-based salesman who sold a popular milkshake mixer nationwide—paid a call on them. The McDonalds required ten mixers when most drive-ins needed only one or two. Kroc saw why they did so much business, and before the year was over, he signed on as the brothers' national franchising agent. To ensure quality, Kroc sold franchises for single restaurants, not for areas, as many chains did.

On April 15, 1955, Ray Kroc opened his own franchised McDonald's restaurant in Des Plaines, Illinois. In 1958, the McDonald's chain sold its 100 millionth hamburger, and the next year, the hundredth restaurant opened near Chicago's Midway Airport. Finally, in 1961, Kroc bought the McDonald's name from the brothers, and opened Hamburger University, granting a bachelor of hamburgerology degree to potential managers. (By 1965, the company had gone public

MCDONALD'S MIDWEST The first McDonald's owned by Ray Kroc opened in 1955 in Des Plaines, Illinois, and copied the California design of that time. The building was decorated with red and white candy stripes. The arches were "golden" with yellow paint: a pair of arches rose through the sides of the roof and a single arch outlined the front sign with a Speedee figure symbolizing quick service. (Speedee was eliminated in 1962, at least partly because he resembled Bob's Big Boy and Speedy Alka-Seltzer.)

Fast and Faster Food

Drive-ins got America used to eating in the car. When the drive-ins faded in the 1950s, self-service fast-food "restaurants"—many franchised chains—took over.

- 1950 Dunkin' Donuts, started by William Rosenberg in Quincy, Massachusetts
- 1951 Jack in the Box, started by Robert O. Peterson in San Diego, California
- 1952 Church's Fried Chicken, started by George W. Church Sr., in San Antonio, Texas
- 1952 Kentucky Fried Chicken, started by Harland Sanders of Corbin, Kentucky; first outlet in Salt Lake City, Utah
- 1953 Burger King, started by Matthew Burns and Keith G. Cramer in Jacksonville, Florida
- 1954 Shakey's, started by Sherwood Johnson and Ed Plummer in Sacramento, California
- 1955 First McDonald's, opened by Ray Kroc in Des Plaines, Illinois
- 1955 Mister Donut, started by Harry Winokur in Revere, Massachusetts
- 1957 Gino's, started by Gino Marchetti in Baltimore, Maryland
- 1958 Pizza Hut, started by Frank and Dan Carney in Witchita, Kansas
- 1958 Burger Chef, started in Indianapolis, Indiana

---

and in 1966 was listed on the New York Stock Exchange.)

Meanwhile, in Sacramento, in 1954 an ex-GI named Sherwood "Shakey" Johnson and his partner Ed Plummer started the first franchised pizza chain. (Johnson got his nickname during a severe bout of malaria, which causes tremors.) Shakey's restaurant was an incongruous combination: the decor was English-style pub, the menu featured dark beer and thin-crust pizza, and the music was supplied by a live Dixieland band. But the chain caught on.

The Sixties: An Age of Contrasts

The curtain opened on the first scene of the decade: Camelot. The new president, John F. Kennedy, and his First Lady were charming the Europeans as well as the Americans. They joyfully refurbished the White House, and invited leading writers and artists of the day to dinners presided over by the eminent French chef René Verdon. World-famous musicians played concerts for them all.

When the curtain fell on the last scene, another new president, Richard M. Nixon, was engaged in peace talks to end the unpopular war with Vietnam that had escalated until U.S. troop strength peaked in April 1969 at 543,400. The nation was in turmoil. John Kennedy, his brother Robert, and civil-rights leader Martin Luther King, Jr., were dead at the hands of assassins. In November 1969, antiwar demonstrations reached a fever pitch when a quarter of a million protesters marched on Washington.

KENNEDY'S FRENCH CHEF When President and Mrs. John F. Kennedy moved into the White House in 1961, they brought René Verdon from France to run the kitchen. Born in France and trained in the classic French apprentice system, Verdon was White House chef until 1965. Afterward, he worked as consultant to the American kitchen appliance manufacturer Hamilton Beach and wrote a cookbook containing his favorite recipes. In April 1972, he realized what he called "every chef's dream" by opening his own restaurant, Le Trianon in downtown San Francisco. (AP Wide World Photo)

At the beginning of the decade, the United States had enjoyed peace for almost a decade despite the cold war with the Soviet Union. During 1961, President Kennedy severed diplomatic ties with Communist Cuba; later, he was embarrassed by the defeat of a U.S.-backed invasion that landed at Cuba's Bay of Pigs. The next year, however, Kennedy faced down Nikita Khrushchev, who was attempting to install offensive missiles in Cuba.

Below the Mason-Dixon line, lunch counters became civil-rights battlegrounds. Four black students from North Carolina Agricultural and Technical College staged the first sit-in at a Woolworth's lunch counter in 1960. By September of the next year, more than 70,000 students—both black and white—had participated in similar sit-ins. Washington, D.C., was the scene of a march in August 1963 of more than 200,000 supporters of civil rights for black Americans. And at last, in 1964, Congress passed a civil rights law giving blacks access to public facilities, including restaurants.

Chagrined by the Soviets' first manned space flight in April 1961, America vowed to send a man to the moon. Throughout the decade, Soviets and Americans exchanged records for the first space walk, first woman in space, longest

ADDING UP EGGS Chickens raised for meat or for egg-laying left the barnyard and moved indoors during the 1950s and 1960s. These chickens, which seem to be looking in puzzlement at the eggs before them, played a part in 1965 agricultural research. Scientists conducted a 280-day test with six strains of hens housed in three ways: one per cage, two per cage, and five in a double-sized cage. The conclusion: hens housed two per cage laid the most eggs.

DOUBLE THE PLEASURE Here's a genuine 1960 newspaper photograph showing what a publicist imagined would be the most elegant main course for a Christmas dinner: two small chickens (known as broiler-fryers in the parlance of the day) roasted and then gussied up with paper frills at the tips of their drumsticks. To add color touches, the platter is decorated with parsley and halves of canned peaches.

duration of flight, first spacecraft rendezvous, and the like, while the world held its breath, watching the proceedings on television. By the time Neil Armstrong took "one giant leap for mankind" in 1969, the country had invested $56 billion in the space race—and technology seemed the answer to all our problems.

PROSPERITY

As the gross national product almost doubled from $515 billion in 1960 to $930 billion in 1969, unemployment fell to 3.4 percent. Americans owned 61 million cars in 1960, but an astonishing 88 million by the end of the decade; meantime population rose from 179 to 203 million. Two-car families became commonplace, and some families—especially those with teenagers—had three or more vehicles. Almost a third of all Americans lived in the suburbs; the nation's median age was 30.2 years, and there were more young families than ever (on an average they had 1.58 children).

With paid vacations of two, three, or even four weeks, Americans had time to expand their horizons with trips to Europe, Latin America, even Asia. Travel abroad increased exponentially, from 676,000 international passengers in 1950, to 1,634,000 in 1960, and—with bigger airplanes and smaller fares—to 5,260,000 by 1970. The list of destinations read like a gazeteer, from Algeria to Zanzibar.

Where time and expense were no object, passengers could enjoy the luxury of an ocean liner; for less money but more time, they could go via tramp steamer. Otherwise, airplanes would whisk them from New York to London in eight or nine short hours, or from Los Angeles to Honolulu in about six hours. Charter planes and "no frills" flights brought the costs down to levels even college students could afford—and by pedaling bicycles they literally could "see Europe for $5 a day."

THE BOOM IN TEENAGERS

The first wave of baby boomers exploded into adolescence just as advertisers recognized their new earning power. Teenagers had allowances or earnings adequate to demonstrate their taste in clothing, music, movies, fast food, cars, and such. Surveys showed that they were a measurable customer base, distinct from their parents. Manufacturers and designers rushed to meet these special demands. Sales skyrocketed while parents bemoaned the "generation gap."

The baby boomers protested against "the establishment" by participating in civil-rights and antiwar demonstrations, or going off to communes. Or they danced the Frug in discotheques, discovered singles' bars, and experimented with marijuana at rock concerts. The excitement and chaos and gaiety of the Woodstock Music and Arts Festival in upstate New York, where 400,000 gathered in the summer of 1969, was a fitting coda to the decade.

College enrollment, which had soared in the years after World War II, doubled in this decade. The economic and social advantages of those college educations provided to their parents by the GI Bill were obvious. This time, most students could afford to pay their own tuition; those who couldn't, found scholarships and financial aid.

The total number of degrees granted increased from 479,215 in 1960 to 833,322 in 1970. And the ratio of men to women

MERINGUE TARTS Ladies' bridge clubs preserved tearoom cuisine after these had fallen victim to fast-food chains. Even if every member of the club were dieting, its luncheon menu included a dessert such as these delicate, baked meringue cases filled with slices of fresh strawberries.

DINNER ON A SPIT As cooks became familiar with barbecue grills and learned how to deal with the coals, the foods they tried began to vary—and grow more sophisticated. One of the most popular kinds of grilled foods was the kabob. Cooks could make it with beef, lamb, pork, even chicken, and such vegetables as tomatoes, peppers, zucchini, and onions in different combinations.

Beef Wellington

The extravagance of the ingredients—a whole beef tenderloin, truffles, Madeira, pâté—gave this entree a glamour few other main courses could boast. In the 1960s "everybody" made it, at least once, despite its complexity and the difficulty of presenting beef at the desired degree of doneness in pastry that was still crisp. The duxelles, sauce, and pastry can be prepared a day ahead, if desired.

DUXELLES
1 1/2 pounds fresh mushrooms, chopped fine
4 shallots, chopped fine
6 tablespoons (3/4 stick) butter
3 tablespoons finely chopped fresh parsley
TRUFFLE SAUCE
2 tablespoons (1/4 stick) butter
1 1/2 cups beef stock
1 tablespoon cornstarch
1/3 cup Madeira
1 truffle, chopped
Salt and pepper
PASTRY
2/3 cup lard
2/3 cup butter
4 cups all-purpose flour
8 to 12 tablespoons cold water
ROAST
1 whole beef tenderloin, trimmed of all fat and tied at tip (about 3 pounds)
Salt and pepper
1/2 cup (1 stick) butter
1 can (5 ounces) pâté de foie gras
1 egg, separated, yolk beaten with 1 tablespoon water

For the duxelles, sauté the mushrooms and shallots in butter until almost dry. Stir in parsley and continue cooking until all moisture is gone. Cover and refrigerate.

For the truffle sauce (SAUCE PERIGUEUX), melt butter in saucepan with stock over low heat. Blend in cornstarch dissolved in Madeira. Stir until sauce thickens, then add truffle and season with salt and pepper. Cover and refrigerate.

For the pastry, cut the butter and lard into the flour with a pastry blender or in a food processor until mixture resembles coarse meal. Add just enough cold water—a tablespoon at a time—to work mixture into a ball. Wrap and refrigerate.

Preheat the oven to 425°F. Bring duxelles, sauce, and tenderloin to room temperature. Season beef with salt and pepper, then rub with butter and roast on rack for 20 minutes or until beef reaches internal temperature of 120°F when tested with a meat thermometer. Set the beef aside to cool to room temperature, but leave oven at 425°F.

Stir the pâté into the duxelles. Moisten lightly with 1 or 2 tablespoons of sauce, then taste for seasoning.

Roll out pastry into a rectangle about 15 inches long and 10 inches wide; it should be large enough to encase the tenderloin. Spread the duxelles over the pastry, leaving a 1-inch margin all around. Place beef upside down on pastry and fold pastry over it. Brush seam and ends with egg white to seal them.

Place tenderloin with seam side down on a large baking sheet. Brush pastry with egg yolk, and prick with a fork to form diagonal lines across wrapping. Bake for 10 minutes, then reduce heat to 375° and bake until crust is golden—about 20 minutes longer.

Let beef stand 10 minutes before carving into 1/2-inch slices. Warm the sauce over low heat and present it with the beef.

Serves 12 generously

---

students changed from about two men for every one woman in 1960 to approximately one for one in 1970.

WOMEN'S LIBERATION

In 1963, Betty Friedan's *The Feminine Mystique* appeared, challenging the social order and accelerating the acceptance of

Salmon Mousse

In a decade of party-giving, hostesses wanted foods like this mousse, which looked elegant and could be prepared in advance.

1 lemon
1 envelope unflavored gelatin
1/2 cup boiling water
1/2 cup mayonnaise
1/4 teaspoon paprika
1 teaspoon dried dill weed
1 can (16 ounces) salmon, drained
1 cup heavy cream
Watercress, for garnish

With a parer, remove a strip of peel about 1/2 inch wide and 2 inches long from the lemon; set strip aside. Halve and squeeze the lemon, then strain juice into a food blender or processor. Sprinkle in gelatin. After it softens in a few minutes, add lemon peel and boiling water and blend until smooth. Add mayonnaise, paprika, dill, and salmon. Blend briefly.

Add cream, 1/3 cup at a time, blending after each addition. Pour into a 1-quart mold, cover, and refrigerate for 4 hours or until firm. Unmold and garnish with watercress.

Serves 4

Quiche Lorraine

Real men ate this rich custard pie in the 1960s, when few of them worried about cholesterol. Quiche was a stylish first course at dinner or main course at lunch. Creative cooks added vegetables such as chopped boiled spinach or sautéed onions, used boiled shrimp or scallops instead of bacon, and substituted cheddar for Gruyère.

6 bacon slices, cut into 1/4-inch pieces
2 eggs, plus 2 egg yolks
1 1/2 cups heavy cream
1/4 teaspoon ground nutmeg
Ground white pepper
3/4 cup freshly grated Gruyère cheese
9-inch partly baked pastry shell

Preheat the oven to 350°F. Fry bacon pieces until crisp; drain on paper towels. In a bowl, beat eggs, egg yolks, cream, and nutmeg. Add a little white pepper, then stir in cheese. Sprinkle bacon into pastry shell and pour in egg mixture. Bake for 30 to 35 minutes or until surface is puffy and a knife inserted into the center comes out clean.

Serves 4 to 6

---

new attitudes. Women formed support groups to talk about being "liberated" from stereotypical roles.

Thousands of women still stayed at home—or at the wheel of the family car, shuttling children to dancing classes and Boy Scout meetings. But about 40 percent of women worked in 1960, taking full-time as well as part-time jobs.

By 1970 almost half of all women worked outside the home—and constituted 37 percent of the U.S. work force. Filling these dual roles was simplified by convenience foods—and by such modern miracles as permanent-press fabrics, which virtually eliminated any need for a family to own an iron.

FINDING JOY IN COOKING

Paradoxically, in a time when precooked frozen entrees were proliferating, food editor Craig Claiborne noted in the *New York Times* that there had never been "such an absorbing interest in fine cuisine in the home as there is in this decade."

Weekdays, putting food on the table was considered "woman's work." To get it

Chicken Breasts Veronique

3 chicken breasts, skinned, boned, and halved
1 teaspoon salt
Ground white pepper
3 tablespoons butter
2 teaspoons chopped fresh tarragon, or 1 teaspoon dried
1 cup plus 6 clusters seedless green grapes
1 cup dry white wine
1 tablespoon flour
1 cup light cream
2 egg yolks, lightly beaten
6 slices toast

Preheat oven to 325°F. Rub chicken breasts with salt and pepper, and brown all sides in butter in an ovenproof skillet. Sprinkle with tarragon, then add 1 cup of grapes and the wine. Bake uncovered for 30 minutes or until chicken is done.
Remove chicken from skillet and cover to keep it warm. Off the heat, stir the flour into the pan drippings, add the cream, then the egg yolks. Stir until this sauce is thick and smooth. Return chicken to skillet and cook over low heat for 5 minutes. Do not let the sauce boil. Serve chicken on toast, garnished with clusters of grapes.
Serves 6

Guacamole

Not only was the avocado delicious to eat, but it had a pit that could be coaxed to sprout and produce a unique, if gangling, house plant. The modern young cook of the 1960s ate it up!

2 large avocados, halved, pitted, peeled, and diced
1 small onion, finely chopped
1 medium tomato, peeled, seeded, and finely chopped
1 teaspoon chopped fresh coriander (cilantro)
1 tablespoon lemon juice
Salt and pepper
Salad greens

Mix the avocado with the onion, tomato, coriander, and lemon juice. Season with salt and pepper. Arrange salad greens on individual plates and spoon guacamole onto them.
Serves 4

Sausage Pinwheels

This "show-off" hors d'oeuvre looks impressive, but is simplicity itself to assemble.

Baking powder biscuit dough, made with 2 cups Bisquick
1 pound ground sausage meat

Roll out dough into two rectangles, each about 8 by 12 inches. Divide meat and spread one half on each rectangle. Starting at the wide end, roll up dough into cylinders about 12 inches long. Wrap and chill for at least 1 hour to make slicing easy.
Preheat oven to 375°F. To bake, cut slices 1/2 inch thick and put on baking sheets. Bake for 15 to 20 minutes or until sausage cooks through and biscuit dough is golden brown. Drain on paper towels. Serve hot.
Makes about 50 slices

---

done on time, she might rely heavily on mixes and freezers for her menus. But on weekends and holidays, families enjoyed cooking as well as eating together. The weekend brunch was born. Men began to do more than grill an occasional steak, and kitchens often were planned so that a husband and wife might cook side by side.

Entertaining became more elegant. Couples formed gourmet clubs for mutual enjoyment of elaborately prepared foods. As with the potluck supper of the 1940s, all the guests cooked something, but a gourmet club meal was carefully and imaginatively planned, and each couple brought a prearranged part of it. Favorite main courses were *Coq au Vin* (cooking with wine was a new technique) and Beef Wellington. Anything with crepes made a classy dessert.

DRESSING UP DINNER When the look of food began to matter almost as much as how it tasted, cooks tried their hands at dishes like this: planked steak topped by a reverent row of sautéed mushroom slices and surrounded by gobs of Duchess potatoes, piped from a pastry bag. (Cheating culinarily, but speedier than starting from scratch, the potatoes could be concocted from an instant variety.)

THE BERRIES OF JUNE What better way to celebrate the first day of summer than with homemade strawberry shortcake smothered with freshly whipped cream. Back in 1963 practically nobody had heard of cholesterol—and shortcake was in demand.

GRILLED FRUIT Once the 1960s cook got the barbecue coals hot, any and every part of the meal might come from the grill. Hors d'oeuvre could be barbecued, stuffed mushrooms or bacon-wrapped clams or oysters. Vegetables like potatoes and corn were cooked alongside salmon or beef steaks. And the triumphant dessert might be kabobs likes these—pieces of fruit that were marinated briefly in honeyed fruit juice, then threaded onto skewers, and grilled five minutes or so. Any firm fruit would serve, including whole strawberries or grapes, cubes of pineapple, segments of tangerine or orange, chunks of banana or apple.

Cooking was an outlet for the creative energies of young housewives who might have felt housebound with only a baby—or 1.58 babies—for company. Author and screen-writer Nora Ephron summed it up, "Everybody loved you for cooking, and they got to eat it at the end of the day."

Kneading bread dough and rolling puff pastry turned out to be easier than anyone had suspected—and much more rewarding. With guidance from *The Art of Fine Baking* by the ebullient Paula Peck, thousands of cooks transformed tons of flour, sugar, butter and eggs into

A SALAD IN A SOUP Loving iced soups as they did, Americans were quick to appreciate the pleasures of Spanish gazpacho. Here, the soup bowl stands in front of a basket holding the kinds of vegetables also in the soup: tomato, pepper, celery, cucumber, scallion, and white onion. Besides the cucumber slices floating on the soup there are ice cubes to keep it frigid.

mountains of tarts, strudels, braided rings, and brioche. Families who had never before heard of *gâteaux* now enjoyed them after dinner.

(When time needed saving, of course, cooks could finish a mix-made *gâteau* with the new canned frostings. And Poppin' Fresh, the Pillsbury Doughboy created in 1965 by Rudy Perz of the Leo Burnett advertising agency in Chicago, reminded them that they could rely on refrigerated dough for biscuits, breads, and cookies.)

AN EXPANDING LARDER

Almost all kinds of familiar vegetables and fruits were available fresh year-round in

Ratatouille

1 medium eggplant, peeled and cut crosswise into 1/2-inch slices
Salt
1 large onion, sliced
2 garlic cloves, chopped
1/4 cup olive oil
2 medium zucchini, cut crosswise into 1/4-inch slices
2 medium green peppers, seeded, cored, and cut into 1/4-inch strips
5 medium tomatoes, peeled, seeded, and cut into chunks
1 tablespoon drained capers
Freshly ground black pepper

Salt the eggplant slices generously and put them between paper towels to drain. Meanwhile, sauté the onion and garlic in the oil until translucent but not brown.

Rinse the eggplant, dry it well, and cut it into cubes. Add eggplant, zucchini, and peppers to onion, cover, and cook over low heat for about 1 hour.

Add the tomatoes and simmer uncovered until mixture is thick. Stir in capers, then season to taste with pepper, and salt if needed. Serve hot or cold.

Serves 4 to 6

Orange and Onion Salad

Improbable as this odd couple may seem, the sweetness of oranges and the tartness of onions blend to make a perfect marriage.

6 navel oranges
6 tablespoons olive oil
1 tablespoon lemon juice
Salt and pepper
2 red onions, sliced thin and separated into rings
Assorted lettuces, torn into pieces to make 6 cups

Working over a bowl to save juice, peel oranges and remove bitter white outer membrane. Slice oranges thin. Mix orange juice with olive oil, lemon juice, and salt and pepper to taste. Toss the greens together in a salad bowl. Arrange orange slices on the greens and top with onion rings. Pour orange-juice dressing over all. Present salad at the table before tossing ingredients together.

Serves 6

the 1960s—but the price might be steep indeed. Although asparagus was more abundant in April and pears in September, most big-city produce counters never lacked such formerly "seasonal" crops. Even in small-town markets, cooks found artichokes, lettuce, strawberries, and tomatoes in every month.

New kinds of vegetables and fruits arrived at markets everywhere. Northerners discovered the delights of Georgia's Vidalia onion. Formerly "ethnic" favorites such as sorrel, leeks, and shallots became generally available. Frieda's Finest, a Los Angeles produce specialty company founded by Frieda Caplan, introduced California brown mushrooms and, in 1962, kiwifruit from New Zealand.

Although fresh produce, especially in its local season, always tasted best—and had more cachet—its frozen counterparts had the intrinsic advantage of being already washed and trimmed. With vegetables such as lima beans, which are so time-consuming to shell, the effort saved was significant. To eliminate more steps, some frozen vegetables came already sauced, and frozen fruits were often presweetened or mixed for fruit cocktail.

Flavorings went beyond the pepper and salt of the 1940s, even the garlic that more courageous cooks began using in the 1950s. In the 1960s, herbs—oregano, basil, tarragon, and thyme among them—came into fashion. Growing them in the backyard garden or a window box was the mark of a dedicated cook.

For kids, and their compliant mothers, Tang instant orange juice powder, introduced in 1958, was becoming the way to start the day. For them, the big news of 1965 may have been the introduction of SpaghettiOs—"the O-shaped spaghetti kids could eat with a spoon."

MEATS AND FISH

Beef was by far the most favored meat, accounting for half the consumption of 145 pounds meat per capita in 1960 and 163 pounds in 1970. But poultry was finding increased acceptance—sales per capita rising from 34 to 48 pounds, mostly of chicken.

Although Vatican II, in February 1966, freed Roman Catholics from the need to abstain from meat on Fridays, old habits seemed to die hard. Fish consumption all during the decade stayed at 14 or 15 pounds per capita per year (a figure that included 4 or 5 pounds of fish caught by sport fishermen). The new industry of "farming" fish, particularly catfish and

---

Sangria

This Spanish drink made from red wine, fruits and sometimes brandy was popularized at the Spanish Pavilion at the 1964 New York World's Fair.

1 bottle dry red wine
2 teaspoons sugar, dissolved in 3 ounces (6 tablespoons) brandy
1 lemon, sliced
1/2 orange, sliced
12 ounces club soda

Stir ingredients together. Taste for sweetness, then add ice cubes and chill for 20 to 30 minutes. In pouring, be sure each glass gets a slice of fruit and ice cubes.
Serves 6

Rediscovering an Old Cuisine

The civil-rights movement fueled enormous interest in "soul food," a term nostalgic northern blacks coined in the 1960s. Originated in the South, soul food was the creation of slaves who had invented it out of leftovers and just about any other edible ingredient they could scrounge.

Over the years, dishes changed; which ones were genuine became the subject of intense arguments and angry letters to the editors of newspapers. As Bob Jeffries declared in his SOUL FOOD COOKBOOK, published in 1969, "All soul food is Southern, but not all Southern food is soul." Meanwhile, cooks both black and white experimented with everything from chitterlings and shin-bone stew to fried chicken and barbecued ribs. Supermarkets were asked to stock vegetables that the recipes called for: black-eyed peas, okra, turnip and collard greens. Sweet-potato pie probably won over the most adherents to the cuisine.

---

trout, ensured cooks of fresh—perhaps live—products.

BEVERAGES

Milk became easier to carry home from the market after the plastic container was introduced in 1964. But milk consumption dropped, and changed character: skim milk and low-fat milk represented less than 5 percent of sales in 1960, but more than 18 percent in 1970. Carnation Milk helped coffee drinkers keep cream on hand when they introduced the dried product Coffee-Mate in 1961.

More families drank wine with food—even when they were not entertaining. And wine became the obligatory offering that dinner guests brought to their hosts; it was often considered necessary to respond to the gift by opening the wine, whether or not it complemented the food. In the then-rigid rules, only red wine was drunk with meat and only white with poultry or fish. The best news of the decade may have been that Americans were establishing many new wineries, not only in California, but also in Oregon, Washington, New York, even Michigan. And American wines were beginning to challenge the imports in quality.

COOKING ON TELEVISION

European cuisines grew in popularity with the help of cooks like Julia Child. Her book, *Mastering the Art of French Cooking*, written in collaboration with Simone Beck and Louisette Bertholle, appeared in 1961. Child's television show, which debuted in 1963 and ran until 1973, aimed to take the mystery out of preparing French foods—and succeeded, largely due to Child's charm and her seemingly casual approach to the subject. The show was an instant hit. When Joyce Chen went on television a few years later to demonstrate Chinese cooking techniques, she was sometimes referred to as the "Chinese Julia Child."

In 1969, a handsome young chef

Salade Niçoise

This is a recipe where cooks could add, subtract, or substitute to taste. Tuna is the one ingredient every cook agreed on. Additions included boiled potatoes, pimiento, roasted peppers, or cooked artichoke hearts, for example. Cherry tomatoes substituted for tomato wedges and rolled anchovies for flat ones.

1 cup olive oil
1/4 cup white wine vinegar
1 small garlic clove, finely chopped
1/2 teaspoon dry mustard
Salt
Freshly ground black pepper
1 pound green beans, freshly cooked
Salad greens
2 cans (7 ounces) tuna, drained and broken into chunks
2 medium green peppers, seeded, cored and cut into thin strips
1 large onion, thinly sliced
2 large tomatoes, cored and cut into wedges
3 hard-cooked eggs, quartered
1 can (2 ounces) flat anchovies, drained and soaked in cold water for 5 minutes
1/2 cup black olives, pitted

Combine oil, vinegar, garlic, and mustard; stir until mustard dissolves. Add salt and pepper to taste. Pour this dressing over beans, and marinate, refrigerated, for about 1 hour.

To assemble salad, line a bowl with greens. Drain beans, saving marinade. Place tuna in bowl. Arrange beans, peppers, onion, and tomatoes around it. Garnish with eggs, anchovies, and olives. Pour marinade over all. Present the salad, then toss ingredients together at the table.

Serves 6

Coeur à la Crème

A sumptuous French treat, this is the perfect foil for fresh berries. Lacking the traditional heart-shaped mold, line any perforated container such as a colander or sieve with cheesecloth.

1 pound cream cheese
1/2 cup superfine sugar
1 teaspoon vanilla extract
2 tablespoons heavy cream, plus 1/2 cup, whipped
Fresh strawberries or raspberries

Soften the cream cheese at room temperature. Beat in 2 tablespoons cream, then fold in whipped cream. Spoon mixture into heart-shaped wicker or porcelain mold lined with cheesecloth. Set mold over pan to catch drippings, and refrigerate overnight. Unmold the heart onto a serving plate and surround it with berries.

Serves 4

---

from Australia, Graham Kerr, went on television as the Galloping Gourmet. Unlike the Child show, which was prepared for public broadcasting and shown in the evening, Kerr's was a daytime show with commercial sponsors. His inventiveness and élan earned him a contract for $4 million for three and a half years. It also entranced viewers, who were devastated when he left television in 1973.

COOKBOOKS

As cooks tried to reproduce the foods they had discovered in restaurants in America or abroad, formal recipes became indispensable. Newspapers increased their attention to food. Magazines attempted to provide readers with answers to their culinary problems; *Gourmet* undertook to get recipes from chefs for dishes its readers wanted to duplicate at home.

Cookbooks sold by the tens of thousands. Cooks started collecting them; cookbooks became bedtime reading. Interest in French food spurred the 1961

CHEF CHARMING During the 1960s, the Australian chef Graham Kerr cajoled and joked his way to television stardom. His daytime show was watched as faithfully as were the soap operas it replaced. Kerr's greatest contribution to American cooking may have been that he gave housewives the courage to use wines in food.

publication not only of the Julia Child book but also *Gourmet's Basic French Cookbook* by Louis Diat and an American edition of *Larousse Gastronomique*, the French cook's bible.

During the decade, books about Italian cooking ran second only to French, but readers found volumes about national cuisines ranging from German and Swedish to Turkish and Indian. In 1968, Time-Life Books initiated the ambitious *Foods of the World* series that would eventually include twenty-seven volumes, produced under the direction of editor Richard L. Williams and Consultant Michael Field. Stressing authenticity, the series not only covered the expected cuisines such as those of France and Italy, but also dealt with food from exotic places like Southeast Asia and Africa.

In addition to bringing out books about national dishes, publishers listed titles on such special subjects as casseroles, stews, brunches, and hors

Fettuccine Alfredo

Although most Americans had not heard of this pasta dish until the 1960s, John F. Mariani's DICTIONARY OF AMERICAN FOOD AND DRINK reports it was created in the 1920s by Roman restaurateur Alfredo di Lellio. Lacking a chafing dish or electric skillet, prepare the fettuccine at the stove and bring it to the table in a heated bowl.

12 ounces fettuccine
Salt
3 tablespoons butter, cut into pieces
1 cup heavy cream
1 egg yolk
1 cup freshly grated Parmesan cheese
Nutmeg, preferably freshly grated
Freshly ground black pepper

Boil fettuccine in a large pot of salted water until barely tender—al dente. Drain fettuccine well and put it in a deep pan or chafing dish or into electric skillet. At table, set fettuccine over moderately high heat, and stir in butter. While it melts, blend in cream, then egg yolk. When fettuccine is hot and evenly coated with cream mixture, stir in Parmesan. Add generous amounts of nutmeg and black pepper, and a bit of salt. Mix well. Serve at once.
Serves 4

Lamb Curry

Cooks in the South began preparing curries in the nineteenth century; one favorite was Country Captain, which flavors chicken with tomatoes as well as premixed curry powder. In the 1960s, most recipes still called for curry powder instead of individual spices. One favorite type gave meat extra tang with apples and lemons.

3 pounds boneless lamb, cut into bite-size cubes
1/2 cup vegetable oil
4 large onions, chopped
6 garlic cloves, chopped
2 tablespoons curry powder
2 lemons, sliced
4 apples, peeled, cored, and chopped
1 1/2 cups chicken stock
1 teaspoon salt
1/4 teaspoon black pepper
2 cups white rice, boiled
Chutney

In a large skillet, brown the lamb in the oil, a small batch at a time. Set lamb aside. Sauté onions and garlic in oil remaining in skillet until soft but not brown. Stir in curry powder and cook over low heat for 5 minutes. Return lamb to skillet and stir in lemons, apples, stock, salt, and pepper. Bring to a boil, reduce heat, cover, and simmer for 1 hour. Check seasoning and add more curry powder, if needed. Simmer 30 to 40 minutes longer, or until meat is tender; lemons and apples will cook down to form a sauce. Serve with rice and chutney.
Serves 6

d'oeuvre. In a 1969 feature in the *New York Times*, Marcia Seligson bemoaned the fact that cookbooks had become big business: "At the moment there are over 1,200 cookbooks in print...In 1968 twice as many cookbooks were published as the year before. Three of the top 10 best-sellers for the year were cookbooks (*Better Homes and Gardens New Cookbook*, which was Number One, *Eat and Stay Slim* and *The Weight Watchers' Cookbook*)." It should be noted that nobody kept track of the growing number of fund-raising cookbooks produced by charities and other social organizations.

COOKING SCHOOLS

Better than learning from a television show or a book was to attend a class where the cook had a real-live instructor

Forager for Food

Euell Theophilus Gibbons, born in 1911 in Texas, had lived as a beachcomber and hobo as well as a teacher, surveyor, and boat-builder before he settled down to write books. His dream was to be a novelist; instead, he became a chronicler of America's bountiful wild food. After STALKING THE WILD ASPARAGUS was published in 1962, he became a hero to naturalists and natural-food proponents alike. His book was treated like a field guide and his poetic writing stirred up interest in the environment while his recipes produced savory foods. Gibbons also wrote of STALKING THE BLUE-EYED SCALLOP (1964), STALKING THE HEALTHFUL HERBS and STALKING THE GOOD LIFE (both 1966); EUELL GIBBONS' BEACHCOMBER'S HANDBOOK and A WILD WAY TO EAT appeared in 1967. Gibbons died at his home in Snyder County, Pennsylvania, in 1975.

---

who could answer questions. During the 1960s, cooking schools grew in number. By the end of the decade there were one or two in most big cities and some small ones. In Manhattan, James Beard and Grace Chu kept on teaching. During 1969, New Yorkers had a choice of fifteen schools ranging from the YWCA's Ballard School to $150 four-hour private lessons with Helen Worth, who also held classes during lunchtime for small groups of businessmen.

LIVING OFF THE EARTH

The most interesting place to find foods, as propounded by Euell Gibbons in his 1962 book *Stalking the Wild Asparagus*, was a cook's backyard. Sunflowers and daylilies, wild berries and nuts were there for the taking, and yielded everything from vegetable dishes to jams and wines.

Young men and women who rebelled against the constraints of living in cities

HEALTHFUL FOOD, 1960S STYLE In a day when mothers taught their children that "an apple a day keeps the doctor away," a Waldorf salad qualified as health food. Invented in the Gay Nineties by Oscar Tschirky, maître d'hôtel at New York's Waldorf-Astoria from 1893 to 1943, the original salad contained apples, celery, and "good" mayonnaise, served on lettuce. By the 1920s walnuts were a standard ingredient. Nobody knows when marshmallows were added, but the children certainly enjoyed them.

THE SIXTIES: AN AGE OF CONTRASTS

Pioneer Environmentalist

"Chemicals are the sinister and little-recognized partners of radiation in changing the very nature of the world—the very nature of life," warned biologist and writer Rachel Carson. Born in 1907, Carson graduated from the Pennsylvania College for Women, Pittsburgh, got a master's degree at Johns Hopkins, and studied at Woods Hole in Massachusetts. From 1936 to 1952, she worked as aquatic biologist and publications editor for the U.S. Fish and Wildlife Service in Washington, D.C. Her first book, UNDER THE SEA, was published in 1942. Her second—THE SEA AROUND US—appeared in 1951 and made her world famous. However, she is best remembered for the 1962 SILENT SPRING, which touched off arguments about pesticides that continue to this day. Carson died in 1964.

---

and working for large companies often considered Gibbons's work a survival guide. Many formed communes and rented or bought farms where they could "get back to nature." Most of these experiments died within a few years, but their supporters became the core of a larger group concerned with the new science of ecology.

Other new cooks formed buying cooperatives to reduce the cost of groceries and develop sources for such "natural" products as whole wheat flour. Rachel Carson showed the dangers of DDT and other pesticides in her epic *Silent Spring* (1962). Herbicides and chemical fertilizers caused concerns too. Food grown organically—that is, without chemicals of any kind—was sought after even if the apples had worms or the carrots were misshapen.

Brown rice and brown bread became the symbols of hip. "Don't eat white; eat right and fight" was an underground slogan directed against Wonder Bread and Cool Whip as well as white-collar society and the White House.

ADDITIVES OR ADULTERANTS

Back in 1958, the Food and Drug Administration had approved use by food manufacturers of additives including several hundred that had been tested and previously sanctioned and about 700 that could be "generally regarded as safe"—the infamous GRAS list. Colorings and flavorings were not the only ingredients approved. There were anti-caking substances that went into sugar and salt to lengthen their shelf life, sequestrants to stop trace minerals from clouding soft drinks or making fats or oils rancid, emulsifiers to help homogenize milk and shortenings, synthetic sweeteners, and more.

During the 1960s, nutrition gained prestige as a science. Consumer groups organized to work for nutrition labeling. The terms "junk food" and "empty calorie" (a calorie containing no nutrients) were coined as disagreement grew about the merits of "chemical" versus "natural" foods. Finally in 1969, the world became alarmed about two additives: monosodium glutamate (MSG), a natural flavor enhancer extracted from seaweed, and a synthetic sweetener called cyclamate.

MSG had been used in Asia for hundreds of years; vegetarians relied on it to add flavor to bland dishes, and other cooks used it to revivify wilted vegetables. But some diners have allergic reactions to MSG. Although commonly known as Chinese Restaurant Syndrome because MSG was favored by Chinese chefs, the allergy is properly called Kwok's Disease for Dr. Robert Ho Man Kwok, who first tracked down its source. Tests in 1969 also led scientists to discover that MSG caused brain damage in infant mice. As a result, baby food manufacturers stopped adding it to their products.

More frightening, perhaps, was the discovery that cyclamates caused cancer in rats. Although doses injected during testing had been massive, cyclamates were ordered off the market in the U.S.

Many scientists questioned the research behind the discoveries about MSG and cyclamates, pointing out that salt was more widely used and more dangerous; that sugar led to obesity; that spinach and rhubarb carry oxalic acid that might form kidney stones. People have been poisoned by or have reacted allergically to everything from almonds to zucchini.

True, products like Twinkies had ingredient lists that read like a chemistry book—sodium acid pyrophosphate or polysorbate 60 don't sound like Mom's cooking. But in a chemist's eyes, food as natural as a melon contained anisyl proprionate and amyl acetate, which would seem just as mysterious to most cooks.

The debates didn't stop in the 1960s, but at the end of the decade, MSG was left in many manufactured foods and was still available retail as a taste powder. Cyclamates have been upstaged now by new synthetic sweeteners.

YELLOW MARGARINE

Truman had removed the federal tax from margarine a decade before, but the governor of Wisconsin still made news when he signed a bill in May 1967, legalizing the sale of yellow-colored margarine in that state. (Back in 1947, selling yellow margarine had been illegal in twenty-two states, but one by one the states had relented. Wisconsin held out longest.)

The Wisconsin State Senator who led the fight against margarine, Gordon W. Roseleip, had agreed to take a blindfold test to prove he could recognize the difference in taste between margarine and butter. He failed, thereby discrediting his cause in the eyes of many of his constituents. However, years after his death, his daughter confessed that the Senator's family had been trying to help control his weight by feeding him margarine at home—without telling him.

SLIM IS BEAUTIFUL

On fashion pages, the lank, leggy look was glorified, bringing with it a diet craze that has not burned out yet. The prize example of femininity was Twiggy (Lesley Hornby),

FROZEN DINNERS FOR DIETERS Jean Nidetch was the best advertisement for the Weight Watchers program she founded. And this 1969 store poster features her—slim and smiling—to announce the company's introduction of low-calorie frozen dinners, a novelty at that time.

WEIGHT WATCHERS

To overcome the problems of going it alone on a diet, Jean Nidetch and Albert Lippert founded Weight Watchers International, Inc. in May 1963. A Queens, New York, housewife, Nidetch had worn a size 44 dress two years before when she went to a Manhattan clinic for weight-loss guidance. To help herself lose weight, she organized a support group by sharing her new knowledge with friends at a weekly meeting in her apartment. By the time she had pared down to size 12, the group had grown to forty members—and Nidetch had developed a unique weight-loss concept. Lippert, who was to become her business partner, had been one of the group and lost 40 pounds; his wife Felice lost 50 pounds.

a sixteen-year-old Cockney with long legs and no bust, who became the star model of the 1960s.

Scores of do-it-yourself books were published about how to lose weight—some featuring off-beat diets consisting chiefly of steak or grapefruit and many failing to provide fundamental dietary elements. Common wisdom was that potential danger from the diets was mitigated by the fact that most provided such uninteresting food nobody would stick to them for long. Unfortunately, dieting did develop into a compulsion for some—especially teenage women—and everyday vocabulary included the words *anorexic*, for persons who dieted to the point of starvation, and *bulemic*, for those who "binged and purged" by overeating, then vomiting.

FITNESS AROUND THE CLOCK The breakfast tray at the Golden Door spa in Escondido, California, came with a "clock" for that day's schedule of exercises, beauty treatments, and massages. The diet was simple and healthful—with an abundance of fresh fruits and vegetables.

KITCHEN CULTURE

The first commercial meeting of Weight Watchers was held in a loft in Queens. Although not advertised, word of mouth spread so far that 400 people attended. Within a few years, former members had purchased franchises and were operating Weight Watchers programs across the country. In 1968, the company introduced four frozen entrees based on sole, flounder, haddock, and halibut. Beef and turkey were added the next year. (By 1990 Weight Watchers had forty-one entrees—everything from Italian cheese lasagna to chicken fettuccine—sixteen desserts and thirteen breakfast items in their frozen food line, and their label appeared on grocery products ranging from bread to yogurt.)

AEROBICS

Watching the outdoorsy Kennedys sail and play touch football, Americans concluded that exercise could be fun. The President's Council on Physical Fitness stimulated interest in sports; calisthenics, and the gymnasiums in which to do them, enjoyed new popularity. And in 1968 Dr. Kenneth H. Cooper, a former major in the U.S. Air Force, wrote *Aerobics*—a best-seller that launched "The World's Most Popular Physical Fitness Program."

The next year Jacki Sorensen choreographed the first aerobic dances when asked to host a television exercise show for the air force base in Puerto Rico where her husband was stationed. Sorensen had been a dancer since childhood and her immediate reaction to Cooper's program was to interpret it in dance. Her routines met favorable response so she continued the dances

THE CHAFING DISH The centerpiece of the 1960s buffet party table was the chafing dish. The flame beneath the bottom pan would keep a treat like Coq au Vin or Shrimp à la Newburg piping hot. And when the time came for dessert, the flame burned bright enough to warm brandy for igniting Crepes Suzette.

until 1971 when she gave her first public courses. By 1980 Aerobic Dancing, Inc., could boast of more than 50,000 students nationwide.

FITNESS SPAS

A classy, and classic, way to get fit was to visit a spa. The archetypal European spa was a resort built near natural mineral waters believed to have a curative effect. (In fact, the word comes from the Belgian resort town called Spa.) Following that tradition, Americans had built such mineral water resort spas as the Greenbrier, at White Sulphur Springs in West Virginia (established just after the American Revolution) and French Lick Springs in Indiana.

Besides soaking in the water or being

Prince of Pots and Pans

During the 1950s, Fred Bridge began to sell professional kitchenware at retail in his New York City store, and home cooks found a diversity of equipment they never dreamed existed. Here at last were utensils and tools in every size, shape, and material: molds for cookies and pastries, pots to hold a cupful or many gallons, slicers and dicers, peelers and graters, cleavers and knives, shredders and strainers. When Craig Claiborne, who was food editor of the NEW YORK TIMES, discovered Bridge, he dubbed him "Prince of Pots and Pans."

---

packed in mud made from it, guests could get massages and beauty treatments, try steam rooms and saunas, and take part in various sports and healthful athletic endeavors.

Fitness spas, however, were modern and came into vogue during the 1960s. The paradigm was Rancho La Puerta at Tecate, Baja California, Mexico, started in 1940 by Dr. Edmond Bordeaux Szekely and his bride, Deborah. (For a time the camp was so rustic that guests were asked to bring their own tents.) The ranch's program was simple: eat natural food, exercise every day, and stay stress-free. As the spa's popularity grew, the Szekelys evolved what would later be called "spa cuisine"—flavorful dishes low in calories and high in nutrients.

The diet and exercise helped guests lose weight in such a pleasant way that dozens of fitness spas—irreverently called "fat farms"—were opened nationwide. Among the new spas was the ultra-sybaritic Golden Door, which the Szekelys opened in Escondido, California (1958). The first developer-inspired spa began in 1962. It was possible for couples to go together to La Costa Resort and Spa near Carlsbad, California, even if one party wanted facials and low-calorie meals while the other preferred to play tennis and enjoy ice cream sundaes. Movie and television stars and directors were enthusiastic supporters of this innovation.

POTS AND PANS

As home cooking grew serious, so did the equipment needed. Sophisticated cooks soon found their pots and pans inadequate for the complicated recipes they intended to follow. Hardware and houseware stores did not carry the fancy baking and dessert molds, flan rings, springform pans, whisks, nutmeg graters, and other specialized equipment. Restaurant suppliers sold many of these items, but they were wholesalers, not retailers, and were ill-prepared—if not downright unwilling—to deal with small orders from amateur chefs.

Soon cooks were discovering stores like the Bridge Company (now Bridge Kitchenware) operated by Fred Bridge in New York City, or Williams-Sonoma run by Charles E. Williams in San Francisco. Bridge started work in the wholesale kitchenware market in 1933. After serving in World War II, he opened his own store and imported much of his kitchenware directly from Europe. When the first amateurs began to cook seriously, Bridge offered them the same equipment he was selling to professionals.

Williams turned a hardware business in Sonoma, California, into a kitchenware store in the early 1950s. Customers persuaded him to move to San Francisco in 1958, where he used the name Williams-Sonoma. Sales boomed during the 1960s and, like Bridge, Williams took frequent buying trips to Europe. The day after a Julia Child cooking show was televised, the shop was crowded with women asking for the pots and pans and other tools she had used. They knew that Williams-Sonoma was the only place in town that carried them.

TEFLON

Teflon-coated cooking utensils were introduced to America's cooks by Macy's, in New York City, on December 15, 1960. Although Teflon plastic was a DuPont creation, the idea of using it on pans was French. In 1956, Marc Gregoire, who called his pans—and company—Tefal, began his business in his garage. At first his wife sold the pans on the sidewalks of Paris. But his success was phenomenal and within a few years he was making pans by the million.

In 1958 a friend of Thomas G. Hardie's gave him an aluminum skillet bought from a Paris shop. The coating inside the skillet eliminated the need for butter in cooking—and made the skillet easier to clean. Hardie, an American journalist, worked for two years to get the

---

Cookware's Cook

Chuck Williams's own enjoyment of cooking was one reason he got into the kitchenware business. Born in Florida, Williams grew up in California. After World War II, he went into the business of building houses in Sonoma because he enjoyed working with his hands. In the early 1960s he bought an old hardware store to remodel as a group of small shops—and he decided to run the one that sold housewares, which soon turned out to be exclusively kitchenware.

Customers from San Francisco who summered in the Sonoma area discovered Williams shop, and urged him to move to San Francisco. When he did, he called his store Williams-Sonoma. In order to find the diversity of kitchenware he wanted, and to get professional-quality pots and pans, Williams began making buying trips to Europe. As his stock and reputation grew—with professional cooks like James Beard as well as with amateurs— he opened additional stores and sold mail order. By 1989, Williams-Sonoma's 118 retail stores included Pottery Barn and Hold Everything outlets and the firm sent out 74 million mail-order catalogs.

THE SIXTIES: AN AGE OF CONTRASTS

FDA to approve the use of Teflon on cookware, and to find a manufacturer to do it. When at long last, a buyer at Macy's put some of Hardie's cookware on sale, not only was Macy's swamped with customers, but stores all over the country wanted the pans.

By the end of 1961, DuPont began to sell Teflon to American manufacturers. Sadly, the Americans went into the business with more enthusiasm than knowledge—and the shoddy merchandise they produced gave Teflon a bad reputation. Over the years, however, Dupont improved the basic coating, and kitchenware manufacturers learned how and where to apply Teflon—and the product took off again, this time to everyone's satisfaction.

MAJOR EQUIPMENT

Manufacturers of kitchen appliances emphasized time-saving and labor-saving improvements to their products. In 1965, for example, Frigidaire introduced a refrigerator that had an ice maker with conveyor cube delivery on its door. In 1969, General Electric had a refrigerator with door dispensers for both ice and water.

Dishwashers improved in capability with rinse and soak cycles, movable racks, and silverware baskets.

The kitchen trash can became obsolete in 1969, when Whirlpool Corporation introduced the very first completely new major appliance in decades: a household trash compactor. The compactor needed emptying, of

THE COUNTER THAT COOKS Much excitement greeted Corning's slick Pyroceram countertop cooking unit when it went on sale in 1966. Here, at last, was a cooktop that blended into the surface of kitchen counters—and smooth burners that could be cleaned with a swipe of the cloth. However, those smooth tops required that pots or skillets have equally smooth bottom surfaces so they would contact burners fully; for that reason, the cooking units were sold with Pyroceram Cookmates pots and casseroles with the bottoms ground and polished "dead flat" to work perfectly.

course, but its capacity for crunching cans, cardboard, and glass was enormous so that job could be put off for days.

In 1963, General Electric developed the pyrolitic, self-cleaning oven; three years later, Modern Maid showed a prototype of a catalytic, continuous-cleaning oven. In 1964 Thermador/Waste King introduced gas and electric cooktops with a "griddle 'n grill." In 1965, Jenn-Air debuted the indoor grill and grill-range.

In 1966, the Pyroceram glass-ceramic top cooking surface was introduced by Corning. To function properly, the slick surface required pans and skillets with comparably slick bottoms, so Pyroceram cookware was sold with the cooktop, and later with Corning's Pyroceram-topped stove.

MICROWAVE OVENS

The most exciting cookery product of the 1960s was the countertop microwave oven. Dr. Percy L. Spencer, a scientist with electronics manufacturer Raytheon, popped corn with microwaves in 1945—and patented the process. Because Raytheon produced magnetron tubes for radar, it was understandable that the microwave oven it introduced for commercial use in the early 1950s would be called a Radarange.

The Radarange stood about 5 feet high and it weighed about 750 pounds. Only restaurants and institutions could accomodate or afford it although, over the years, Raytheon brought out better and better models for less and less money—$3,000, $2,000, $1,250.

The first microwave designed for home use was introduced by Tappan in October 1955. It was fitted into a 40-inch free-standing case or could be used as a wall-mounted built-in; the cost was $1,295. In 1956, Hotpoint showed a competitive unit. In 1963, General Electric introduced a stove with both conventional and microwave ovens. Their designers assumed that the cooks would want the

DIAL A MEAL The Radarange microwave oven of the 1950s (below left) was designed by Raytheon for use in restaurants, hospitals, and similar institutions. Its price was a hefty $3,000. By the time Amana introduced a countertop microwave for the home in 1967 (below right), it had a price tag of less than $500.

LASAGNE LIKE MAMA MADE During the 1960s, Americans discovered that there was more to Italian food than spaghetti and meatballs. Lasagne was adopted early because it produced a hearty one-dish main course that could be made with various meats and cheeses to suit any family's taste and pocketbook.

microwave oven for roasting bulky foods such as turkey and leg of lamb. To provide deep penetration to cook these foods quickly, the oven operated on a different microwave frequency from that adopted by Tappan and Hotpoint. The GE innovation didn't sell—and they switched to the standard frequency.

Not until 1967, after Amana Refrigeration, Inc. had become a Raytheon subsidiary, would microwave ovens be really affordable for home use. That year Amana produced a 115-volt countertop model for just $495. Litton brought out a low-cost oven a year later. Interest in microwaves started soaring—and hasn't stopped yet.

SMALL APPLIANCES

America's love affair with portable electric kitchenware went on without slacking in the 1960s. The Salton Hotray—an electrically heated tray that was handsome enough to be placed on the dining room sideboard—was on every hostess's Christmas wish list in 1960. The toaster, which hadn't done much except pop up toast for several decades, merged with the countertop oven in General Electric's 1961 toaster oven.

Most small appliances, however, did only one job. For stir-frying, the ancient Chinese wok was electrified. So were coffee grinders and percolators. In 1967, Salton produced an egg poacher and two years later a yogurt maker. The cook's problem became where to put all these so-called helpers. Many times the answer was a garage sale.

SUPERMARKETS

Markets got bigger and sold more kinds of food with every passing year. Trading stamps, as a sales incentive, reached their zenith in 1967. Three out of four supermarkets issued them—even A & P and Safeway, which had resisted the trend, began to use stamps in the early 1960s. About $825 million worth of stamps changed hands in 1967—more than twice the total for 1956. Housewives could collect their premiums at 2,500 to 3,000 redemption centers nationwide.

But supermarkets still considered stamps costly, and they were eager to find other ways to attract customers. In 1968, Jack Hooley found an answer when he opened a warehouse store in the Minneapolis suburb of Fridley. Its entry (insiders referred to it as "Power Alley") was lined two stories high with special purchases.

The "warehouse store," which sold most foods at lower prices than supermarkets, dispensed with all decor and most service. (Like the original Piggly Wiggly, the warehouse store had service in the meat department.) Canned and boxed foods were left in open cartons. No effort was exerted to carry every flavor of soup or size of cereal box. The customer was expected to make compromises—and to bag his or her own groceries. The idea worked. The warehouse-store shopping carts were wider than usual to encourage more purchases, and the customers filled them.

Not all supermarkets pared down to bare essentials. Some went in the opposite direction to give customers more service. They expanded their nongrocery sections to sell complete cosmetic selections, automotive supplies, dishes, pots and pans, even articles of clothing. Other opened in-store delicatessens, bakeries, flower shops, or restaurants.

EATING OUT

Despite interest in French food at home and in restaurants, and the expansion of American schools for professional cooks, the majority of first-rate chefs still trained in Europe. Restrictions on immigration created problems for those who were foreign born and wished to work in

---

Mr. Omelet

No fancy fund-raiser, after-theater supper, or public relations party held in Manhattan during the 1950s or 1960s was quite complete without Rudy Stanish's omelet bar, where he produced a made-to-order omelet for each guest. As a chef to wealthy families—Palm Beach in winter, Newport in summer—he perfected the art of turning out delicate, fluffy omelets almost as fast as guests could order them. At the top of his form, he did four per minute. When TIME reported his feats in 1968, Stanish was working weekdays as chief chef at Wall Street's Goldman, Sachs brokerage firm and moonlighting as Mr. Omelet on weekends. According to the magazine's editors, Stanish was "a veritable CHEF D'OEUF, the best omelet maker in the land, maybe even in the world."

America—and for restaurateurs like Roger Fessaguet of La Caravelle in New York who had to deal with a severe shortage of chefs. Sadly, for restaurant-goers, too, many chefs chose to work for the food industry where their wages were higher than La Caravelle would pay. After the death of Henri Soule in 1966, Le Pavillon on Fifty-seventh Street closed its doors, still the only American restaurant to have ever been considered worthy of a three-star rating by Michelin Guide inspectors.

The foreign cuisine second only to French was Italian—whether in elegant restaurants featuring veal scallops or in neighborhood spaghetti joints. Americans took the pizza into their hearts, and both independent and chain pizza parlors sprang up all over the country. Exotic Hawaiian and Polynesian restaurants with Saturday night "luaus" drew crowds. Scandinavian restaurants appealed to diners at lunch and dinner with smorgasbords. Old-style German restaurants, many dating back to the nineteenth century, had faithful followings. Japanese restaurants—even the rare sushi bar serving raw fish and seafood—found an audience in the big

A REVOLUTIONARY RESTAURANT The first revolving restaurant in the United States was in Hawaii. The first in the contiguous states was at the top of the Space Needle (below). It opened April 21, 1962, and was the hit of the Seattle World's Fair. Glass elevators took diners up 500 feet to the restaurant; glass windows all around gave fabulous views as the restaurant made a complete 360° revolution each hour. The Space Needle has become a permanent Seattle attraction; the restaurant prides itself on its Pacific Northwest cuisine, emphasizing fresh seafood of all kinds—salmon, halibut, scallops, crab, prawns, and shrimp among them.

cities, where some Chinese cooks started to offer Hunan and Szechwan dishes.

Restaurants with discotheques were the craze in New York City. Folk music was the drawing card in San Francisco. Women were not merely allowed but encouraged to visit bars without escorts. Capitalizing on that freedom, Butch McGuire and Gene Sage opened the first singles' bars in Chicago. In New York City in 1965, Alan Stillman opened the original TGI Friday—the prototype "fern bar" with hanging plants, brass railings, oak floors, and Tiffany lamps. TGI Friday has been held responsible for a "greening of American restaurants." Plants certainly sprang forth in restaurants all over.

Aiming to please men—although women were welcome with male escorts—Hugh Hefner and Arnie Morton opened the first Playboy Club in Chicago; Playboy West on Sunset Boulevard in Los Angeles soon followed. Diners bought memberships entitling them to keys to the clubs, which soon were opening nationwide.

STEAKHOUSES

Steak was still the all-American food, and a dinnerhouse restaurant was a popular place to eat it. (Typically, these establishments opened at 5 P.M. Few—if any—served lunch.) More informal than the traditional white tablecloth restaurant, a dinnerhouse was likely to have an English pub or Colonial American decorating motif. *Institutions* magazine dubbed the decor "Meat and Potatoes Tudor." The dinnerhouse served a short menu—often no more than steak, lobster, and salad. The idea for a salad bar may not have started with dinnerhouses, but it certainly got wide exposure there, as did the turf-and-surf entree combining a steak and a lobster tail.

Pioneered in Waikiki, the first dinnerhouse on the mainland was the Steak Pit in Aspen, opened July 4, 1960. In 1962, the Chart House chain was founded in Rancho Mirage, California; in 1964, the Cork 'n Cleaver opened in Scottsdale, Arizona; in Dallas, in 1966, Norman Brinker opened the Steak & Ale—its decor inspired by the movie *Tom Jones*.

For spectacle as well as steak or seafood, diners could visit Benihana of Tokyo, where chefs cooked the food in front of them with a swashbuckling slashing of cleavers; the first opened in New York in 1964. For more modest prices, Bonanza Sirloin Pit (1962) and Ponderosa (1964) chains claimed the budget market.

FAST FOOD

By the beginning of the 1960s, Americans ate about 40 percent of their meals away from home—sometimes a brown-bag lunch at the desk, but with increasing frequency a lunch bought in a restaurant, school or company cafeteria, soda fountain, drive-in, coffee shop, or fast-food outlet. As women with children started working, families began to eat dinner at fast-food restaurants.

The number of fast-food restaurants nearly tripled during the 1960s, while "Mom and Pop" restaurants closed. Franchising enabled fast-food chains to expand the number of outlets with little money and lots of speed. McDonald's had 200 units in 1960; by 1969 it had 1,500. Kentucky Fried Chicken grew from 200 to 1,800. The highways leading into towns were crowded with self-service fast-food outlets for hamburgers, fried chicken, tacos, pizza, "donuts," and ice cream.

Joining an already overflowing "strip" was Hardee's, a chain of franchised outlets established by Wilbur Hardee in Greenville, North Carolina, to sell 15-cent hamburgers. More upscale was Arby's, a chain of roast-beef restaurants begun in Boardman, Ohio, near Youngstown by Forrest and Leroy Raffel (Raffel Brothers, or R.B.s).

Flamboyant is the kindest word for the neon signs, striped walls, A-frame shapes, and zigzag roofs of many fast-food restaurants during the 1950s and early 1960s. Their bright lights and colors made them unwelcome in most neighborhoods. To discourage loitering, interiors were small—in the mid-1950s, a standard Burger King measured 22 by 25 feet—and customers rarely found any seating.

By the end of the 1960s, however, the

THE KENTUCKY COLONEL During the 1920s and 1930s, Harlan Sanders's small restaurant in Corbin, Kentucky, grew so famous that Governor Ruby Laffoon dubbed him a Kentucky Colonel—a title Sanderss used proudly. When a new highway bypassed Corbin, he closed his restaurant and in 1952 began franchising his recipe for fried chicken. By 1964, the colonel had more than 600 outlets in the United States and Canada, and sold his interest for $2 million.

novelty of eating in the car had worn off. In response, Burger King incorporated a dining area in its new restaurant prototype in 1967. Other chains, including McDonald's, took to the style so that families could eat in comfort—and teenage customers were less likely to congregate noisily outdoors. At the same time chains subdued their signage and building architecture to some degree.

The Seventies: Turbulent Years

On April 22, 1970, the country celebrated the first Earth Day. It became the symbolic first step on a back-to-nature trip for the decade. The baby boomers had grown up and gone to college. Now they made it clear that the 1970s were not going repeat the errors of the past.

Some sociologists borrow words from a Tom Wolfe essay to label the 1970s the "Me Decade." Indeed, judged by the fancy-free proliferation in credit cards, the country had grown more acquisitive and narcissistic than ever before. Some could afford it: the gross national product more than doubled from slightly more than $1 trillion in 1970 to $2.5 trillion in 1979. Some only hoped.

The decade started badly. Vietnam War hysteria was at its height in 1970. The tragic killing of college protesters at Kent State University generated distrust that turned into cynicism with Watergate, Nixon's resignation, and the humiliating evacuation of U.S. civilians from Saigon on April 29, 1975, while Communist forces finally took over South Vietnam.

Then, almost magically, the tall ships sailed into New York harbor as an elegant symbol of the Bicentennial of 1976, giving Americans a collective reason to celebrate. Interest in American history led cooks to explore traditional regional and local culinary customs. The country was reminded of its strengths and was proud of its exploration of space as both *Viking I* and *Viking II* set down successfully on Mars.

During the 1970s, Americans took up all sorts of causes, from vegetarianism to saving baby seals. They went to discos and the King Tut exhibit. Dress codes faded like the designer blue jeans that became a unisex uniform. They put CBs in their cars and messages on their T-shirts. They made more trips overseas than ever before—the number building

INSCRUTABLE CHOPSTICKS When President Richard Nixon visited Premier Chou En-lai in Shanghai in 1972, banquets were held in his honor. However, Nixon was expected to eat with chopsticks—implements he apparently regarded with some puzzlement. In the United States, meanwhile, cooks got caught up in the excitement of using woks and bamboo steamers to prepare dishes as authentic as those Nixon ate. (AP/Wide World Photo)

from about 5 million to more than 8 million—and nearly half visited Europe.

Women, in particular, discovered new aims. They entered the work force in unprecedented numbers and excelled in jobs not traditionally women's work. In 1972 the Senate approved a constitutional amendment banning discrimination because of sex; then the fight for state ratification began. In 1973, the Supreme Court invalidated state abortion laws, and set off another kind of fight.

The year 1974 marked a watershed, when more women entered the work force (52 percent) than stayed at home. By the end of the decade almost 58 percent of all women had jobs outside their homes, and constituted nearly 42 percent of the national labor force. These were not "girls" working for a year or two to kill time before marriage; nor were they "old maids" grateful for a paycheck with which to pay the rent. These were ambitious women—women to be reckoned with. By the end of the decade, they held 25 percent of all management jobs.

HOME COOKING

The 1960s cook had been enthusiastic. The 1970s cook was sophisticated as well. Reading, travel, and cooking classes (firsthand or on television), helped him or her master many of a chef's basic skills; the cook's repertoire included numerous dishes from Europe, Latin America, and Asia.

Chicken Kiev

This classic Ukrainian dish is made more flavorful with herbs and lemon juice.

12 tablespoons (1 1/2 sticks) butter
1 teaspoon finely cut chives
1 teaspoon finely chopped fresh parsley
1 teaspoon lemon juice
Three 1-pound whole chicken breasts, skinned, boned, and halved
Salt and white pepper
Flour
2 eggs, lightly beaten
2 cups fine dry white bread crumbs
Vegetable oil, for deep-frying

Knead the butter with chives, parsley, and lemon juice until thoroughly blended. Shape the butter into 6 cylinders, then freeze. Place each boned breast-half between pieces of wax paper and pound lightly into a cutlet about 1/4 inch thick. Sprinkle with salt and white pepper. Center a cylinder of butter on it and fold over one long side, then the short ends. Cover them with the other long side. Roll each breast in flour to coat it lightly. Then dip in egg and roll in crumbs. Refrigerate breasts for 2 or 3 hours to let coating become firm.

Pour oil into a pan to depth of about 2 inches—enough to immerse the breasts—and heat it to 360°F. Deep-fry 2 or 3 breasts at a time for 5 minutes, or until golden brown. Drain on paper towels. Serve hot.

Serves 6

Artichoke Spread

Where did it come from? Nobody knows. But in the 1970s almost every hostess used a version of this concoction as a spread for crackers or a dip for chips.

2 10-ounce packages frozen artichoke hearts, thawed
2 cups mayonnaise
2 cups grated Parmesan cheese
Paprika

Preheat the oven to 350°F. Squeeze the excess water out of the artichoke hearts. Chop them fine and mix them with the mayonnaise and 1 1/2 cups of the cheese. Put the mixture into a baking pan. Smooth the top: sprinkle with the remaining cheese and with paprika. Bake for 10 to 15 minutes or until bubbly.

Makes 5 to 6 cups

TIDIER TURKEYS The Thanksgiving turkey—and just about every other candidate for oven roasting—got easier and faster to prepare when Reynolds Oven Cooking Bags were introduced in 1970. The transparent, heat-resistant, nylon-film bags would cook meats, poultry, or fish together with vegetables for a "one-pot" meal, and hold in juices so both the pan and the oven stayed clean. When microwaves became popular, the bags proved safe in them, too.

The stockpot on the stove held homemade broth and the sourdough bread came fresh from the oven. More serious cooks often outdid their French counterparts: they made their own pastries, pâtés, and sausages—foods any Parisian would assuredly buy at a patisserie or charcuterie.

Americans' insatiable interest in creative cooking led them to see entertaining

THE SEVENTIES: TURBULENT YEARS

Gravlax with Mustard Sauce

The delicate, spicy flavor of this Scandinavian hors d'oeuvre made it a favorite of American hostesses.

1/4 cup sugar
1/4 cup coarse salt
2 tablespoons white peppercorns, crushed
2 pounds center-cut salmon fillets, with skin on
2 bunches fresh dill, coarsely chopped
MUSTARD SAUCE
1/4 cup prepared dark mustard
1 tablespoon dry mustard
1/2 cup vegetable oil
1/4 cup chopped fresh dill
2 tablespoons distilled white vinegar
2 tablespoons sugar

Wash the fillets. Place 1 fillet, skin side down, in a glass or ceramic dish. Combine sugar, salt, and peppercorns. Rub half of this mixture into the fleshy side of fillet. Sprinkle chopped dill generously on top. Rub remaining sugar and salt mixture into flesh side of second fillet. Place second fillet, flesh downward, over first one. Sprinkle remaining dill on top. Cover tightly. Place a board over the fillets and weight it down. Refrigerate salmon for 2 or 3 days; every 12 hours, turn fillets and baste with liquid from dish.

For sauce, mix ingredients in a blender or food processor until smooth. Taste and correct seasonings. Chill overnight to blend flavors.

To serve, remove salmon from marinade and scrape away seasonings. Pat fillets dry with paper towels. Place fillets skin side down on a cutting board. Holding the knife diagonally, carve fillets crosswise into thin slices, lifting them away from the skin. Arrange the GRAVLAX on a serving platter and present accompanied by sauce.

Serves 8 to 10

Seviche

The lime or lemon juice cooks the scallops. Any raw, firm fish, or briefly-boiled shrimp can replace all or part of the scallops.

1 pound scallops
1 cup lime or lemon juice
1/2 cup finely chopped onion
2 tablespoons finely chopped red or green bell pepper
1 tablespoon finely chopped fresh hot red or green chili pepper
1/4 cup chopped fresh parsley
1/4 cup vegetable oil
Salt and pepper
1 large avocado, halved, pitted, peeled and diced

Wash scallops and cut large ones into halves or quarters. Pour lime or lemon juice over scallops and marinate at room temperature for about 1 hour. Drain scallops, discarding juice. Add onion, peppers, parsley, oil, and salt and pepper to taste. Refrigerate until chilled—at least two hours. Before serving, stir in avocado.

Serves 4

---

as a means of self-expression. Every occasion and hour of the day could be party time—anniversaries, birthdays, and holidays set off brunches, lunches, cocktail parties, dinners, and midnight suppers, exploding like a string of firecrackers.

Each party let a cook show off his or her talents, and worldliness. As cocktail accompaniments, fussy little canapés were dislodged by wheels of Brie or huge, dramatic wedges of Stilton or Monterey Jack, presented with homemade breads and toasted crackers. Or tiny tea sandwiches might spill from the cornucopia created by hollowing out an oversized loaf of bread.

The raw vegetables served with dips were now called *crudités*, and probably included mushrooms, edible-podded

FRESH PASTA Rolling out pasta got easier when cooks discovered the machine that chefs used for the job. With its heavyweight rollers the dough is kneaded, then flattened to the desired thickness before being cut into noodles of uniform narrow or broad widths. (Photograph courtesy The Chef's Catalog).

peas, and strips of fennel and bok choy as well old standbys like carrot and celery sticks.

Dinner parties were held in the dining room—or what passed for one in modern houses. Hostesses brought out damask tablecloths; the china matched, the silver was sterling, the glassware was crystal and sparkled.

By curious contrast, family meals got more casual. Nobody thought it strange if dinner was a series of "sittings"—with latecomers heating leftovers in the microwave.

The 1970s woman with a job as well as a home to run was smart enough to make compromises, whatever her claims as a gourmet. When time was short, desserts could be found in a bakery or a box; although a cake mix wasn't going to yield a product as wonderful as Mom's, neither did it fall in the oven. Hams injected with flavorings and water might not match those cured in a smokehouse, nor did they need to be soaked overnight. Tomatoes picked "green ripe" and shipped cross-country did not equal vine-ripened specimens, but they were available year-around; for sauces, canned tomatoes worked well.

French Potato Salad

The light dressing of stock, oil, and vinegar was a revelation to 1970s cooks who believed potato salad and mayonnaise were inseparable.

1/4 cup beef stock
1/2 cup olive oil
1/4 cup white wine vinegar
1/2 cup chopped red onion, or scallions with 2 inches of green tops
2 tablespoons chopped fresh parsley
1/2 teaspoon dry mustard
Salt and pepper
2 pounds unpeeled red or yellow new potatoes, washed

Mix the stock, olive oil, vinegar, onion or scallions, parsley, mustard, and salt and pepper to taste. Set aside. Boil potatoes in lightly salted water for 10 to 15 minutes or until barely tender—firm not soft. Drain potatoes and—as soon as they cool enough to touch—slice into a serving bowl. Stir stock and oil mixture well, then pour over potatoes and toss them together gently. Serve at room temperature. Serves 6

NOUVELLE CUISINE

In 1972, French food critics Henri Gault and Christian Millau started a culinary revolution that reverberated across the Atlantic when their new magazine, *Le Nouveau Guide Gault-Millau* introduced their readers to *la nouvelle cuisine*. Although Americans were taken by surprise, French chefs had watched classic cookery changing subtly for several decades.

After World War II ended, the grandest concoctions of *la grande cuisine* seemed excessive. French restaurants simplified their menus, and chefs used the old-fashioned *farcis* (fillings), heavy cream-laden sauces, and flour-based purees sparingly, if they used them at all.

The master chef of the 1940s and 1950s—Fernand Point of La Pyramide restaurant in Vienne—still turned out

Orange Souffle

A traditional dessert souffle incorporates a cream sauce containing flour to lend body to the egg mixture. This more delicate version is supported only by the air beaten into the eggs; it must go into the oven as soon as it is assembled. After the souffle bakes, sifting confectioners' sugar over it glazes the top instantly with a thin coat of caramel.

Butter
1 1/2 cups granulated sugar
4 egg yolks
1 tablespoon orange-flavored liqueur
1 teaspoon finely grated orange peel
1 teaspoon vanilla extract
6 egg whites
Confectioners' sugar

Preheat oven to 350°F. Butter bottoms and sides of 6 individual 4-inch souffle dishes. Using 1/2 cup granulated sugar, coat buttered surfaces; discard sugar remnants.
Combine remaining 1 cup granulated sugar with egg yolks and beat for 15 to 20 minutes, until the mixture is thick, cream-colored, and pale yellow. Gently blend in liqueur, orange peel, and vanilla. In separate bowl, beat egg whites for 5 minutes or until very stiff but not dry. Fold about one-fourth of egg whites into egg yolk mixture. When well blended, fold in remaining whites. Spoon into prepared dishes, filling them about three-quarters full. Bake for 20 to 25 minutes or until souffles are risen and lightly browned.
Immediately sift confectioners' sugar over the souffles. Serve at once.
Serves 6

exquisite delectations like *foie gras en brioche* and salmon with champagne sauce, poaching the fish in wine, mushrooms, and pureed tomato, then glazing it with a dollop of hollandaise. But Point also lightened the sauces he concocted, and reduced the cooking time for vegetables such as asparagus so they were left with a bit of crunch.

Point was a superb teacher as well as a culinary genius. Among the graduates of his kitchen was Paul Bocuse, who launched his own restaurant in 1962 at Collonges-au-Mont-d'Or near Lyons—and by 1965 had won the ultimate reward: three stars from the Michelin guide. Bocuse followed his master's lead toward simple, light cookery. He sauced foods with *beurre blanc* (whipped, melted butter) or pan juices thickened not with flour but with pureed vegetables. He abbreviated the cooking time not only for vegetables but also for fish. The freshness and perfection of ingredients were more imperative than ever, as he began to cook food more quickly.

Soon other chefs joined Bocuse in his revolt against *grande*: Roger Vergé of Le Moulin de Mougins, Jean and Pierre Troisgros at Roanne, Alain Chapel of Chez La Mère Charles outside Lyons, Paul and Jean-Pierre Haeberlin of Illhaeusern, Jean Delaveyne of Camélia at Bougival, Louis Outhier of L'Oasis, and Michel Guérard at Eugénie-les-Bains. All contributed ideas and invented new recipes in their mutual effort to revitalize French cookery.

Gault and Millau were the intellectuals as well as the promoters of *la nouvelle cuisine*, explaining its aim as naturalism. In their influential and sprightly *Guide Gault-Millau*, they disparaged rich and processed foods, and praised light, fresh-tasting ones. Honesty in cooking was what they were after. Bocuse, himself, did

---

France's Apostle of Fine Food

The most famous French chef of the 1970s, Paul Bocuse went on a cook's tour of the world that ended in Paris at the Elysée Palace. There French President Valéry Giscard d'Estaing awarded him the Legion of Honor. Bocuse had served his apprenticeship with Fernand Point at La Pyramide restaurant in Vienne, before opening his own restaurant at Collonges-au-Mond-d'Or near Lyon. In 1961, his restaurant earned one star from the Michelin guide; in 1962, it received two stars; finally, in 1965, it got three stars. Besides running his restaurant, Bocuse led the young French chefs who were simplifying classic dishes to create a NOUVELLE cuisine. To spread the message, Bocuse had gone on international teaching tours, visiting the United States as guest chef, and overseeing a restaurant in Tokyo and a cooking school in Osaka. With his travels and writing, Bocuse became the first "celebrity chef." (AP/Wide World photo)

A Peripatetic American Original

Credited as one of the creators of "California Cooking" or the "New American Cuisine," Jeremiah Tower (left) was born in the United States, then educated in England and the United States, earning a B.A. from Harvard and a M.Arch. from Harvard Graduate School of Design. Tower began his culinary career as chef and partner of Alice Waters at Chez Panisse in Berkeley. Later he worked in England and France, and in the 1980s became the owner-chef of Stars restaurant in San Francisco. His thorough understanding of traditional European cuisine and America's regional fare has spurred his culinary creativity. Tower is a recognized authority on barbecue cooking, even tasks like barbecuing a spitted suckling pig. (AP/Wide World Photo)

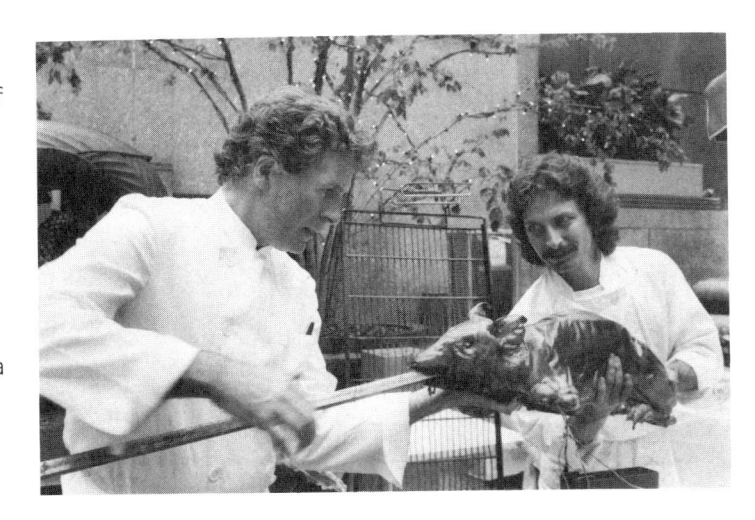

---

more to spearhead a new approach to cooking. He also set a new professional style for chefs: Paul Bocuse was the first "celebrity chef." Unlike chefs of an earlier generation who rarely left their kitchens except for occasional bows, Bocuse regularly strolled into the dining room to talk to guests. He wrote books and hired a public-relations agent to publicize them, and—of course—him. He visited the United States frequently and acted as "guest chef" for special occasions. He appeared on the cover of *Time* magazine.

With help from fellow chef Roger Vergé and the Parisian pastry chef Gaston Lenôtre, he planned the in-flight menus for Air France, and set up the French restaurant at Disney World in Florida. Bocuse lent his name to a Beaujolais wine label. He taught cooking classes in Japan, where he was a partner in an Osaka hotel school.

New York magazine food critic Gael Greene dubbed him poetically, "The lion of Lyons, gastronomic comet." In 1974 France's President Valéry Giscard d'Estaing rewarded Paul Bocuse with the Legion of Honor.

CUISINE MINCEUR

Michel Guérard took Bocuse's ideas one step further with *cuisine minceur*, "the cookery of slimness." While maintaining flavor, Guérard cut calories. He banished butter, oil, cream, starches, and sugar—except the natural sugars in fruits—from the kitchen. Then he baked, poached or steamed foods—using herbs instead of fats to heighten the taste.

California's Culinary Star

Alice Waters has been called the "Mother of New American Cuisine." Her Chez Panisse restaurant in Berkeley, California, celebrates the bounty of locally grown products with a menu of elegant and imaginative concoctions. Waters got a degree in French cultural history from the University of California at Berkeley. Travels in Europe inspired her to open her restaurant in 1971, and there she has inspired a host of culinary stars who worked with her. Among them are Joyce Goldstein (owner/chef of Square One, San Francisco), Mark Miller (owner/chef of the Coyote Cafe, Santa Fe, New Mexico), Annie Somerville (chef at Greens in San Francisco), Jeremiah Tower (owner-chef of Stars, San Francisco), and Jonathan Waxman (former owner/chef of Jams, New York City).

For delicacy, Guérard searched out miniature or immature vegetables, or cut full-sized ones into julienne. He became a culinary artist in his arrangement of foods on a serving plate. Bocuse was quoted as saying, "For the first time, cuisine and dieting are no longer contradictory.".

THE AMERICAN WAY

During the 1970s, amateurs as well as professional cooks in the United States, tested both *nouvelle cuisine* and *cuisine minceur*. The kitchen work wasn't easy, but these healthy approaches to food jibed with the American trend toward natural foods, low in calories but high in pleasure.

Cooks sliced poultry paper thin, julienned meats, and carved spiral designs in mushroom caps. They tried their hand at boiling meat and vegetable stock to reduce it to a syrupy sauce, and they dressed salads with simulated *crème fraîche*, made by adding buttermilk to whipping cream to give it a faintly sour flavor.

Americans also produced an innovation of their own: "California cuisine" based on local foods and minimum cooking. Typically, an assembly of vegetables and poultry, fish, or lean meats was steeped in an herbed marinade, grilled or steamed until barely done, then served with a spicy tomato *salsa*, a garlicky *aïoli* mayonnaise, or a flavored butter. Not only was the technique easy and the result healthful, but foods could be endlessly varied to suit the cook or the season.

Why California? First, because cooks like Alice Waters and Jeremiah Tower who worked there had the imagination to create exciting dishes from whatever foods the markets offered. And, perhaps more important, because the technique's success depended on preserving the flavor integrity of superb raw ingredients, which were more readily available from California growers than any other U.S. source during the 1970s.

Radicchio and Arugula with Warm Mushroom Dressing

To prepare the arugula, trim leaves, wash, spin dry, and tear them into bite-size pieces. With radicchio, separate the leaves before trimming, cleaning, and tearing them.

- 1/2 cup olive oil
- 2 tablespoons white or red wine vinegar
- 1 teaspoon lemon juice
- 1 teaspoon Dijon-style prepared mustard
- Salt and pepper
- 1 small head radicchio, leaves separated, trimmed, washed, dried, torn into bite-size pieces
- 1 bunch arugula, trimmed, washed, dried, torn into bite-size pieces
- 1/2 pound mushrooms, wiped clean, trimmed and sliced thin, including stems

Mix oil, vinegar, lemon juice, and mustard. Taste and correct seasonings; add salt and pepper, if needed. Let dressing stand at room temperature for 1 or more hours, stirring it occasionally, to let flavors blend.

Just before serving, arrange radicchio and arugula on 4 salad plates. Pour dressing into skillet and set over moderately high heat. Stir in mushrooms and sauté them for 5 minutes or until they are tender and delicately browned. Immediately pour mushrooms and dressing over radicchio and arugula. Serve while still warm.

Serves 4

Baked Couscous with Fennel

- 4 cups chicken stock
- 2 1/2 cups couscous (about 1 pound)
- 1 fennel bulb, trimmed, cored, and sliced thin
- 2 tablespoons vegetable oil
- 1/2 cup raisins
- 1/2 cup blanched almonds
- Salt and pepper

Preheat oven to 350°F. Bring stock to boil. Stir in couscous, remove from heat, cover, and let stand 5 minutes. Transfer to bowl. Fluff couscous with fork. In large oven-proof skillet, sauté fennel in oil for 4 or 5 minutes until it softens slightly. Remove from heat and add raisins, almonds, and salt and pepper to taste. Stir in couscous. Cover skillet and bake for 30 minutes, until flavors blend and fennel is tender.

Serves 6

Grapes Juanita

The easiest of elegant desserts, named for a now-forgotten Juanita.

- 2 pounds green seedless grapes, stems removed
- 1 cup sour cream
- 1/2 cup brown sugar
- 1 tablespoon finely grated orange peel

Mix grapes, sour cream, and brown sugar in a serving bowl. Refrigerate for about 2 hours. Sprinkle orange peel on top before serving.

Serves 6 to 8

THE EXPANDING LARDER

Like French cooking, French foods were treated with reverence by Americans. In the early 1970s, importers were profiting from thirty brands of canned *foie gras* and twenty brands of canned snails. At the same time, convenience foods got more so: in 1970, General Mills introduced five flavors of Hamburger Helper; in 1972, they added Tuna Helper. All the cook added was ground beef (or tuna) and water. Dinner was ready in less than twenty minutes. In 1973, Stove Top stuffing mix debuted from General Foods; Good Seasons Toss 'n Serve salad makings were distributed nationwide that year.

SWEET AS SNAP PEAS What a crowd-pleasing addition to the plate of crudités around a dip! The sugar snap pea lived up to its name, with an almost sugary sweet flavor. It had an edible pod as snow peas did, but the snap pea's pod was as plump as that of any garden pea.

As olive oil and vinegar became totems of culinary chic, the greens they dressed changed from the old familiars like Bibb and romaine to newly stylish *arugula* (rocket), *radicchio* (red chicory), dandelion, and sorrel. Young, newly picked spinach proved surprisingly tasty when raw. Fresh herbs found their way into more salads when they were cultivated by truck farmers and grown in greenhouses.

Fresh fruit was available to be eaten or drunk on a daily basis. The first carload of oranges had been shipped by rail from California to the East Coast in 1876. One hundred years later, Americans were buying about 15 million tons of fresh citrus fruit from Florida and Texas as well as from California.

Both fresh fruits and vegetables increased in variety as Asian, Caribbean, and Latin American immigrants became farmers—and customers: daikon (large Japanese white radish), bamboo shoots, plantain (starchy bananas), snow peas, breadfruit, taro root, papaya, mango, litchi, and loquat. A boon for home vegetable gardeners in 1979 was W. Atlee Burpee Company's national introduction of seeds for the sugar snap pea, developed by Dr. Calvin Lamborn.

The sugar snap's edible pod, unlike that of the snow pea, was plump, and the pod and contents had an unmistakable sweet taste. Most important, perhaps, it was a food fashion statement only gardeners could make.

By the middle of the decade, butter and margarine had reversed their roles in the American diet. Margarine consumption was about 4 pounds a person in 1940, and became 11 pounds in 1975. Butter dropped from almost 17 pounds in 1940 to 4 pounds in 1979.

The annual American consumption of meats—beef, veal, pork, lamb, mutton—reached its zenith in 1971 at 156.7 pounds per capita. That figure included 83.4 pounds of beef. Although Americans began to eat less meat thereafter, beef consumption rose until 1976, when it peaked at 94.4 pounds per capita. By 1979, total meat consumption was 144.8 pounds, 78 pounds of which were beef.

Grilled Butterflied Lamb

Cooked indoors under the broiler or outdoors over coals, leg of lamb became popular when cooks found butchers would bone and butterfly it. The meat cooked more evenly than it would with the bones left in—and nobody needed to be embarrassed about carving the lamb.

5-pound leg of lamb, fat trimmed, boned and butterflied, scored and lightly pounded for uniform thickness
4 tablespoons olive oil
2 large garlic cloves, minced
1 tablespoon dried thyme
1 teaspoon ground black pepper

Cut 1-inch deep slits into surface of lamb on both sides. Combine 2 tablespoons oil with garlic, thyme, and pepper. Press seasoning mixture into slits. Wrap lamb and refrigerate overnight. Bring lamb to room temperature about 1 hour before grilling. Rub meat with remaining oil. Grill 4 to 6 inches from heat for 10 to 15 minutes on each side or until meat thermometer inserted into center registers 125°F for medium rare. Transfer to platter. Let meat stand 5 minutes before cutting into thin slices.
Serves 6

Grace's Spareribs with Curry-Apricot Glaze

No matter how sophisticated the American cook became, an almost insatiable sweet tooth kept fruit-flavored glazes popular for barbecues.

1 cup chopped onion
1 garlic clove, chopped
2 tablespoons vegetable oil
1 tablespoon curry powder
1 cup apricot nectar
3 tablespoons honey
3 tablespoons cider vinegar
1/2 teaspoon Tabasco sauce
4 pounds pork spareribs, trimmed and cut into 2-rib or 3-rib pieces

Sauté onion and garlic in oil for 5 minutes or until soft but not brown. Add curry powder and cook, stirring constantly, for 1 minute. Mix in apricot nectar, honey, vinegar, and Tabasco. Simmer for 10 minutes, stirring often to prevent sticking.
Arrange spareribs on rack set 4 to 6 inches above coals of barbecue grill. Cook ribs for 15 minutes on each side. Brush with glaze. Turning ribs often and brushing on more glaze, grill them 45 minutes longer or until pork is cooked through.
Serves 4

In 1976, the Department of Agriculture turned the meat industry upside down when it introduced new grading standards for beef. These reduced the amount of marbling (flecks or veins of fat) required for the top grades of Prime and Choice, and multiplied the number of beeves (young steers) eligible for such desirable grades. The decision pleased cattlemen, who could expect higher prices for those cattle, and also appealed to consumers worried about cholesterol.

Pork consumption rose during the

CHICKENS BY THE THOUSANDS While demand for broilers grew at the grocer, chicken coops increased in size until they became houses that could hold 10,000 to 20,000 birds. Wood chips underfoot kept the houses clean; heaters suspended from the ceiling (left) provided warmth. "Layers," grown for egg production not for meat, were kept in cages two or three tiers high to facilitate collecting eggs; those houses for layers sometimes held as many as 50,000 birds. (Photograph courtesy of U.S. Department of Agriculture)

decade, from about 62 to 64 pounds per capita. Veal, lamb, and mutton were prized by gourmet cooks and by such ethnic groups as Germans, Greeks, and Italians. Other Americans ate them rarely. During the decade consumption fell about 50 percent; by 1979, veal sales per capita were about 1.7 pounds, and lamb and mutton together totaled 1.3 pounds.

FLOCKS OF CHICKENS

As the sales of "red meat" went down, those of poultry rose. Turkey producers saw to it that the cook could buy the birds year-around, not just at Thanksgiving and Christmas, and could pick only the parts needed: breast, wings, drumsticks. Sales increased from 8 pounds per person in 1970 to 9.9 pounds in 1979.

The big winner, though, was the chicken salesman. Consumption zoomed from about 37 to 48 pounds of chicken per person during the decade—figures that include birds sold to fast-food outlets as well as to home cooks. Most of the birds were "broilers"; chicken for roasting and stewing got scarce.

Labels appeared on "brand-name chickens" as poultry production became big business. In the 1940s, Jesse Jewell, owner of a feed store in Gainesville, Georgia, had sold chicks to growers and bought back the live, finished birds. Thus began the development of "integrators," who coordinated all stages of production from chick to cook. Thousands of small operators were absorbed by businesses that boasted retail sales in the billions of dollars.

In the 1960s, Holly Farms started selling chickens already packaged and identified with labels. When Frank Perdue went into the business, he used a wing tag to mark his "golden" birds (colored by eating dried, ground marigold petals mixed into their feed). Soon all the major integrators were putting their labels on their birds.

At the same time, chicken parts increased in popularity until they represented half of all chicken sold for home use. Butchers were delighted to let somebody else halve or section the birds for fastidious cooks, and welcomed chickens that arrived at the supermarket market already cut-up and packaged.

WHAT TO DRINK?

A bottle of sparkling water on the table was an important status symbol. Imported beers came to be seen as a badge of sophistication, and selections of these beers greatly increased. The traditional European beers competed with brews from Denmark, Japan, China, and India. Although brewed—as American beers were—by descendants of German and English immigrants, the beers of these countries had kept the rich malty flavor no longer found in most U.S. products. Overall U.S. beer consumption went from 18 gallons apiece in 1970 to 24 gallons in 1980.

For millions of Americans, though, the preferred dinner beverage was wine, much of it made in the United States. During Prohibition, American vineyards were neglected; after repeal in 1933, the Depression had slowed their renaissance. In the 1930s, American wine authority Frank Schoonmaker persuaded some California vintners to give up French generic names such as Burgundy and call wines after the varieties of grapes from which they are made—Reisling and Zinfandel, for example. This "varietal" labeling—75 percent of a wine consisted of the named variety—finally became popular in the 1970s when two-thirds of American wine was made in California.

However, the effects of the temperance movement lingered. Although wine consumption was increasing, a U.S. Department of Agriculture survey showed that a third of Americans did not drink wine at all. Some eschewed wine for religious or personal reasons, but most because they knew little about wine and were reluctant to try it.

Indeed, just 68 percent of American adults (76 percent of men, 61 percent of women) drank any kind of alcoholic beverages in 1974. The strong spirit of choice was vodka, which had been practically unknown until the 1940s, when the Soviets were wartime allies and it was chic to drink Moscow Mules made with vodka and ginger beer, or screwdrivers made with vodka and orange juice. During the 1950s, vodka began to replace the gin in martinis. Finally, vodka overtook gin altogether, and outsold bourbon in most states. (In 1979, Americans drank 35.5 million cases of vodka, about 28 million cases of bourbon, and 18 million of gin.)

The consumption of carbonated

Vintage American Wines

Although Americans had been making wine since Colonial days, Prohibition and the Depression closed most wineries. Vineyards were neglected. When wine-making was resumed, producers often had to start from scratch. From the 1930s through the 1950s American wines tended to be blends or "generics" because they carried names referring to their color (Mountain White) or to French or Italian prototypes (Burgundy or Chianti). Since many of these came in big bottles, they were often called "jug wines"—a term now considered pejorative. However, some makers also used a single variety of grape alone—or with minimal blending— to produce a so-called "varietal" wine such as Pinot Noir or the uniquely American Zinfandel.

By the 1960s and 1970s, wine-making burgeoned in the United States, especially in California where the climate and soil were eminently suited to growing the grapes needed. Scores of wineries were established and California produced millions of gallons of wine, much of it still generic, but increasing quantities of varietals, many with vineyard designations on their labels to further distinguish them.

For the avante garde, modern technology developed machines to pick grapes and stainless-steel tanks to hold their pressed juices or "must" inside double jacketed shells containing refrigerant. But traditional vintners stuck with hand-picking and aged their wines in oak casks kept in cool cellars.

Acres of vineyards established about 1868 cloak the fields and hills beside the road leading to the Glen Ellen Winery.

Harvest worker loads a truck with Zinfandel grapes for the Louis M Martini Winery.

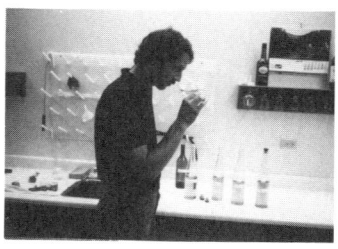

Winemaker evaluating the latest vintage at the Louis M Martini Winery.

Michael and Louis P. Martini taste a barrel sample of the latest vintage.

Guests enjoy California-fresh food and complementary wines at the Robert Mondavi Winery.

THE SEVENTIES: TURBULENT YEARS

Aileen's Honey Graham Bread

Quick-rising yeast both speeded and simplified bread making. This recipe produced the kind of wholesome loaves appreciated by a generation concerned about nutrition as well as good flavor.

5 1/4 cups all-purpose flour
1 cup whole-wheat flour
1 cup graham cracker crumbs
2 teaspoons orange peel
2 teaspoons salt
2 packages quick-rising yeast
1/2 cup water
2 cups orange juice
1/4 cup honey
2 tablespoons (1/4 stick) butter

Set aside 1 cup all-purpose flour. In a large bowl, mix remaining 4 1/4 cups all-purpose flour, the whole-wheat flour, cracker crumbs, orange peel, salt, and quick-rising yeast. In a saucepan, heat water, orange juice, honey, and butter until it registers 125°F on a candy thermometer. Stir orange juice mixture into flour mixture.

Stir in only enough of the reserved 1 cup flour to make a soft dough. Turn out onto a lightly floured board and knead until smooth and elastic, about 10 minutes. Cover, let rest 10 minutes.

Divide dough in half. Roll each half into a 7 by 11-inch rectangle. Roll up each from the short end into a loaf; pinch seam and ends to seal. Spray two 8 1/2 by 4 1/2 by 2 1/2-inch loaf pans with vegetable cooking spray. Place loaves, seam sides down, in pans. Cover with clean cloth. Let rise in warm, draft-free place until doubled in bulk—about 40 minutes.

Preheat oven to 375°F. Bake loaves in oven for 35 minutes or until they sound hollow when tapped. Remove from pans; cool loaves on racks.

Makes 2 loaves

---

beverages exceeded that of coffee by 1976 and soda became the principal between-meals drink, partly because it was easily available, partly because bottlers advertised so aggressively.

MILK

Adults as well as children continued to drink milk, although from 1970 to 1979 total per capita sales fell from about 125 to 110 quarts. Furthermore, tastes shifted as Americans began to worry about fatty foods; in the same period low-fat and skim milk consumption almost doubled, from about 23 to 42 quarts a year.

By 1976 only 7 percent of the nation's milk was being delivered to the customer's door. The housewife bought most of her milk, along with the rest of her food, at the supermarket. Store-bought milk had been an innovation in the early 1900s—a convenience for emergencies. But when refrigerators could keep milk in perfect condition for a week or more, the expense of daily delivery was unnecessary.

For convenience, cooks and shoppers alike looked to large containers, and in 1962 a gallon-size plastic bottle was introduced. A decade later almost all gallon and half-gallon milk containers were plastic, although quarts, pints, and half-pints continued to be laminated or paraffin-coated paper.

HEALTHFUL FOODS

The *Wall Street Journal* reported in 1970 that there were 1,500 to 2,000 health food stores in the United States. By 1973 the number was 3,000, and growing. New York City alone had over 175 stores featuring 36 natural foods. Combined with health food restaurants, the business had grown by 1979 to $1 billion annually.

Health food stores had been around since Dr. Sylvester Graham opened one in the 1830s. Graham believed in a diet of "fruits, nuts, farinaceous seeds and roots"; his enduring legacies are graham crackers and graham, or whole-wheat, flour. Among his followers were Dr. John Harvey Kellogg and his brother Will, who invented "granula" and wheat flakes, and Charles W. Post, who devised the grape nuts he first marketed as a cure for appendicitis, loose teeth, consumption, and malaria.

Over the years health-food apostles could be both sensible and nonsensical. Adolphus Hohensee, popular in the 1940s, put great faith in garlic as a cure-all. Gayelord Hauser's *Look Younger, Live Longer* led the nonfiction bestseller list in 1951; he convinced Greta Garbo—among others—that skim milk, yogurt, wheat germ, brewer's yeast, and blackstrap molasses were wonder foods. In 1958, Dr. D.C. Jarvis (an ophthamologist) published *Folk Medicine: A Vermont Doctor's Guide to Good Health*; he swore by apple cider vinegar.

The leading miracle food of the 1970s probably was honey, recommended for sore throats, coughs, colds, but also for ulcers, even cancers. Honey with or without comb, plain or blossom flavored, was served up on slices of whole wheat bread and became the sweetener for herbal teas as well as for cooking and baking.

But the most talked about natural cure was proposed by Linus C. Pauling, who had won Nobel Prizes for both chemistry and peace. In 1971 he announced that massive doses of vitamin C would prevent and cure colds. He recommended taking vitamin pills as well as eating citrus fruits and drinking citrus juice.

Each new theory created a modest

Granola with Fruit

This healthy combination was served as a snack or doused with milk to be eaten as a breakfast cereal. The types of nuts and fruits were varied.

1 1/2 cups quick-cooking rolled oats
1/2 cup chopped unroasted peanuts
1/2 cup chopped blanched almonds
1/2 cup wheat germ
1/2 cup golden raisins
1/2 cup cut-up dried peaches, apricots, or bananas
1/2 cup honey

Preheat the ovento 400°F. Combine oats, peanuts, almonds, and wheat germ in a shallow baking pan about 15 by 10 inches. Stirring once or twice, bake for 10 minutes or until lightly browned. Transfer to a bowl and stir in fruits. Drizzle honey over mixture and stir to blend well.
Makes about 4 1/2 cups

stir. And every big city and college town supported a store where devotees could buy the necessary products for cooking healthily at home—shopping, perhaps, while sipping on carrot juice.

NATURAL FOODS

The rebellion against the conventional food establishment that started in the 1960s found a sympathetic audience in the 1970s. Getting back to nature seemed a pretty good idea to the general public. Environmentalism and concern about pollution led a new generation of cooks to look on wheat germ and bean sprouts with kindness, and to gladly pay premium prices for natural, organically grown foods.

These were the keystone of Jerome Irving Rodale's publications—including *Organic Gardening and Farming* and *Prevention* magazines. Adelle Davis, the doyenne of health food nutritionists, also insisted on foods grown without "chemical fertilizers"; she deplored refined sugar, pasteurized or homogenized milk, food additives, even unfertilized eggs.

Bread, as a symbol of life, was a focal point of a natural diet. Of course it should be made with the whole grain; the crustier the loaf, the better. Rye bread, pumpernickel bread, black bread—all were desirable. The very term "white bread" became pejorative.

At the supermarket the hottest cereal was granola, a modern and considerably more appetizing form of the "granula" that Dr. Kellogg served at his Battle Creek, Michigan, sanitarium years before. The original formula called for stale bread, toasted in the oven, then ground. In the 1970s, the typical granola contained rolled oats, wheat germ, nuts, dried fruit, honey, and coconut. After 1975, children could munch on granola bars—a snack with no additives or preservatives.

Another beneficiary of the new approach to diet was the herbal tea company, Celestial Seasonings, founded by Mo Siegel in 1970. It leapt from health food store to supermarket until, by 1978, the firm employed 200 people and grossed over $9 million a year.

Yogurt was still considered "good for you" just ask those Georgians and Azerbaijani somewhere in the southernmost reaches of the U.S.S.R., who ate it daily and lived for 100 years or more! In the mid-1970s Americans were eating yogurt at the rate of 2 pounds apiece each year; fruit flavors made it more palatable and a Swiss jelling technique made its texture more appealing. That year frozen yogurt appeared—and became a runaway bestseller. Here, at long last, was a dessert as healthful as it was tasty.

Jane E. Brody's "Personal Health" columns inaugurated in the *New York Times* in the 1970s helped Americans to understand healthful diets and exercise plans (her very first column dealt with jogging). A science writer at the *Times* for eleven years, Brody's broad knowledge and expertise enabled her to report on subjects ranging from emotional problems to high-carbohydrate diets.

As the decade went on and the flower children matured, those who had stayed on the communes made jams for supermarkets or sold brown bread at the farmers' markets that were springing up

Making Nutrition Taste Good

Scientist and journalist Jane Brody paid attention to flavor and thus played a major role in convincing Americans that they would enjoy eating a balanced diet. Her weekly NEW YORK TIMES column "Personal Health" is syndicated nationwide; she writes frequently for FAMILY CIRCLE magazine and is the author of several books including JANE BRODY'S NUTRITION BOOK (1981) and JANE BRODY'S GOOD FOOD BOOK (1985). Brody was born in 1941, earned a B.S. in biochemistry from the New York College of Agriculture at Cornell in Ithaca, New York, and an M.S. in science writing from the University of Wisconsin in Madison. After working as a reporter for the MINNEAPOLIS TRIBUNE for two years, Brody went to the TIMES in 1965. Her column debuted in 1976.

---

in cities of all sizes. By then the healthful eating habits they had espoused were being accepted everywhere. Even Los Angeles and Manhattan had markets where farmers could sell their wares directly to cooks and their families.

CONSUMERISM

Truth—and details—in labels became the rallying cry for cooks and diners alike. A food product did not have to list its ingredients on its label if it conformed to the U.S. Food and Drug Administration's "standard of identity"—meaning that it contained the ingredients usual for that category; ice cream, for example, was to consist of milk (or cream), sweetener, flavoring, and coloring. Obviously this system allowed for great diversity in contents of different products. (How much butterfat in the milk used in the ice cream? What amount and type of sweetener? Which flavorings and colorings?)

Consumer awareness, heightened by Ralph Nader's bird-dogging and congressional committee investigations, brought enough pressure to bear so that the FDA met them partway. In 1974 they ruled ingredients must be listed in descending order of weight—a system that at least gave the shopper hints about the ratio of sugar to grain in breakfast cereal.

Throughout the 1970s, chemical scare stories spread: DDT in animal fat (use of DDT was banned in 1972), mercury in fish, arsenic in chicken feed. In January 1972, saccharin was removed from the GRAS (Generally Regarded As Safe) list. But no toxicity was ever proved and saccharin was never taken off the market. The possible danger of nitrates and nitrites in products such as bacon and ham was examined throughout the decade, with little conclusive result. However, the coloring Violet I, used to stamp grades on meat, was banned in 1973—not much of a triumph because the stamps were usually put on fatty parts of a carcass, and cut off by the butcher or cook.

Restaurateur Nonpareil

The guiding spirit behind the renaissance of Rockefeller Center's Rainbow Room, Joseph H. Baum invented the much-copied custom of waiters and waitresses introducing themselves to diners. In 1960, when Baum opened the luxurious Tower Suite restaurant at the top of the 48-story Time-Life Building in New York, he assigned a "butler" and "maid" to each table—and the butler announced his first name and declared he was "your butler today (or tonight)." Baum grew up in the restaurant business in Saratoga Springs, New York, studied the subject at the Cornell University School of Hotel Administration, and has since turned it into a high art, directing and creating restaurants from New York and Boca Raton to Los Angeles and Appleton, Wisconsin. Baum was a pioneer in the development of theme restaurants—Roman, Mexican, Italian, English—and in menus that stressed fine foods made from quality ingredients, including fresh herbs, baby vegetables, unusual fish and seafoods. He was an early enthusiast for regional cooking and American wines.

THE KITCHEN

The dream kitchen of the 1970s was stocked with tin-lined copper pots. And everyone who deserved to be called a cook had an assortment of whisks, including—of course—a huge balloon whisk for beating egg whites in the requisite copper bowl.

The Cooks' Catalogue, published in 1975 by Beard Glaser Wolf Ltd. was 565 pages long. To create the volume, cooking experts James Beard and Burton Wolf, and designer-cook Milton Glaser, together with food editors Barbara Kafka and Helen Witty, enlisted information from dozens of consultants and writers. The catalogue seemed to show, and explain, every kind of gadget and small appliance imaginable—but in 1977, the team topped their original

GOURMET BADGES Proof positive of status as a gourmet cook during the 1970s was possession of a copper bowl AND a balloon whisk. When used correctly, the whisk-bowl combination produced airier beaten egg whites than any other equipment could—even an electric mixer. And what would a souffle be without fluffy egg whites to puff it up? (Photograph courtesy of The Chef's Catalog).

THREE GENERATIONS OF LABELS When the Joseph Campbell Preserve Co. introduced its tomato soup in 1897, they put a giant beefsteak tomato on the label. After the turn of the century, the company dropped the word "preserve" from their title, and in 1905 replaced the tomato with the medal Campbell's had been awarded at the Paris Exposition of 1900. The current label was designed in the 1970s. The medal remains, but the word Tomato is in a typeface that makes it stand out as never before in sharp contrast to the white background.

Cookery's Genie

When Carl Sontheimer put the first Cuisinart food processor on the market he started a culinary revolution. Techniques that most home cooks avoided—mincing nuts and making mayonnaise, for example—became easy. Pie or cookie dough was now simple to put together. Not only did this incredible device mix ingredients for yeast bread in moments, but it also could knead the dough. As cooks explored the possibilities of this remarkable man's product, their culinary horizons widened and they wrote new recipe books to celebrate.

THE SEVENTIES: TURBULENT YEARS

ZIPPING UP SANDWICHES The first zipper-seal sandwich bags were Dow's Ziploc brand which came out in 1975, three years after Dow originated zipping storage bags. The easily opened and closed sandwich.holders needed no tape or folding to keep in the flavor and freshness of sandwiches, brownies, and other totable foods.

accomplishment with *The International Cook's Catalogue.*

Amateur cooks spent thousands, even tens of thousands, of dollars remodeling their kitchens, sometimes incorporating adjacent rooms to get additional space. Designers made careers out of doing or redoing kitchens; special stores carried only kitchen cabinets and countertops.

The mid-kitchen "island" was a stylish and workable way to accommodate countertop cooking or an extra chopping block. The butcher's maple-block counter so desirable in the 1960s was supplemented now with a marble or granite counter to provide a suitably cool surface for rolling out pastry and fondant.

If the kitchen—and budget—were large enough, the stove would be a professional chef's range, which might have six or more burners, a griddle-broiler, and two ovens. Some cooks got an indoor charcoal-broiler and a plate warmer.

MOTHER'S LITTLE HELPERS

The most revolutionary kitchen tool of the century—certainly the one that caused the most hubbub—was the Cuisinart food processor. Unlike other multipurpose devices that called for a cabinet-load of attachments, the Cuisinart had two disks and two blades that accomplished everything from chopping, slicing, shredding, and pureeing to beating and kneading foods.

The man behind the excitement was Carl Sontheimer, a physicist, inventor, and passionate cook. Sontheimer had retired at the age of fifty-three, and in 1971 was in Paris looking for kitchen products he could franchise in the United States. There he discovered the roly-poly Robot-Coupé, manufactured for restaurant use. During the next two years, he modified the blades and disks, making the machine simple and safe for amateur use, before he introduced it here in 1973.

Originally the processor cost $175. Sales were slow until 1975 when *Gourmet* magazine ran an article, complete with recipes, on "The Phenomenal Food Processor." The rush to buy one started.

Fabled cooks such as Julia Child raved about the processor. It became the new hallmark of the gourmet cook. One busy dealer, Kitchen Bazaar in

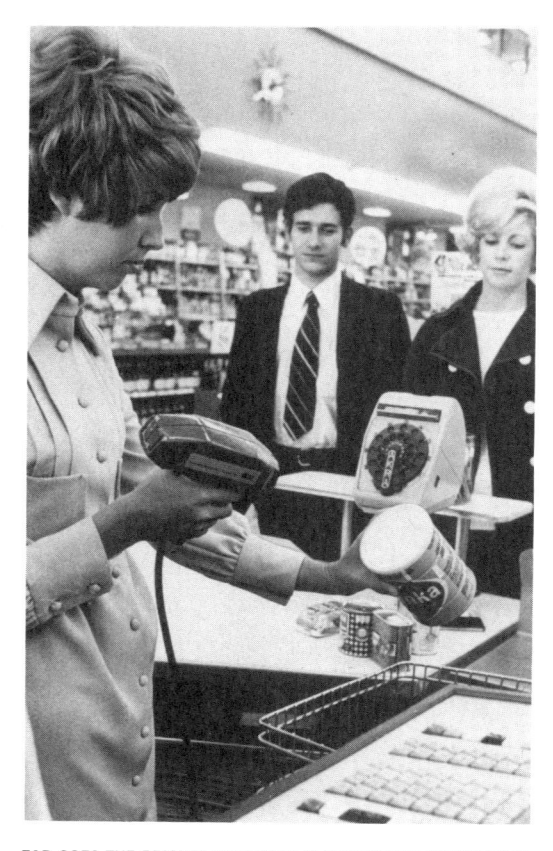

ZAP GOES THE PRICE It seemed as if Buck Rogers had invaded the supermarkets when a checkout clerk used a hand-held scanner that looked like a ray gun to read the prices on food items. Not only did the scanner enable the clerk to ring up prices on the register faster than he or she could by hand, but it kept a constant record of the market's inventory.

Cashing Coupons

Susan J. Samtur was in the vanguard of cooks who learned they could use manufacturers' coupons to reduce grocery bills and—in some cases—get cash refunds. Her book CASHING IN AT THE CHECKOUT was a guide to realizing the biggest possible returns from coupons, and it caught the attention of several television show producers. Here, she appears on the "Gary Collins Hour" show to display the result of one shopping trip and explain how her system worked.

Washington, D.C., produced cookbooks especially for Cuisinart. Within a few years, processors were available from Farberware, Waring, General Electric, Hamilton Beach, and the French company Moulinex. Yet in 1977, when all manufacturers together sold 500,000 processors, half of them were Cuisinarts.

Coffee-making changed, too. The electric coffee percolator that had dominated breakfast tables across America for decades went to the thrift shop in the 1970s. The manufacturers of Mr. Coffee electric percolators switched styles. Their new drip-coffee makers produced better-tasting brews more quickly and easily by boiling the water in one compartment and piping it into another, where it would drip over the grind into a serving pot. In some models a timer could be set the night before so coffee would be ready to drink first thing in the morning.

FOOD COOPERATIVES

Between 5,000 and 10,000 nonprofit food coops formed in towns across the country during the 1970s. They were seen as a way of fighting the inflation of the times, but were also meant to encourage organic farmers and to provide a reliable supply of "counterculture" foods such as whole grains, brown rice, and herbal teas. They are said to have grossed about $500 million a year—a substantial sum, but only 2 percent of the nation's $29 billion food budget.

These were no-frills stores with food still in the wholesaler's shipping cartons or farmer's bags. The coop founders' hope was that they could sell food cheaply. However, they could not buy foods in large enough quantity to get the kind of discounts given to supermarkets, and consumer enthusiasm for coops waned with the decade.

SUPERMARKETS

A 1972 *Supermarket News* survey found that 50 percent of American shoppers did their marketing in a single weekly trip. Their choices were broad: most markets had about 8,000 items. They abounded with special-interest sections: shelves of Asian foods like bamboo shoots and sesame oil across from Latin American tortillas and salsas. Low-calorie foods were grouped together with water-packed fruits and vegetables; down the aisle might be carob powder, whole-grain flours, sunflower seeds, and dried apples.

Nonfood items had always offered supermarkets larger profit margins than food, so stocks of tobacco, health and beauty aids, drugs, cleaning products, and small housewares rose consistently after World War II. By 1977, jumbo stores accounted for one-third of all supermarket sales and provided one-stop shopping for clothing and auto supplies along with bread and breakfast cereals.

By the mid-1970s the supermarkets themselves were having money problems. The low profit margins on which food sales operated left little room for competitive pricing. The only segment of the retail food industry that grew significantly in the 1970s was the late-night convenience store, which did 30 percent of its business in beer and cigarettes. Because of an increase in convenience stores, however, supermarkets extended their own hours until many were open twenty-four hours a day and seven days a week.

The trading stamp had lost its allure by the 1970s, so stores battled with manufacturer's coupons—staging "double coupon" or "triple coupon" value days. Sorting, saving, and exchanging coupons became a kind of cottage industry, with newsletters and books—the best known of which was *Cashing in at the Checkout*, written by Susan J. Samtur with Tad Tuleja and published in 1979.

COOKING SCHOOLS

Whatever culinary mysteries a cook wanted to explore, he or she could find lessons taught in a local school. Every town had one or more gourmet cooks willing to share knowledge for a price. In large cities, a student could choose from among dozens of schools, including specialists in bread or candy making, or cuisines as exotic as Moroccan. Cooks discovered that not all Italian food started with pasta; in the north, rice dominated. France's cuisine varied from one region to another—from the apples and cream of Normandy to the olives and lamb of Provence.

Glowing newspaper and magazine accounts of the banquets given for, and by, Nixon during his landmark 1972 trip to China were reflected in a surge of students at classes in Chinese cooking in the early 1970s. Every year during the mid-1970s, the China Institute in New York City was conducting twenty-eight classes with twenty in each class every year—and turning students away. (By

CULINARY MASTERS Two of America's favorite cookbook and food writers—James Beard and Craig Claiborne—share a joke before a luncheon held on January 19, 1976, as a part of the celebration of the U.S. Bicentennial. (Photograph by Irving Newman)

Bagna Cauda

This is an extremely rich version of a dip for crudités. It was an Italian import of the 1970s.

4 tablespoons (1/2 stick) butter
8 flat anchovy fillets, chopped fine
1 teaspoon finely chopped garlic
2 cups heavy cream, boiled until reduced to 1 cup
Crudités: carrot and zucchini sticks, broccoli florets, celery strips, mushrooms, and the like

In a small casserole over an electric hot tray, candle warmer, or spirit lamp, melt the butter without letting it brown. Stir in the anchovies and garlic, then the reduced cream. Bring sauce to a simmer before using it as a dip for the vegetables.
Makes 1 to 1 1/2 cups

1980, classes had dwindled to a handful.)

In 1975, the English food authority Anne Willan founded La Varenne, a bilingual school of French cooking, on the left bank of Paris. Named for the most important chef of the seventeenth century and the author of the first modern French cookbook, the school was staffed by French chefs—but patronized chiefly by Americans.

COOKBOOKS

After years of reading recipes where ethnic foods were "adapted" to suit American tastes, home cooks found a new faithfulness to sources in the books of the 1970s. The writer's aim now was to make it possible for the jet-age gourmet to reproduce, with reasonable accuracy, the foods he or she had eaten on recent travels.

The 1970s was a golden age of cookbooks. Not only were hundreds written every year, but the quality of the writing

Steak au Poivre

Pan-broiling gave steaks the crisp, brown exterior and tender, pink interior restaurants achieved with their superheated grills. Freshly cracked peppercorns added zest.

3 pounds boneless sirloin steak cut 1 1/2 inches thick
2 tablespoons black peppercorns, cracked with mortar and pestle

Sprinkle half of the pepper on a work surface, and press steak into it. Push remaining pepper into top surface of steak with heel of your hand. Let steak rest at room temperature for about 30 minutes before pan-broiling.
Rub bottom of a heavy iron skillet with fat trimmed from the steak, or coat it with a film of oil. Set pan over high heat; lightly sprinkle with salt. When pan feels hot and salt begins to brown, add steak. Broil about 10 minutes on each side for medium rare meat.
Serves 6

Pesto Sauce

2 cups fresh basil leaves
3 garlic cloves, chopped
Coarse salt
1 cup grated Romano cheese, or mixed Romano and Parmesan cheeses
1 tablespoon pine nuts (optional)
Olive oil

Tear several basil leaves to pieces in a mortar, add a little garlic and salt, and pound with pestle. Gradually add more basil and garlic until mixture is reduced to a pulp. Then work in cheese amd add nuts, if desired. Dilute sauce with olive oil to achieve desired consistency.
Makes 2 to 3 cups

---

and the cooking was higher than ever. Among the outstanding volumes were

Vitello Tonnato

A rich, rustic Italian version of veal with tuna sauce. In France, the veal is braised with white wine and vegetables, then cooled and coated with mayonnaise that has been flavored lightly with tuna and anchovies.

2 cans (7 ounces) oil-packed tuna, preferably in olive oil
1 can (2 ounces) flat anchovy fillets
4 tablespoons olive oil
5-pound veal leg, boned and tied (about 3 1/2 pounds)
2 medium onions, chopped
2 celery ribs, chopped
2 carrots, chopped
1/4 cup chopped fresh parsley
1 bay leaf
1 teaspoon dried thyme
Fresh ground black pepper
2 cups chicken stock
4 tablespoons lemon juice
2 cups mayonnaise
2 tablespoons capers
Lemon slices or wedges, for garnish

Drain oil from tuna and anchovy cans into a large, heavy casserole. Stir in olive oil. Over moderately high heat, brown veal, turning it often. When it is lightly colored all over—about 15 minutes— lift out veal by its strings and set it aside.

Pour off all but about 2 tablespoons of oil remaining in casserole. Add onions, celery, and carrots and cook, stirring often, for 5 minutes or until vegetables are soft but not brown. Stir in tuna, anchovies, parsley, bay leaf, thyme, and pepper. Add chicken stock and 2 tablespoons lemon juice. Stir to dissolve browned bits from bottom of casserole, and bring mixture to a boil. Add veal, reduce heat to low, cover casserole, and simmer veal for 3 hours.

Transfer veal to a plate, cover, and refrigerate. Simmer tuna and vegetable mixture uncovered, stirring often, for 10 minutes or until reduced to approximately 4 cups. Pour into bowl and cool to room temperature. Puree mixture in a blender or, by batches, in a food processor. Cover and refrigerate.

To make tuna sauce, stir remaining lemon juice into mayonnaise. Add 2 tablespoons of puree, taste, and stir in more puree if desired. Add capers.

Cut strings off veal, slice meat thin, and arrange slices on a serving platter. Spoon half the sauce over the veal and garnish platter with lemon slices. Pass the remaining sauce in a bowl.

Serves 8 to 10

---

such now-classic titles as *Mastering the Art of French Cooking, Volume II* by Julia Child and Simone Beck; *The French Menu Cookbook* and *Simple French Food* by Richard Olney, *Culinary Classics and Improvisations* by Michael Field; *La Méthode* and *La Technique* by Jacques Pépin; and *The Saucier's Apprentice* by Raymond Sokolov. *Better Than Store-Bought* by Helen Witty and Elizabeth Schneider Colchie showed cooks how to produce such staples as ketchup and peanut butter. For bakers, the selections included *The Complete Book of Breads* by Bernard Clayton, Jr., and *Maida Heatter's Book of Great Desserts*. In praise of American food, cooks found *The Taste of Country Cooking* by Edna Lewis and *James Beard's American Cooking*. Alan Davidson finished his remarkable *North American Seafood*. Among the many celebrations of foreign cuisines were *Florence Lin's Regional Cookbook*, *The Cuisine of Hungary* by George Lang, *An Invitation to Indian Cooking* by Madhur Jaffrey, *The Classic Italian Cookbook* by Marcella Hazan, and *Couscous and Other Good Food* by Paula Wolfert.

A Food Writer Without Peer

No food writer has received, or deserved, more acclaim than M.F.K. Fisher, shown in the kitchen of her Sonoma Valley, California, home. Born Mary Francis Kennedy in Albion, Michigan, Fisher spent most of her childhood in Whittier, California. She attended Illinois and California colleges before spending three years in France at the University of Dijon. SERVE IT FORTH, her first book of gastronomical writings, appeared in 1937. Regularly thereafter she has regaled, educated, and enchanted readers with vivid evocations of foods, markets, and restaurants—and recipes for everything from PETITS POIS À LA FRANÇAISE to crackling bread. (AP/Wide World Photo)

MAGAZINES

Americans' increasing preoccupation with cookery, and the boom they were creating in the cookbook business, encouraged publishers to start food magazines. In 1975, Knapp Communications launched *Bon Appétit* as a monthly. Three years later, Michael and Aline Batterberry started *The International Review of Food & Wine*, and Carl Sontheimer brought out *Cooking*.

Despite its fancy title, *Bon Appétit* magazine had started out humbly in Kansas City around 1955 as a promotional booklet made up of recipes and ads, and was distributed free through liquor stores. The Pillsbury Company bought it in 1970 and turned the booklet into a bimonthly magazine. After Knapp bought it and put it on a monthly schedule, *Bon Appétit* got a new staff and a complete make-over. In 1975, its circulation was about 250,000; by 1980, it had skyrocketed to more than 1 million.

The International Review of Food & Wine met with more difficulty. Although it had more than 300,000 paid-up subscribers at the start, advertisers did not support it. Its circulation more than doubled, but its publication stopped—temporarily—after its December 1979 issue. *Cooking*, which soon changed its name to *The Pleasures of Cooking*, was an upscale magazine, aimed at the devoted amateur; the price was high and the circulation low, but it stayed in business through the decade.

Yakitori

Asian foods became popular in the 1970s as the formerly exotic ingredients got to be increasingly available. This simple grilled, skewered chicken could be made with sherry and ground ginger, but shopping in ethnic markets was part of the pleasures of discovering new cuisines. SAKE and MIRIN are rice wines; the mirin is faintly sweet.

3 tablespoons SAKE, or substitute dry sherry
1 tablespoon Japanese soy sauce
2 teaspoons sugar
1 teaspoon finely chopped fresh ginger, or substitute 1/2 teaspoon ground ginger
8 chicken livers, trimmed of fat
2 whole chicken breasts, halved, boned, skinned, and cut into 32 1-inch pieces
8 scallions, including 3 inches of green stems, cut into 24 1-inch pieces
TERIYAKI SAUCE
1/2 cup MIRIN or substitute dry sherry
1/2 cup Japanese soy sauce
1/2 cup chicken stock, fat skimmed off
1 cup rice, cooked

Marinate chicken livers for 4 hours at room temperature or overnight in refrigerator in a blend of SAKE, 1 tablespoon soy sauce, sugar, and ginger. Soak 12 small wood or bamboo skewers in water for several hours.

To cook, drain livers and halve them. String 4 livers on each of 4 small skewers. String 4 pieces of chicken breast and 3 of scallion alternately on 8 remaining skewers, beginning and ending with chicken pieces.

Make teriyaki sauce by mixing MIRIN, 1/2 cup soy sauce, and stock. Brush skewered livers and chicken with sauce, then grill under broiler or above coals—about 3 inches from heat—for 3 minutes. Turn skewers, brush livers and chicken with sauce again and grill 3 to 5 minutes longer. When done, livers and chicken meat will be firm and slightly browned; their juices should run clear when a piece is pricked with a knife tip.

Accompany YAKITORI with small bowls of plain, cooked rice.

Serves 4

A NEW MAGAZINE MAKES ITS DEBUT In spring 1978, Aline and Michael Batterberry introduced The International Review of Food & Wine. On the cover was a myriad of spring vegetables; inside were articles by important writers along with news of the latest trends in cooking and dining.

ELEGANT DINING

For two-income families, eating dinner in restaurants became almost a necessity. Many families took it for granted. Restaurants were the place to meet friends and to entertain both socially and for business. Credit cards were the way to pay, with the tab going to Diners Club, American Express, Master Charge (founded in 1966), or Visa—the name that the BankAmericard program adopted in 1977.

French *grande cuisine* still dominated the fancy restaurants and hotels. Windows on the World, at the top of the World Trade Center in New York City, opened on April 12, 1976, under the direction of Joseph H. Baum to become the best-known and largest grossing single restaurant in the world. (Between 1974 and 1977, Baum opened twenty-two eating places in the World Trade Center, these ranged from the elegant Windows to fast food operations.)

Size was not the aim for everybody. Among those were chef Sally Darr, who started the exquisite French restaurant La Tulipe, and John Clancy, who opened the eponymous seafood dinnerhouse Clancy's—both in Manhattan. Paul Prudhomme and his wife Kaye founded K-Paul's in New Orleans; Alice Waters established Chez Panisse in Berkeley.

The multiplication of restaurants gave new importance to the restaurant critics in big cities across the map. New York, Washington, Chicago, Dallas, Los Angeles, and San Francisco all had newspaper critics, and some of the cities also had magazine critics. (The most famous and clever of these probably was Gael Greene, who made food "sexy" and treated restaurant news like gossip-column items.)

In 1978, when the Internal Revenue Service tightened rules for deducting lunches and dinners as business expenses, there was a moment of panic. President Carter deplored the custom of writing off three-martini lunches. Unchastened, restaurateurs and customers alike soon went back to their spendthrift ways.

The preppies' favored restaurants were casual and welcomed singles. They also were likely to be decorated with an English pub, Victorian, or art deco theme. TGI Friday's—the archetypal fern bar with plants hanging from the walls and ceilings—went national in the 1970s, emulated by R. J. Grunts, Houlihan's, and Bennigan's.

The dinnerhouses with their steaks and prime ribs flourished. But so did individually owned ethnic restaurants, which increased so fast that by 1973 they represented about 11 percent of all eateries. Businessmen visiting from abroad wanted to be able to eat familiar dishes. Japanese visitors asked for, and got, sushi bars. The wealthy Mexicans demanded Spanish-inspired dishes—worlds away from the tortilla concoctions that Americans previously thought comprised that cuisine.

Furthermore, the immigration reform act of 1965 had done away with the quota system and most immigrants now came from China, Thailand, Vietnam, Korea, Italy, Portugal, Greece, Mexico, and the Caribbean. All these groups wanted restaurants that served their native food. For example, the overwhelming number of Chinese restaurants in the past had been owned by Cantonese, who came to the U.S. early, and they served Cantonese food. Now there were Chinese restaurants with Peking, Hunan, and Szechuan menus.

As the newcomers gained wealth, the restaurants that served them became more elegant or moved "uptown." Some ethnic restaurants adjusted their menus to please American tastes, but others held to their food traditions and often found them widely accepted.

DIPPING STORES

Before World War II, ice cream consumption barely reached 10 quarts per person. Afterward, the figure was quickly doubled.

Home freezers made it possible to store ice cream in quantity and serve it for desserts or snacks at any time. In 1975, sales peaked at 20 gallons (or 80 quarts) for every American man, woman, and child.

Part of the new enthusiasm for ice cream was due to the increase in so-called dipping stores that offered dozens of delectable flavors. Howard Johnson had built an ice cream stand in 1925, and soon developed a chain renowned in the Boston area. However, in 1929 Johnson broadened his sights and turned his stands into restaurants.

The most important dipping-store pioneer was Baskin-Robbins. In 1945, Burton Baskin and Irving Robbins opened the Snowbird Ice Cream Store in Glendale, California, offering twenty-one different ice cream flavors. By 1954, they adopted thirty-one as a standard number of flavors, and put the number in their logo (Baskin 31 Robbins). As fast-food restaurants took over the lunch business, drug stores closed their fountains, and Baskin-Robbins prospered

Trying to capitalize on the nostalgia for "the good old days" that was induced by the Bicentennial, entrepreneurs

ICE CREAM IN 31 FLAVORS Starting with one "Snowbird" ice-cream store Irving Robbins, and his brother-in-law Burton Baskin developed a chain of franchised dipping stores with nearly 1,000 outlets nationwide by 1970. Baskin-Robbins had conceived the idea of selling thirty-one flavors, one for each day of the month, in 1953. At that time the number 31, enclosed in a circle, became part of their logo. Although Baskin-Robbins' repertory now includes 625 different ice creams, only 31 are made and sold on any given day. (By 1990, Baskin Robbins had more than 3,000 stores, with about a third of those in Canada, Europe, Asia, and the Middle East.)

staged a revival of the nineteenth century ice cream parlor during the late 1970s. The parlor decor was complete from the striped awning outside to bentwood or wire-backed chairs and tables inside. A long marble counter provided a stage behind which a soda jerk performed. But prices were high and sales too disappointing to keep the parlors alive for long.

EATING OUT ON A BUDGET

During the 1970s just about everybody went out to eat sometimes. On any given day about a third of the population spent about a third of the nation's food dollars on restaurant meals. By 1978 dinner made up about 40 percent of those meals.

Most people preferred a medium-priced "tablecloth restaurant" for their evening meal, and a small town might still support a locally owned restaurant with a mimeographed menu featuring sandwiches, fried fish, and roast chicken with stuffing. Nevertheless, most Americans insisted on patronizing take-out and sitdown fast-food restaurants.

Between 1958 and 1972 the number of chain restaurants and drinking establishments almost doubled while owner-operated establishments declined by one-third. The top hundred chains accounted for 25 percent of the commercial food service in 1970, 40 percent in 1978 and 50 percent by 1982. One-third of the $23 billion those hundred firms took in during 1977 went to five companies: McDonald's, Kentucky Fried Chicken, Pillsbury (owner of Burger King and Steak and Ale), International Dairy Queen, and Big Boy.

McDonald's alone grew from 1,592 to 5,747 units in the decade. Sales of McDonald's food went from $587 million in 1970 to $5.4 billion in 1979. Burger King grew from 240 to 1,850 units; Kentucky Fried Chicken went from 3,722 to 6,091 units.

The rising star of fast-food was Wendy's, which was founded in 1969, expanded to 4 units in 1972 and swelled to 1,818 units by 1979. Wendy's owed part of its success to the drive-through windows it first installed in 1971. Customers found windows convenient; Wendy's saved both parking lot and indoor eating space. Within a few years, the other chains knocked out walls to follow suit.

Network television was at the peak of its popularity, and the chains advertised lavishly. They also lengthened their menus. The old standbys chicken, steak, and burgers lost little in popularity, but when customers ate out more often they wanted more selections. Fish appeared in hamburger restaurants. Roast beef sandwich chains began frying chicken and grilling burgers. Chicken chains added side dishes.

The Egg McMuffin debuted in 1973. By 1977, McDonalds—and the competition—were serving a complete line of breakfast sandwiches and biscuits for eating on the run. (Perhaps literally. A Yankelovich poll found that 40 million Americans, nearly one-fifth of the population, claimed to be occasional or regular joggers.)

The all-you-can-eat salad bar that some chains added in the 1970s appealed especially to health-conscious customers—although the bar was often loaded with mayonnaise-drenched appetizers and salads in addition to basic vegetables and toppings. (Restaurants were not the only places to find salad bars. By 1979, about 35 percent of all school lunchrooms featured them.)

Deep-frying was popular in the 1970s because restaurants finally had the automatic timers and lifts to produce perfect French-fried potatoes or batter-fried vegetables such as onion rings. To make the fried food seem more healthful, cooks left skins intact on French fries. Eventually somone tried frying the potato peels alone: a new snack was born.

The Eighties: Health and Wealth

In the 1980s, fitness became a thriving industry. Americans jogged, ran, walked, exercise-cycled, lifted weights, and spent weekends at the tennis court or golf course. Nutritionists became media stars as research showed how fat, cholesterol, sodium, fiber, and calcium could affect widespread health problems like heart disease, cancer, and osteoporosis. Concern for the environment included discussion of local air quality as well as the clear-cutting of distant forests.

Still, conspicuous spending was very much in style: "If you've got it, flaunt it" seemed to be everybody's motto. The gross national product zoomed to $5.3 trillion. Lots of people prospered; the average annual pay in 1989 was $22,567. Wall Street was a money machine. The top 20 percent of wage earners received $85,000 or more annually. More than 100,000 millionaires were minted during the decade.

Ronald Reagan had been swept into the presidency in 1980 vowing to stop inflation and attack crime. The first goal was eventually accomplished, but crime problems lingered—even escalated, partly because of the new crack form of cocaine. In 1984 he turned more of his attention to international affairs after a visit to China. The next year—for the first time in six years—leaders of the United States and the Soviet Union met for talks that Reagan called "a fresh start." (About 13 million of his countrymen and women also traveled abroad that year.)

Americans were enthralled by space shuttles and *Star Wars*. The watchword was *high-tech*—computers went into the classrooms and satellites beamed television programs into living rooms. Mail seemed quaint when letters came by Fax and replies were phoned to answering machines. Long-playing records became obsolete as Americans bought CD players for their homes and cars, and put on Walkman earphones when they jogged.

AEROBICS AT PALM SPRINGS Fitness guru Sheila Cluff (center front) sets a healthy pace in exercise and diet. Cluff pioneered the teaching of "cardiovascular," later called "aerobic," dance in 1957. In 1977, she turned a 1920's hotel in the resort town of Ojai, California, into a spa called The Oaks; she opened The Palms at Palm Springs (above) in 1979.

Then the Dow dropped more than 500 points on October 19, 1987, and investors beat a fast retreat. Insider trading and junk bonds began to dominate the headlines. With the economy slowing down, a couple frequently needed two jobs to achieve the upwardly mobile life style that one wage earner had provided two decades earlier.

Still this didn't appear to bother the yuppies and dinks (young urban professionals and double-income/no-kids families) who cheerfully followed the "foodies" (restaurant critics and other food writers) from one culinary fad to another.

Tex-Mex or Southwestern food was stylish for a while. Jalapeno peppers turned up in everything except apple pie; blue corn tortillas were on menus across the country. Next, Cajun food had its turn. The hero was Paul Prudhomme, creator of blackened redfish—fillets dusted with spices, then quickly seared in a hot skillet.

The technique won both praise and criticism, but achieved such popularity that it put the redfish on the Endangered Species list. Over time emulators produced blackened swordfish, blackened bluefish, even blackened scallops.

Thai and Vietnamese dishes became the next rage. *Toute le monde* sipped delicate fish broth flavored with lemon grass, crunched deep-fried shrimp, or dipped skewered and grilled morsels of beef or pork into spicy sauces.

Nouvelle cuisine was defined and redefined, juggled and varied. California cooking became a major influence on writ-

65 Years Young

The title of America's best-known cook goes to Betty Crocker, who has symbolized General Mills products for decades. In fact, she's older than General Mills itself: her name was first used in 1921 in replies to entries in a contest sponsored by Washburn Crosby Company, a forerunner of General Mills. The name Betty was chosen because it sounded friendly; Crocker honored the first flour mill in Minneapolis, where Washburn Crosby was located. From 1924 to 1948, radios broadcast the "Betty Crocker Cooking School of the Air" to over a million listeners, but she didn't get a face until Hilda Taylor painted her portrait in 1936 for use in Gold Medal Flour advertising—and eventually its packages. Over the years Betty Crocker has been painted six more times to reflect changing American styles and attitudes. The latest version was done in 1986 by New York artist Harriet Pertchik, who depicted a Betty Crocker most cooks then could identify with—a working woman who was as much at home on the job as in the kitchen.

1936

1955

1965

1968

1972

1980

1986

THE EIGHTIES: HEALTH AND WEALTH

Anita's Chicken Fajitas with Fresh Tomatoes

Fajitas swept through Tex-Mex restaurants in the 1980s. A Southwestern equivalent of kabobs, fajitas are marinated strips of beef or chicken grilled with vegetables and served with shredded cheese, sour cream, and avocado.

1/2 cup dry white wine
1/3 cup lime juice
1 teaspoon grated lime peel
1 teaspoon crushed garlic
1/2 teaspoon salt
1/2 teaspoon ground red pepper
1 1/4 pounds boned, skinned, and halved chicken breasts, cut into strips
3/4 cup sliced onion
3/4 cup sliced green bell pepper
3/4 cup sliced yellow bell pepper
3 large, fully ripe tomatoes (about 1 1/4 pounds), cut into wedges
6 7-inch flour tortillas, warmed
Shredded Monterey Jack or cheddar cheese
Sour cream
Avocado slices or guacamole

In a shallow pan, combine wine, lime juice and peel, garlic, salt, and red pepper. Stir in chicken, onion, and peppers; let stand for 20 minutes. Preheat broiler to hot.

Using a slotted spoon, remove chicken, onion, and peppers from marinade, and arrange in single layer on broiler pan. Broil 3 to 4 inches from heat until chicken is opaque on one side, about 2 minutes. With a spatula, turn chicken and vegetables. Place tomatoes on broiler pan. Broil until chicken is cooked through, about 2 minutes longer. Serve in tortillas, accompanied by cheese, sour cream, and avocado.
Serves 6

Salad with Baked Goat Cheese

8 ounces goat cheese (chévre), cut into 12 rounds
1/2 to 3/4 cup olive oil
2 teaspoons dried thyme
6 slices day-old bread with crusts removed, cut into cubes
1 cup soft bread crumbs
Salt and pepper
THYME-FLAVORED VINAIGRETTE
1/2 cup olive oil
1 teaspoon dried thyme
1/4 cup balsamic vinegar
Salt and pepper
3 small heads Bibb, Boston, or red leaf lettuce

Marinate the cheese overnight in 1/4 cup oil mixed with 1 teaspoon thyme. Heat 2 tablespoons of the remaining oil; brown the bread cubes, a handful at a time, adding oil as needed. Drain these croutons on paper towels and set them aside.

Preheat oven to 350°F. Mix bread crumbs with remaining 1 teaspoon thyme and salt and pepper to taste. Drain the cheese, reserving the marinade. Roll cheese rounds in flavored crumbs, set in shallow dish, and bake for 7 or 8 minutes, or until lightly browned.

Meanwhile for the vinaigrette combine the oil and thyme with the balsamic vinegar. Add reserved marinade and season to taste with salt and pepper. Place lettuce in a large bowl, add vinaigrette and croutons, and toss well.

Arrange lettuce salad on 6 serving plates. Place 2 cheese rounds on top of each salad. Serve at once.
Serves 6

---

ers and restaurauteurs (often one and the same, as more chefs put their recipes in print.) Cross-cultural influences were important: Asian sesame oil gave body to French sauce, ginger spiced Italian soup, pound cake was made with polenta.

By the end of the decade, fickle restaurant-goers were seeking out diner food—or its French and Italian equivalents, *bistro* and *trattoria* food. Just as clothing and furniture styles of past decades were

Gratin of Potatoes and Carrots

Scalloped potatoes became a dinner party favorite in the 1980s as cooks found cream or a blend of milk and cream was an effortless way to ensure a golden crust. Gratins were made of potatoes used alone or in combination with other root vegetables such as the carrots here or celery root, parsnips, or Jerusalem artichokes.

1 garlic clove, halved
Butter
1 to 2 cups light or heavy cream
1 1/2 pounds boiling potatoes, peeled and sliced thin
1/2 pound carrots, peeled and sliced thin
1 cup shredded Gruyère cheese
Grated nutmeg
Salt and pepper

Preheat oven to 350°F. Rub bottom and sides of shallow oval gratin dish or deep 10-inch pieplate with garlic; discard clove. Butter dish generously. Arrange about half of potato and carrot slices in buttered dish. Season with lots of nutmeg; add salt and pepper to taste. Scatter 1/2 cup cheese over slices. Arrange remaining potato and carrot slices on top and sprinkle with remaining cheese. Pour in enough cream to barely cover potato and carrot slices. Bake for 1 hour or until vegetables are tender and have absorbed all liquid. The top should be golden brown.
Serves 4

Jícama Rémoulade

Although it looks like a turnip, the Mexican jicama tastes and crunches like a water chestnut when served raw. Here it substitutes for celery root in a variation of céleri-rave rémoulade.

1 cup mayonnaise, preferably homemade
1 tablespoon Dijon-style prepared mustard
1 teaspoon lemon juice or wine vinegar
2 to 4 tablespoons heavy cream
Salt and pepper
1 pound jicama, peeled and cut into thin julienne strips
1 tablespoon chopped fresh parsley, preferably flat-leaf parsley
Lettuce leaves

Combine mayonnaise, mustard, and lemon juice or wine. Add enough cream to make this sauce flow slowly from a spoon. Season to taste with salt and pepper. Add jicama julienne and stir until well-coated with sauce. Cover and let flavors blend for 30 minutes at room temperature, or for 3 or 4 hours in refrigerator. Spoon onto lettuce leaves and sprinkle with parsley.
Serves 4 to 6

WHO ATE WHAT WHEN

Busy life-styles, and a plethora of convenience foods, conspired to drive Americans out of both the kitchen and the dining room. A 1988 survey reported that only 60 percent of families ate together at least once a day. The old-fashioned picture of mom, dad, and the kiddies around a heavily laden dinner table was fading fast.

Because of jobs, school, clubs, or social activities, families ate in shifts or on staggered schedules. Breakfast was a bowl of cereal or a waffle heated in the toaster. Lunch was a sandwich or soup. Getting dinner meant microwaving a frozen entree or

revived, so were the comfort foods of the "retro cuisine" associated with them. For baby boomers who led the trend, the most comforting foods were those they remembered from their childhood in the 1950s and 1960s.

leftover, or finding a burger at a fast-food restaurant. ("Warming" and "heating" became new methods of cooking.)

Even when families gathered at the table, about a third ate haphazard meals assembled from cans and the freezer. However, the rest ate meals cooked from scratch; about half of these enjoyed "gourmet dishes"—sometimes defined as foods containing mushrooms or wine—and the rest indulged in old-fashioned American favorites like ham steak with yams or fried fish and hush puppies. (In the East, families ate more broiled foods, fewer fried foods, than other regions did. Everywhere, most cooks avoided dishes that took more than thirty minutes' preparation.)

Gracious dining had suffered a terrible blow when television appeared. Even if a cook took pains to prepare food carefully, by 1988 about one half of all adults would watch television while they ate dinner. The ratio rose to two-thirds among those who dined alone.

HOME COOKING

With more convenience foods and more microwaving, many cooks began to consider themselves "assemblers" rather than "creators." However, as *Fortune* magazine noted in 1980, "the same working mother

A MICROWAVABLE MENU By the end of the 1980s, traditional canned and frozen foods gave way to more convenient microwavable products. This display featured soups, a soup-and-cheeseburger combination, a fish sandwich, a bagel sandwich, a vegetable sidedish, and apple dessert: the makings of a three-course meal that could be "cooked" in minutes. Because the packages included disposable containers, only spoons and forks needed washing after dinner.

A Culinary Melting Pot

Any doubt that American cooks were responding to the food fashions and fads being advertised and promoted during the 1980s was erased by General Mills' 1990 Pantry Survey. The ten items most Americans kept on hand were ketchup (100 percent); prepared mustard, vegetable oil, and cinnamon (99 percent); margarine (98 percent); packaged spaghetti (96 percent); seasoned salt, chili powder, potatoes, and soy sauce (94 percent). An eclectic group, to say the least. The survey did not report how often any of these items were used, although the assumption was that cooks considered them all essential.

Sausage and Cheese Pizza

When the food processor proved able to knead bread dough, everybody could produce pizzas.

SAUSAGE AND CHEESE TOPPING
1 pound sweet Italian sausage
1 onion, sliced thin
2 tomatoes, peeled, seeded, and coarsely chopped
1/2 pound mozzarella cheese, grated (about 2 cups)
1/2 cup grated Parmesan cheese

PROCESSOR PIZZA DOUGH
1 package active dry yeast
1/2 teaspoon sugar
2/3 cup lukewarm water (110°F.)
1 1/2 to 2 cups all-purpose flour
1 teaspoon salt
2 teaspoons olive oil

2 tablespoons cornmeal
Olive oil

For the topping, remove and discard sausage casings. Stirring frequently to prevent lumps, fry meat in a skillet over moderate heat for 10 minutes; no trace of pink should remain. Drain well and cool.

Sauté the onion in the fat remaining in the skillet until slices are soft, about 10 minutes. Drain and cool.

For the dough, stir yeast and sugar into warm water; set aside until mixture foams, about 10 minutes. Place 1 1/2 cups flour in a food processor, turn machine on, and pour in yeast through feed tube. Process about 45 seconds. When dough pulls away from sides of bowl, add salt and oil. Process about 60 seconds. Dough should leave sides of bowl, but will be soft. (If dough sticks to bowl, add more flour by tablespoonfuls and process 10 seconds after each addition.)

Transfer dough to a lightly oiled bowl and turn to coat all sides with oil. Let dough rest for 5 minutes. Preheat oven to 450°F. Roll out dough. If using pan, oil it, strew with cornmeal, and slide dough onto it. Brush dough with oil and sprinkle evenly with sausage, tomato, and onion, then mozzarella and Parmesan. Place pan on lowest oven shelf or use peel to slide pizza onto baking stone. Bake for 20 minutes, or until cheese melts and crust browns.

Serves 4 to 6

HOME-STYLE PIZZA After Americans adopted pizza as a national food, cooks tried producing the pie at home. Making the dough and topping was easy, but getting a crispy crust was tricky until kitchenware dealers began selling baking stones that heated evenly to the high temperature of a pizzeria's brick hearth. For safety, cooks also could buy a wooden pizza peel—like the ones professionals used—with tapered front and side edges that would slip under the pie to slide it onto and off of the stone. (Photograph courtesy of The Chef's Catalog)

Mesclun Salad

The most interesting salads combine baby leaves of different flavors—sour and sweet, peppery and bland. Caution: do not use leaves from plants treated with insecticide or herbicide.

4 cups MESCLUN: young leaves of assorted greens such as arugula, curly endive, dandelion, lamb's quarters, nasturtium, oak leaf lettuce, and watercress
4 radishes, leaves trimmed and bulbs thinly sliced
1 tablespoon finely cut chive stems
Chive or nasturtium blossoms, if available
VINAIGRETTE
1/4 cup olive oil
1 tablespoon balsamic vinegar
1 teaspoon Dijon-style prepared mustard
Salt and pepper

Arrange MESCLUN in a serving bowl. Scatter radish leaves and slices over it. Add chives. Whisk oil, vinegar, and mustard together; taste and season with salt and pepper. Pour vinaigrette over salad. Toss ingredients together. Garnish with chive or nasturtium blossoms, if using.

Serves 4

---

who repairs to McDonald's three times a week may settle down on the weekend for a bout of gourmet cooking."

When Saturday came, cooks happily made cheese and baked breads and cakes for their families and friends. Home canning came back in style—not to save money but as a response to concerns about taste and nutrition. Making a batch of marmalade or strawberry jam proved remarkably easy, and rewarding.

Cooks felt freer—courageous enough to use ingredients in ways that would please them, not suit some special code. In the 1970s, foreign foods were faithfully reproduced. In the 1980s, cooks took liberties with dishes—creating vegetable lasagne and fish sausage, for example—and presented their improvisations confidently. Thus couscous was no longer an "ethnic" food served up with self-conscious flourish, but a side dish that might accompany anything from broiled fish to sautéed chicken.

Light and simple were the order of the day. Reflecting concern for health as well as calories, Americans cooks cut down on red meat and eggs, and increased their use of fish, skim milk, and fresh fruits and vegetables. New American cooking was typified by main-course salads (sometimes warm) and by barbecues, which came back in fashion with the discovery of mesquite, an ugly southwestern shrub that added a musty flavor to the coals. By the end of the decade, pecan branches and grapevines were more sought-after than mesquite.

A virtual bouquet of flowers appeared on platters and dinner plates. Roses, nasturtiums, daylilies, violets, and blossoms of such herbs as chives, basil, and sage were all edible. Cooks used them as garnishes and in salads, alone or with other ingredients. Gardeners were at an advantage, being able to control the spraying of plants so the nosegay would be chemical free. Just in time, Americans learned the French word *mesclun* for a mixture of wild and cultivated herbs, lettuces—and flowers.

Olive oil—extra virgin, virgin, first-press, cold-press—was discussed as passionately as wine. Pickles were put up in herbed and fruit-flavored vinegars produced in the kitchen keg (maybe an old wine keg converted for the purpose).

Although women did the cooking in

most families (86 percent of the time according to a Food Marketing Institute survey), in younger households one in ten primary food preparers was a male and in almost a third, the children helped. An American Frozen Food Institute survey found that 61 percent of pre-teen children prepared one or more meals on their own each week.

When entertaining, cooks embellished meals with soup and salad, and baked special cakes or froze ice cream. But on a day-to-day basis menus became simpler: fewer first courses, fewer side dishes, and—despite America's sweet tooth—fewer desserts. The trend away from elaborate meals was confirmed by a General Mills study that indicated Americans ate an average of 2.5 food items at lunch or dinner, whether at home or in a restaurant.

EXPANDING LARDER

In France, *nouvelle cuisine* had brought a change in the way food was cooked. In the United States, the major impact of the revolution was on the freshness and variety of ingredients that cooks sought. Jonathan Waxman who, with Melvyn Master, is credit-

SIN-FREE SWEETS As Americans began to take nutrition more seriously, manufacturers responded with foods that would fit into ever stricter diets. The mixes for these desserts and muffins, for example, contain none of the cholesterol that many people with heart trouble worry about, and remarkably little of the fat and calories anyone overweight should avoid.

Pasta Primavera

PRIMAVERA refers to spring, but cooks made this dish any time of year—improvising with whatever fresh vegetables and herbs were available.

1 cup tender green beans, cut into 1-inch pieces
2 small zucchini, sliced
2 small yellow squash, sliced
1 cup thinly sliced carrots
1 cup cauliflower florets
8 ounces spaghetti
2 garlic cloves, finely chopped
1 tablespoon olive oil
1/8 teaspoon crushed red pepper flakes
1/4 cup chicken stock
1/4 cup chopped fresh basil leaves
1/4 cup oil-packed sun-dried tomatoes, cut into strips
3 tablespoons grated Parmesan cheese
1/4 cup chopped fresh parsley

Steam the vegetables until crisp-tender, drain, and set aside. Cook the spaghetti according to package instructions. Drain and set aside.

In a large pan, sauté the garlic in olive oil until golden. Stir in pepper flakes, then chicken stock, and simmer for 1 minute. Stir in basil and vegetables. Add spaghetti and toss all the ingredients together thoroughly.

Arrange pasta on a serving platter. Garnish with sun-dried tomatoes, and sprinkle with cheese and parsley. Serve at room temperature.

Serves 4

ed with introducing California cooking to Manhattan at their restaurant Jams summed it up this way: "Jams is simple. And simplicity is the hardest thing to achieve. It means finding the very best of everything."

The French had always prized superior raw materials, so finding them in Lyons or Paris was nothing special. However, the American food industry, which prided itself on being able to ship foods by refrigerated truck or train, and bring "fresh" vegetables into every corner of the country, often delivered week-old lettuce and month-old carrots. Chain supermarkets preferred buying in bulk to dealing with local truck farmers; thus, in New Jersey—the "Garden State"—stores sold California peaches while the Jersey crop was being picked. In the United States, it was as much a challenge to get just-picked corn and strawberries as to locate newly laid eggs or to find free-range chickens or fish and shellfish not frozen for shipping.

During the 1980s, fresh ingredients were exactly that. Farmers' markets proliferated and greengrocers stocked locally grown fruits and vegetables. The quality of produce became the criterion by which most shoppers chose a supermarket. And there the produce sections obligingly stretched out to include dozens of salad greens (some of which were actually red or sported red or bronze ruffles) and miniature vegetables like tiny carrots and eggplants that were no bigger than a finger.

Frieda's Finest saw to it that the cook could have tomatillos and cactus pears from Mexico and Japanese enoki mushrooms. Her wares still had the most informative labels, but an increasing number of packers and importers were putting brand names on fruits and vegetables, including sweet corn.

Spaghetti squash, whose mild-tasting inner strands resembled pasta when

---

Frieda's and Karen's Finest

Starting in 1962 with only California brown mushrooms to sell, Frieda Caplan founded a produce specialty company in Los Angeles. The name she gave it—Frieda's Finest—represented her attitude toward her wares. Soon cooks across the country were hunting for places where they could identify the mushrooms and other unusual produce that bore Frieda's informative, purple labels. Frieda brought the first fuzzy New Zealand kiwi fruit to the U.S. She introduced passion fruit, spaghetti squash, purple potatoes, cactus pears, and kabocha squash. By 1989, Frieda's Finest, renamed Frieda's of California, was selling about 250 different exotic kinds of produce. Frieda had become Chairman of the Board and Chief Executive Officer of the firm in 1986 when her eldest daughter Karen (right) was named its President.

Golden Dried-Tomato Soup

In the 1980s, gourmets discovered the dried tomatoes that Mediterranean peasant cooks had used for centuries. During the peak of the season, cooks and farmers alike spread vine-ripened tomato halves in the sun to dehydrate them for winter use—a processs that concentrates their sweet flavor.

1 butternut squash (about 2 pounds)
1 onion, sliced
1 tablespoon vegetable oil
1 cup (1 1/2 ounces) dried tomato halves
2 1/2 cups water
1 cup milk
1 tablespoon chopped fresh basil, or substitute fresh parsley
Salt and pepper
GARNISH:
12 dried tomato halves
1/4 cup sour cream
1 tablespoon milk

Preheat oven to 400°F. Cut stem end from squash and halve lengthwise. Place in shallow baking pan; add 1/2-inch water. Bake until fork-tender—45 to 60 minutes.

Meanwhile, in 3-quart saucepan, cook onion in oil over medium heat about 5 minutes or until tender, but not browned. Stir in tomato halves and 2 1/2 cups water. Bring to boil; then simmer 5 minutes. Set aside to cool.

For garnish, pour boiling water over 12 dried tomato halves. Soak for 2 or 3 minutes, drain softened tomatoes and set aside. Thin sour cream with 1 tablespoon milk. Set aside.

Discard seeds from cooked squash. Scoop squash pulp into container of electric blender or food processor. Add contents of saucepan. Blend until smooth. Return to saucepan. Mix in 1 cup milk and chopped basil; simmer 3 minutes. Thin with additional water or milk, if desired. Season to taste with salt and pepper. Serve hot, garnishing each bowl with 1 tablespoon sour cream and 3 softened tomato halves.

Serves 4

---

cooked, and licorice-flavored fennel, which looked like bulbous celery, appeared in seed catalogs and supermarkets. Familiar vegetables in unexpected colors—red cauliflower, white eggplants, or yellow beets—had been sold only in ethnic markets before, now everyone could get them.

Fruits that had never been seen beyond the tropics, or the fanciest of metropolitan greengrocers, appeared in small-town stores: pomegranates and passion fruit, lush papayas, mangos tasting like ripe peaches, armored cherimoyas with custard-soft flesh, waxy-skinned carambolas (starfruit).

Mushrooms were displayed in profusion. In 1970, Americans ate only 1.3 pounds apiece each year, but by 1989 they were gobbling up 3.5 pounds. Fresh tomato consumption (including those picked green as well as local crops) jumped from about 12 pounds per person per year in 1970 to 18 pounds by the end of the 1980s, presumably reflecting concern with health as well as calories.

Sun-dried tomatoes were received with such enthusiasm that they became a cliché. Blue cornmeal upstaged the white and yellow kinds. Raspberry vinegar or pungent balsamic vinegar were mixed with walnut oil to dress salads.

SEASONINGS

Fresh herbs became increasingly available for longer seasons. And exotic herbs like lemon grass took root in American cooking as it spread from Asian grocery specialists to supermarkerts.

Green peppercorns appeared, followed by red peppercorns. (Actually, the latter were the fruit of the Brazilian pepper tree also known as the Christmasberry or Florida holly, a species not related to the true pepper plant *piper nigrum.*)

As highly seasoned cuisines like Cajun, Mexican, and Chinese became more popular, spice sales more than doubled from 1970 to 1990—reaching 762.1 billion pounds. In 1989 American cooks spent an estimated $2 billion on dried herbs and spices, according to the American Spice Trade Association.

Spice blends dated to the eighteenth century, when Indian dealers catered to British customers with already-ground spices in mixtures called curry powder. Predictably, premixed spices such as seasoned salt, Cajun spices, crab boil, and barbecue seasonings had enormous appeal because their names explained their purpose—and the cook did not need to worry about getting proportions of spices right or, indeed, measuring them at all.

CHEESE

During the Christmas season in 1980, a supermarket in Chicago sold four tons of Brie—a triumph for importers who had found Americans slow to shift from familiar cheddars to exotic kinds of cheese. However, cheese consumption was on the rise; in 1966 it hovered between 9 and 10 pounds per person each year and twenty

CHEESE FOR EVERY TASTE Not only did Americans eat more cheese than ever in the 1980s, they also made and ate more varieties. This sampler shows ten best sellers: in the back row, from left, are Edam, Gouda, Muenster, and blue cheese; in the middle row, are Provolone, Parmesan (grated), Swiss, another Provolone, Colby, and white cheddar; in the front row are cheddar slices and yellow cheddar.

Soufflé Sponge Roll with Nut Filling

Fashionable as a first course at dinner or a main course at lunchtime, this soufflé was baked twice—in a jelly-roll pan, then on a serving platter. Before being rolled, the souffle could be spread with softened liver pâté, minced chicken mixed with mayonnaise, or softened cream cheese beaten with minced pimientos or hot chili peppers.

SPONGE
2 tablespoons (1/4 stick) butter
2 tablespoons all-purpose flour
1 cup milk
5 eggs, separated
1/2 cup grated Parmesan cheese
FILLING
1 to 1 1/2 cups ricotta cheese
1/4 cup grated Parmesan cheese
1/4 cup chopped walnuts or pecans
1/2 teaspoon grated nutmeg
TOPPING
2 tablespoons (1/4 stick) butter
2 tablespoons grated Parmesan cheese

Butter or oil an 11 by 17-inch jelly-roll pan. Line with buttered wax or parchment paper. Preheat the oven to 350°F. For sponge, melt 2 tablespoons butter in a large pan. Stir in flour, then add milk and stir until this sauce thickens and boils. Remove pan from heat to cool sauce. Beat in egg yolks and 1/2 cup Parmesan cheese. Beat whites until stiff; fold them into sauce mixture. Spread in the prepared pan and bake for 15 minutes or until puffy and golden.

For the filling, beat together 1 cup ricotta and 1/4 cup Parmesan. Stir in nuts and nutmeg. If filling is too thick to spread, add more ricotta.

When soufflé is baked, cool slightly, then turn it out onto wax paper. When completely cooled, spread surface with filling and roll up soufflé starting from one long end.

Just before serving, preheat oven to 350°F. Place the roll on an ovenproof platter. Pour melted butter over and sprinkle with Parmesan. Bake for 5 to 10 minutes, or until crusty and heated through. Cut into 1/2-inch slices.

Serves 8 to 10

---

years later it more than doubled to 23 pounds.

Although processed American cheese for grilled sandwiches and mozzarella for pizzas dominated, imports found a bigger place on the cheeseboard. Sales rose from 170 million pounds in 1968 to 274 million pounds in 1989. And chèvre—the goat cheese once considered too pungent for American tastes—became a status symbol of the 1980s.

For many people, the stylish images of cheese and white wine before dinner, or cheese and fruit afterward, also overcame any lingering doubts about fat and cholesterol counts.

PASTA

Ubiquitous. Everywhere everyone was making or eating pasta. Cooks could buy it fresh or dried in more than 400 sizes and shapes: flat, round, tubular, fluted, or fancifully formed into butterflies, shells, rings, or alphabet letters. Domestic consumption in 1989 topped 4 billion pounds—approximately 18 pounds for every American man, woman, and child.

Americans had known pasta since *Yankee Doodle Dandy*, but they rarely ate much of it except in spaghetti and meatballs or macaroni and cheese. In the 1960s and 1970s, growing interest in

Hamburger Steaks with Goat Cheese

During the 1950s, putting Roquefort cheese on top of—or inside—hamburgers was considerably terribly chic. By the 1980s, it was goat cheese that proved the cook was a gourmet.

2 pounds lean ground beef
4 tablespoons soft goat cheese
4 slices French or Italian bread, toasted in the oven (optional)

Preheat broiler. Divide beef into four portions and shape each one into a patty. Press a 1-tablespoon lump of cheese into the center of each patty, completely enclosing it with beef. Broil patties about 4 inches from heat, for about 5 minutes on each side for medium-rare meat. Serve on top of, or beside, toasted French bread, if liked.

Serves 4

A PANOPLY OF PASTAS From squiggles to shells, elbows to squills, pasta came in endlessly varied shapes and sizes at supermarkets nationwide by the 1980s. Although some cooks insisted on making their own, most of the 17.7 pounds that each American ate during 1989 was store-bought, and at least 90 percent of it was made in the U.S.

Italian cuisine gave pasta new appeal. Its diversity was bewitching. As demand increased, though, local pasta makers disappeared to be replaced by regional and national brands; only about forty plants in the United States made pasta in the 1980s. Less than 10 percent of sales represented imported pasta, most of which came from Italy although Americans toyed with Asian and Middle Eastern forms.

Fresh pasta—some flavored and colored with vegetables such as carrots or spinach—became widely available in supermarkets.

New kinds of pasta machines enabled cooks to produce pasta at home with a minimum of effort. Serving green fettuccine or shells was fashionable, but not quite as splendid as presenting hot dishes or salad combining colors: green with white for "straw and hay," pink with both green and white for "rainbow" effects.

FAREWELL TO RED MEAT

Red meat lost sales to poultry during the decade, reflecting a widespread acceptance of nutritional guidelines calling for diets with less fat, less cholesterol, and less salt. In 1987, the U.S. Department of Agriculture changed beef grades again. This time the government altered only names, changing Good (which ranked third after Prime and Choice) to Select.

The hope was that a new name would get more supermarkets and butchers to stock the grade, and would coax more shoppers into buying this leaner, less-marbled beef. Cattle ranchers and dieters cheered while steak-lovers groaned.

By then, annual per capita con-sump-

Beef on a Big Scale

When cowboys drove enormous herds of steers from Texas up the Chisholm trail to Abilene, live cattle were shipped by rail to wherever meat was needed. But after Gustavus Swift began the use of refrigerated railroad cars in 1877, packers started to slaughter cattle at central yards and ship only carcasses, thus saving money for everyone—packer, butcher, and cook alike. Chicago, the hub of many railroads, became meat packer to the nation,

Before World War II, most cattle went from the plains states' ranches to the cornbelt states where they fattened for several months. Next the cattle traveled to farmer-feeders near the major meat packers, where 150 or so at a time were "finished" in feedlots before being sent to the stockyards. The packers slaughtered the cattle and sold the carcasses to regional wholesalers, who divided or "broke" them into halves or quarters for re-sale to retail butchers or to institutions. (After a carcass went from Chicago to a New York wholesaler, its halves or quarters might then be shipped to Miami and Cleveland.)

During the 1950s and 1960s, the center of U.S. population moved westward. Rather than ship cattle east, Currier Holman and A. D. Anderson decided to move their packing operation west and established Iowa Beef Processors in rural Dennison, Iowa. Other packers followed their lead.

Over the years, packers moved even farther west to the plains states. By the end of the 1980s nearly half of all beef cattle were produced in Nebraska, Texas, Kansas, and Colorado. Although most feedlots handled less than 1,000 cattle at one time, some were enormous, like the one below, and could hold more than 32,000 cattle.

In the 1960s, I.B.P. also had pioneered the sale of "boxed beef" to supermarkets. Instead of buying whole carcasses, stores could order "primal" or "subprimal" sections that would yield the retail cuts that would sell best. (A loin is an example of a primal cut; butchers slice it into sirloin, strip, and tenderloin steaks.) Supermarkets, and their customers, benefited because they did not need to buy, or pay for the shipping of, whole carcasses; local butchers only had to cut wholesale pieces into retail ones. At the end of the 1980s, most packers sold boxed beef—that by then was shipped in vacuum-sealed plastic pouches.

tion of red meats had declined to a tad above 135 pounds. Beef sales were at about 73 pounds per capita—eclipsed by poultry sales at 78 pounds, of which 63 pounds were chicken and 15 turkey. (The evident turn-around did not accurately reflect what was eaten: the boneless equivalent of beef sold in 1987 was about 69 pounds, while chicken was about 43 pounds and turkey close to 12.)

Duck Breasts with Raspberries

In some cases, butchers sell duck breasts separately. Otherwise, use a boning knife to cut wings and legs from whole ducks. Then cut along each side of the breastbone to free the meat. Keeping the knife blade close to the ribs, use short strokes to remove each breast in one piece. Set wings, legs, and body aside for another use.

4 boneless duck breast halves, skin and fat removed
1 tablespoon vegetable oil
Salt and pepper
1 cup red wine vinegar
1/4 cup sugar
1 cup fresh raspberries, or substitute 10-ounce package frozen raspberries, thawed and drained

Sauté duck breasts in oil over moderate to moderately high heat—turning them often—for about 10 minutes or until they become just firm and juices run clear when they are pierced with knife tip. Transfer breasts to warmed platter, sprinkle with salt and pepper, and cover to keep them warm.

Deglaze skillet with wine vinegar, stirring to scrape up all brown bits. Cook until vinegar is syrupy and reduced to about 1/2 cup. Stir in sugar, then add raspberries. When raspberries are coated with sauce, remove skillet from heat. For each serving, slice a duck breast across the grain into 4 or 5 pieces and arrange them on a warmed plate. Spoon raspberry sauce over duck slices.

Serves 4

Buffalo Chicken Wings

Janice Okun, food editor of the BUFFALO NEWS, New York, supplied this authentic recipe.

BLUE CHEESE DIP
1 cup mayonnaise
1/2 cup sour cream
1/4 cup crumbled blue cheese
1/4 cup chopped fresh parsley
2 tablespoons chopped onion
1 garlic clove, chopped
1 tablespoon lemon juice
1 tablespoon distilled white vinegar
Salt and pepper
Cayenne pepper

20 to 25 chicken wings
Vegetable oil, for deep-frying
SAUCE
1/4 to 1/2 cup (1/2 to 1 stick) butter
1/2 to 1 bottle (2 1/2 ounces) Frank's Louisiana hot sauce

Celery sticks

Make the dressing ahead to chill for at least 1 hour. In a bowl, blend the mayonnaise, sour cream, and blue cheese. Stir in the parsley, onion, garlic, lemon juice, and vinegar. Taste and season with salt, pepper, and cayenne.

Cut wings in half and remove wing tips. Deep-fry the wings, about half of them at a time, in hot oil until they are crisp and golden brown—about 10 minutes. Drain wings well. Meanwhile, melt 1/4 cup butter in a saucepan. Add about 1/2 bottle hot sauce; stir until blended. Taste sauce. To make it milder add more butter; to make it hotter add more hot sauce.

Place chicken wings in a large container with a cover. Pour sauce over wings and mix well. Serve wings warm, accompanied by celery sticks and dip. Dunk wings and celery in dip as you eat. Provide lots of napkins.

Serves 4 to 6

A BIRD IN EVERY POT

In 1962, 17 percent of chickens were sold cut up; in 1989, 79 percent. The retail cost of these broilers was near $16 billion. Even turkeys brought in $5 billion, and some of these carried brand names like those on chickens.

The plump capon, like the stewing hen, became a *rara avis*. Few markets were even willing to special-order it. Just a handful of farmers bothered with what seemed in the 1980s to be a costly process of first castrating male chickens, then keeping them supplied with corn for four to five months.

Duck became everybody's darling in the 1980s. By the decade's end retail sales were about $100 million. Previously, the Long Island Duckling (in fact, a duck given a more euphonious name by some long-forgotten advertising man) had been most often roasted whole and served, as likely as not, à la orange, cherry, kumquat, or grape. Although the roaster's goal was crispy skin enclosing moist meat, in most homes the skin turned out flabby and the meat dry.

Then some clever cook discovered that the breast—really the only edible part anyhow—could be removed, sautéed to perfect doneness, and sliced to spread out in a fan for serving. Usually, the duck still arrived at the table with fruit; raspberries now were the first choice.

(Oddly, the goose was not redeemed in like fashion, despite its similarity to duck. The best hope for the goose was the technique popularized by Julia Child of steaming and braising the bird—duck or goose—before browning it in the oven.)

DESIGNER WATER

During the 1980s, Americans had their pick of hundreds of different bottled waters—perhaps as many as 600—from just about every part of America and Europe, including Transylvania. These were consumed before, during, and after meals. They became between-meal refreshers. While many were purer-than-pure still spring water (or tap water masquerading as such), others bubbled. Some were flavored with fruits or vegetables.

The most stylish sparkling water of the decade was Perrier, which got a set-back in 1988 when a North Carolina laboratory found traces of benzene (a possible carcinogen) in samples of it. Although the traces were miniscule, the Perrier company immediately recalled nearly 72 million bottles.

Perrier discovered the source of the benzene in filters used for the natural carbon dioxide gas that gave their water its bubbles. The problem was soon corrected, and the springs at Vergeze, France, reopened. The *nouvelle* production bottles were labelled "natural mineral water," not "naturally carbonated water" in response to the FDA contention that although the water might be carbonated when brought up from underground, its bubbles had to be removed before it could be safely bottled—then it was recharged with natural CO_2.

By the time the fuss was over, Evian had supplanted Perrier as America's top-selling imported bottled water. The little green bottle of Perrier was stilled considered toney on the East Coast, but in San Francisco and Los Angeles it had been replaced by more recherché waters such asa Levissima and Ram-Losa.

BEVERAGES

Bottled water wasn't the only beneficiary of the national preoccupation with health and fitness. By the end of the 1980s, Americans drank enough fruit juice and juice drink to serve about 30 quarts a year to every man, woman, and child. Concerns about health also explain why they preferred low-fat and skim milk (consuming more than 60 quarts) to whole milk (about 50 quarts).

During 1989 the beverage industry spent almost $1.5 billion for print, television, radio, and other kinds of advertising and promotions. Among the "other" were the fees paid to television and movie producers to introduce brand-name products into their sets where they would be seen as part of a table setting or room decoration.

(If $1.5 billion seems outrageous, even unbelievable, here's how it broke down: regular soft drinks, $288 million; diet soft drinks, $140.4 million; bottled water, $19.5 million; wine $90.8 million; distilled spirits, $272.2 million; beer, $677.2 million. Coca-Cola Classic alone spent $66 million and Diet Coke $52 million. Advertising paid off. According to Beverage Industry magazine, an American drank more gallons of soft drinks than of tap water—46.6 to 37.3 gallons.)

At the decade's end, 75 percent of all wine drunk in the United States was American made, and the domestic vintages cost as much as the imports. California, which could boast of more than 600 wineries, 150 of them in the Napa Valley alone, produced the lion's share. But the quality of American wines from every part of the country increased along with the enthusiasm of wine lovers. Wine substituted for the preprandial cocktails of earlier days, sales increasing to more than three gallons annually per capita. (Strong spirits consumption dropped from about 3 to 2 gallons per capita during the decade.)

For those who wanted a sweet or distinctly fruit-flavored drink, the bottled wine cooler replaced the bar-made wine spritzer. Even with coolers, close to 75 percent of the wine drunk in America was consumed by 5 percent of the population.

MICROBREWERIES

Beer was as popular as ever during the 1980s. Almost 400 brands of foreign beer were available, including such exotic imports as Club beer from Ghana and Trader from Kenya. But these began to lose cachet as microbreweries opened across the country, providing Americans with rich local brews.

During Prohibition, most hometown breweries had gone out of business. Afterward, changes in technology—pasteurization, refrigeration, and the like—made it costly for small brewers to compete with the large ones, which soon became regional distributors and eventually national brands. During the 1940s and 1950s, customers seemed to be impressed with standardized and mass-produced light lagers. Imports satisfied those beer lovers who demanded maltier taste, or insisted on ale or stout.

Then, in 1965, Fritz Maytag took over the failing Anchor Brewery in San Francisco and popularized Steam Beer, a nineteenth century nickname for a draft beer brewed without ice. "Steam" referred to the pressure of carbonation that developed in the barrels, making the beer difficult to control and serve—and reminding early

THE MODEL MICROBREWER When Fritz Maytag took over San Francisco's foundering Anchor Brewing Company in 1965, he turned it into the paragon of innovative, upscale microbreweries. Although its production remained miniscule compared to that of nationally advertised firms, in 1989 Anchor made about 58,000 barrels of beer of half a dozen or so different types including porter, barley wine, and a clove-scented yuletide ale.

Californians of the pressure in a steam engine's boiler.

When Maytag made a success of his brewery, others were opened on the West Coast. But not until 1977, when the federal government legalized home brewing of up to 800 gallons per family, did beermaking become popular and spur widespread development of the microbrewery industry. By then the quality of information and ingredients had improved enough so that small brewers could count on good results.

By definition, a microbrewer's production is small. Anchor pumped out 58,000 barrels of various beers in 1989. (By comparison, Anheuser-Busch pumped out about 170,000 barrels a day.) The microbrewer aimed not at quantity but quality, and usually experimented with different styles of beer. In addition to Steam Beer, Anchor produced Liberty Ale, Anchor Porter (a dark beer), Old Foghorn (an aged barleywine akin to ale), and a spicy Christmas Ale.

Depending on state law, microbrewers would package the beer in kegs or bottles, and sell it to consumers, retailers, or wholesalers. Although some sixty-four microbreweries were in operation by the decade's end, they still represented less than 1 percent of the beer market.

TRENDS IN FISH

Bland-tasting fish with white flesh were American favorites as consumption increased to 16 pounds per person in 1989—a national total well over 6 billion pounds. Fish sales rose to more than 15 pounds a year for each American by the end of the decade; adding the usual estimate of 5 pounds of sport fish apiece, the total consumed is above 20. Young adults, twenty to thirty years old, ate 40 pounds a piece—almost twice the average consumption.

Lean fish fillets sold best to all segments of the market, partly because they were high in protein but low in cholesterol, partly because they could be cooked in less than thirty minutes, making them the perfect choice for hectic schedules.

Trendy varieties included "trash fish" that fisherman previously had considered unsaleable, such as shark, skate, and monkfish—an incredibly ugly specimen the French call *lotte*, which tastes like the similarly unattractive lobster. Hitherto unheard-of fishes such as New Zealand's orange roughy appeared in supermarkets nationwide.

FARMING FISH

The U.S. appetite so exceeded its haul of wild fish that up to 60 percent of those fish served were imported. And American aquaculture became big business, with about 12 percent, or 750 million pounds, of the fish eaten in 1989 coming from farms. Instead of netting or hooking their catch, the "fishermen" grew it like a crop, raising fish

---

Catfish with Mustard-Dill Sauce

4 tablespoons clarified butter
Salt and pepper
4 catfish fillets
2 tablespoons finely chopped shallots
2 tablespoons dry white wine
1 tablespoon Dijon-style prepared mustard
1 cup low-fat milk
Hot pepper sauce
1 teaspoon fresh lemon juice
2 teaspoons finely cut fresh dill, or 1 teaspoon dried dill
1 lemon, cut into 8 wedges

Melt the butter in a large skillet. Salt and pepper the catfish fillets lightly. Sauté fillets for 4 or 5 minutes on each side, or until fish is opaque. Transfer fillets to a warmed platter and cover with a tent of foil to keep the fish warm.
In same skillet, sauté shallots for 2 minutes, or until translucent. Stir in wine, mustard, milk, and a dash of hot pepper sauce. Simmer until sauce thickens enough to coat spoon. Stir in lemon juice and dill. Spoon a circle of sauce on each dinner plate and place a fillet on top. Garnish with lemon.
Serves 4

ELEGANCE WITHOUT CHOLESTEROL Dieting need not mean flavorless or boring foods. A case in point: this fillet of farm-raised catfish is bathed in a tangy Scandinavian-style sauce of mustard and dill, and accompanied by curls of paper-thin cucumber slices.

FARMING FISH What look like acres of water turn out to be catfish farms. Mississippi alone has about 90,000 acres of ponds fed by underground wells that are home to an estimated 625 million catfish. The fish are harvested with seines when they are eighteen months old and weigh a respectable 1 to 1 1/2 pounds apiece.

either in tanks or ponds, or in pens set out in coastal waters.

Aquaculture had been practiced in China 3,500 years ago, and was well known to ancient Greece and Rome. The earliest evidence of modern-type farms comes from first-century B.C. accounts by the Roman historian Pliny, who describes "fish reservoirs" a nobleman kept at his summer estate.

Contemporary techniques, of course, are more sophisticated and farmers usually specialize in one crop. Catfish accounts for half of all U.S. aquacultural production. In 1990, total harvest was close to 360 million pounds—three-fourths of which came from Mississippi, where brand-name catfish originated and the average pond was a massive 17 land acres in area and 7 feet deep.

Belzoni, Mississippi, has named itself the Catfish Capital of the World. It applauds that title every spring with a catfish festival and, at what is undoubtedly the world's largest fish fry, serves thousands of catfish to tens of thousands of happy diners.

Aquaculture also yielded 57 million pounds of rainbow trout (mostly from Idaho), 11 million pounds of salmon (Washington and Maine); and about 6 million pounds of tilapia, a mild-flavored fish with white meat grown in California.

Shellfish, too, were being farmed: crayfish in Louisiana—about 95 million pounds; clam, mussel, and oyster meats totaling at least 30 million pounds. Farmed shrimp was imported, chiefly from Ecuador, and farmed frogs' legs from Japan.

Many other species of fish and shellfish were being experimented with: striped bass, sea scallops, lobsters, blackcod, and abalone. The Japanese are working on a technique for training certain fish to lead "wild" fish toward bait; the United States has had similar experiments with fish farming.

FARMS

By the 1980s, less than 2 percent of the U.S. population (about 6 million people) fed Americans better and at lower cost than

A RURAL IDYLL America's lush farmland lured pioneers westward to plant crops and raise cattle—and settle the continent from "sea to shining sea." Although some years might be bad, others would be bounteous enough to keep the farmer's hopes high. And by the 1980s up-to-date equipment took much of the drudgery out of the jobs of tilling, planting, cultivating, and harvesting. (Photograph courtesy of John Deere)

farmers and ranchers in any other part of the world could feed their own people. By the end of the decade, over half of all farmland was still owned by individual farmers. The family farm, with three generations pitching in to get chores done, survived. Corporate ownership was prohibited in the Dakotas, Iowa, Kansas, Nebraska, and Oklahoma. Nonetheless, more than three-fourths of America's 2.25 million farms produced incomes less than $40,000 a year, so those farmers depended on outside work for survival.

Institutional investors directed many of the largest, most technologically advanced farms. About 15 percent of the farms took in almost 75 percent of all farm sales. For these agribusinesses, world markets were critical because American agriculture exported about one-third of what it produced.

Like the chicken farmer before him, the hog farmer tried to "industrialize." Although most hogs still were only one part of a diversified farm operation, others were bred, born, and fattened for sale in what have been called pork factories. Anywhere from 5,000 to 15,000 hogs might be housed together with the temperature, daylight, rations, even reproductive cycles meticulously controlled. In some, the hog never saw the sun or set hoof on soil from birth until market day six months later.

Even the farmer who raised only 400 to 500 hogs at a time—along with growing wheat, corn, and perhaps cattle—housed the animals in heated, insulated buildings with cement flooring.

With *big* generally treated as synonymous with *better*, the so-called old-time varieties of plants and animals became more rare. Both plants and animals were judged by productivity and marketability. If plants failed to yield generous crops or didn't look as good as they tasted, they disapppeared from fields. Two-thirds of U.S. corn, for example, came from six varieties, although hundred of varieties once existed; two thirds of all rice came from four varieties. Livestock and poultry fared no better if they matured slowly, laid few eggs, or were slow to reproduce.

The inevitable shrinking of the gene bank resulting from these policies worried horticulturalists and zoologists, who began to take measures to preserve some samples of discarded varieties or types. Without a wide array of genetic alternatives, a disease or pest might destroy American herds or wipe out its crops, as the root louse *Phylloxera vastatrix* ravaged European vineyards in the 1860s. In Margaret Visser's insightful *Much Depends on Dinner*, she noted that "Uniform crops are easy sow, easy to harvest, easy to sell. Machines like, demand, and produce uniformity. But nature loathes it: her strength lies in multiplicity and in differences. Sameness, in biology, means fewer possibilities and, therefore, weaknesses."

Meanwhile, consumer and environmental groups were working on a number of fronts to ban the use of pesticides and

---

Brave New Gardens

Disease-resistant, insect-tolerant plants may be here soon if biotechnologists have their way. And the National Science Foundation is working on the development of fifty-four potential new crops for U.S. farms. Out of the more than 110,000 known plant species in the world, nearly 80,000 are edible—yet human beings use only about 3,000 of them. Thirty species supply more than 95 percent of our calories; wheat, rice, and corn alone account for more than half.

Among the promising new species for American cooks and gardens, the NSF includes half a dozen native vegetables: familiar-sounding wild rice and unfamiliar buffalo gourd, grain amaranth, tarwi, quinoa, and marama bean. Buffalo gourds are squashlike; the edible seeds are 35 percent protein and 34 percent oil; the starchy roots reach 60 pounds but must be soaked in saltwater to remove their bitter taste. Amaranth was a major grain crop of the Aztecs and Incas when the Spanish arrived. Its grains are higher in protein than cereal grains—and contain the key amino acid, lysine; their leaves resemble spinach.

Tarwi and quinoa are other Incan crops, still grown in Latin America. The protein-rich seeds need soaking to remove the bitter outer coating. Marama bean resembles the peanut in nutritional value and is as protein-rich as soybeans. The beans taste like cashews when roasted. The roots may be roasted like sweet potatoes.

herbicides they believed could endanger foods and/or contaminate ground water. The manufacturers insisted that the existing regulations on chemicals ensured their safety—and chemicals were needed to eliminate weeds and insects. Antichemical groups asserted that pests could be dealt with by natural methods, which would prove cost-effective and profitable. The individual farmer, of course, chose sides for himself.

Pasta and Walnut Fruit Salad

1/2 pound medium-sized pasta shells
1 cup nonfat plain yogurt
1/4 cup frozen orange juice concentrate, thawed
2 oranges, peeled, sectioned, and skin removed
1 cup red seedless grape halves
1 cup green seedless grape halves
1 apple, cored and chopped
1/2 cup sliced celery
1/2 cup walnut halves

Cook pasta shells according to package directions. Drain. In large bowl, blend yogurt and juice concentrate. Stir in shells. Add orange sections, grapes, apple, celery, and walnut halves. Toss together. Serve at room temperature, or cover and refrigerate to serve chilled.
Serves 6 to 8

(About 1 percent of all fruits and vegetables were organically grown in 1989; it was predicted that by 1999, the figure would be 10 percent.)

DIET AND NUTRITION

Americans were obsessed during the 1980s with healthful eating. Comparing their cholesterol counts was small talk; so was gossiping about the latest changes in the rules. Caffeine was out, then in again; oat bran was in, then out, and in once more. For a time olive oil was acclaimed because it would lower cholesterol levels, but by 1989 the wonder oil was canola, which is pressed from rapeseed.

In 1983 sugar was said to cause diabetes, heart disease, appendicitis, and ulcers. Three years later the FDA absolved it of blame except for contributing to tooth decay.

At the decade's end the secretary of health and human resources ruled that all claims linking a food product's ingredients to the prevention of disease must be deemed scientifically valid by his department. Evidence supported only a few: foods rich in calcium help prevent osteoporosis; reduced salt intake helps prevent high blood pressure; reduced fat intake and/or eating foods rich in dietary fiber might reduce the risk of cardiovascular disease and cancer.

Meanwhile, health-conscious diners claimed they wanted high-fiber, vitamin-rich, low-calorie, low-fat, reduced-salt food. Food manufacturers obliged them with a deluge of "lo" and "lite" products ranging from soft drinks to beers, from mayonnaise to ice cream. The words *no cholesterol* turned up on labels for everything from soups to cake mixes.

Tabbouleh

Middle Eastern peasants, who ate cracked wheat as a staple, would have been stunned to find this simple cold dish considered high fashion. However, whole wheat, nuts, and raw vegetables made tabbouleh delicious and crunchy—and a healthy substitute for potato salad.

1 cup bulgur (cracked wheat)
1/3 cup lemon juice
1/4 cup almond or olive oil
Freshly ground black pepper
1 cup quartered cherry tomatoes or tomato chunks
2/3 cup sliced scallions
2/3 cup chopped almonds
1/2 cup lightly packed chopped fresh parsley
2 tablespoons chopped fresh mint
6 romaine lettuce leaves

Measure the bulgur into a large bowl. Pour boiling water over bulgur just to cover. Set aside about 30 minutes, or until water is completely absorbed. In another bowl, blend lemon juice and oil; season with pepper. Stir in tomatoes, scallions, almonds, parsley, and mint. Add bulgur and toss thoroughly. Cover and refrigerate at least 2 hours. To serve, spoon bulgur mixture onto romaine leaves.
Serves 6

Yogurt Cheese with Parsley

For use as an hors d'oeuvre spread, the cheese might be flavored with whatever fresh herbs were at hand—dill, thyme, basil, or rosemary, for example. For topping a dessert, the cheese might be mixed with oil of peppermint drops or with a dab of almond or vanilla extract.

32 ounces plain, low-fat yogurt
1/4 cup olive oil
2 tablespoons chopped fresh parsley, preferably flat-leaf parsley
1 garlic clove, chopped
Freshly ground black pepper
Toasted crackers

Line colander with double thickness of cheesecloth and set in deep pot or bowl. Put yogurt inside cloth and cover tightly. Refrigerate overnight. Gather edges of cloth and squeeze out remaining liquid. Transfer cheese to bowl, cover, and refrigerate until ready to use. (Keeps 1 week.)
Divide cheese into 4 portions and shape into patties. Place in shallow dish. Stir oil together with parsley and garlic; add pepper to taste. Pour seasoned oil over yogurt, cover, and marinate at least 4 hours in refrigerator. Bring to room temperature for about 30 minutes before serving on small plates, accompanied by toasted crackers.
Serves 4

Of the $290 billion spent on retail food in the United States, an estimated 20 percent—some $58 billion—went for "lo," "lite," or "diet" foods. Fresh fruits and vegetables were not counted in the total.

By the 1980s, more than 8,000 health food or natural food stores, which had sales in excess of $4 billion, supplied an enormously varied fare. Tofu and bean sprouts were still there, along with fresh yogurt and whole grains. But in addition the grocery

Oven-Fried Green Tomatoes

In the B.C. (Before Cholesterol) tradition, green tomatoes were fried in bacon fat and served coated with a sauce made by deglazing the skillet with heavy cream. During the 1980s, tomatoes—like chicken pieces—were "oven-fried." Winter's firm, ripe tomatoes might substitute, but in the green stage tomatoes have a special, spicy taste.

Nonstick pan spray or 1 tablespoon   vegetable oil
2 eggs
2 tablespoons cider vinegar
1/4 teaspoon cayenne pepper
1 cup cornmeal
Salt and pepper
3 large green tomatoes, trimmed and cut into 1/2 inch slices

Preheat oven to 400°F. Coat a large baking sheet with nonstick spray, or brush with oil. Set aside. In small bowl, beat eggs with vinegar and Cayenne. Mix cornmeal with salt and pepper to taste. Spread meal on plate. Dip one tomato slice at a time into eggs to coat it, then into cornmeal to cover both sides. Place slice on baking sheet. Bake for 10 minutes, turn slices over and continue baking for 10 to 20 minutes longer or until tomato slices are tender and golden brown. Serve hot.

Serves 3 or 4

Chocolate Torte

During the 1980s, chocolate became such a passion among cooks and diners that whole cookbooks were written about it—and enthusiasts launched the magazine, CHOCOLATIER. Among the most popular chocolate desserts was the flourless, or nearly flourless, torte. Like Viennese DOBOS TORTE, this version benefits from being served with dollops of whipped cream.

8 ounces semisweet chocolate, cut into pieces.
8 ounces (2 sticks) butter, cut into pieces
2 teaspoons vanilla extract
6 eggs, separated
1 cup superfine sugar
1/4 cup flour
1 cup heavy cream, whipped and sweetened

Preheat oven to 325°F. Melt chocolate and butter over simmering water or very low heat. Stir in vanilla. Set aside to cool. Butter and flour a 9-inch round cakepan with 2-inch sides; line bottom with buttered waxed paper.

Beat egg yolks with superfine sugar until pale and thick, 15 to 20 minutes. In separate bowl, beat egg whites until peaks form, about 5 minutes. Gently fold flour into egg yolk mixture; add chocolate. Stir heaping spoonful of egg whites into yolk mixture to lighten it; then fold remaining whites into yolks. Pour batter into cake pan. Bake until center of cake is moist, but not runny—about 35 minutes. Edges will be firm and center somewhat soft.

Cool cake completely in pan. Loosen sides with knife. Invert cake onto serving plate. Garnish each serving with whipped cream.

Serves 6 to 8

---

had organically grown vegetables and fruits, hormone-free chickens, nitrite-free sausages and bacon, and preservative-free drinks.

Although Americans talked a good game about nutrients, many wanted to eat their cake—and skip it, too. A man would put Sweet 'n Low in the coffee he drank while eating a frosted doughnut. A woman would have a green salad with lemon juice for dressing at lunch, then order an ice cream sundae as dessert.

In 1985 the sales of low-calorie sauces or dressings and artificial sweeteners increased 10 percent. Also in 1985, Dove Bars went on sale nationally, to the delight of chocolate lovers everywhere. And prestige ice creams with a butterfat content of

Farm Support at the Grass Roots

During the mid 1980s, organic farmers in New England borrowed a new marketing system from Western Europe and Japan. Called Community Supported Agriculture, it was based on selling "shares" in crops; shares were payable in advance, thus permitting farmers to buy seeds, livestock, and feed without borrowing money from a bank. In return, shareholders received fresh fruits, vegetables, and livestock directly from the farmer and spent less than they would have to in stores. For example, at one farm in Maine, where shares cost $450 per adult, community members got a grand total of 650 pounds of produce—one or two bags of assorted freshly picked and organically grown vegetables every week from June through September. Besides produce or livestock, shareholders might get herbs, flowers, even honey or cider. By 1990, almost 100 CSA projects were operating in the U.S.—including farms in Michigan, Wisconsin, Oklahoma, and California.

---

15 to 20 percent (10 to 16 percent in traditional ice cream) increased sales by 20 percent. In 1986, Americans spent $3.3 billion on potato chips—thin, thick, ridged, natural, or flavored—but always salted. And they bought about $7 billion worth of ready-to-eat cereals, many sweetened with the equivalent of 1 tablespoonful of sugar per serving.

A 1989 Gallup poll of 1,225 adults showed 44 percent thought their diets were very healthful; 48 percent settled for somewhat healthful. Even so, 63 percent said they worried a great deal or a fair amount about the healthfulness of the food they ate. Nearly half believed they did not eat enough fish and seafood and one-third admitted to not eating enough fresh fruits and vegetables. As for overindulging, 31 percent admitted to eating too many sweets, 23 percent too much red meat, 20 percent too much snack food such as chips and crackers. Cynics sneered that American interest in eating a healthful diet was a mile wide and an inch deep.

SPA FOOD

Spa food, elegantly known as *cuisine minceur* when the recipes came from France's Michel Guérard, was high style. At the beginning of the decade, only three or four dozen spas existed in the United States. By the end of the decade an American could choose from among about 165 spas in the United States and as many again abroad, at prices ranging from less than $200 a week for the Spartan approach to fitness to $4,000 a week for sybaritic self-indulgence.

The spa programs might include mountain biking, walks in the woods, shiatsu massage, aerobics, or mud-wrap facials—but were almost sure to feature gourmet low-cholesterol meals.

Like *nouvelle cuisine*, spa cooking started with fresh ingredients. Vegetables and fruits dominated; one rule of thumb was that three-fourths of a diner's plate at any meal should be covered by plant foods, with seafood or meat or dairy foods occu-

Spa Cuisine

Persian Pancakes with Cinnamon Filling demonstrate that the spa food at Rancho La Puerta could be tempting to look at as well as low in calories. Two of the crepe-like pancakes plus filling represent 120 calories, a quarter-cup of fresh raspberries add 17 or 18 more calories. By comparison, one serving of raspberry shortcake has about 350 calories. Here's the Rancho recipe:

Persian Pancakes

2 eggs
1/2 teaspoon canola oil
1/4 teaspoon ground cinnamon
1/4 teaspoon grated nutmeg
1/2 cup whole-wheat flour, preferably stone-ground
1 cup nonfat milk
Vegetable spray for pan
Cinnamon Cheese Filling
Fresh raspberries

In a bowl, whisk eggs, oil, cinnamon, and nutmeg together. Add flour, then whisk in milk and blend thoroughly. Refrigerate 2 hours. Heat 5-1/2-inch nonstick crepe pan; coat with vegetable spray. Pour in about 2 tablespoons of pancake batter, tilting the pan in different directions to cover bottom evenly. Cook 1 minute on each side. Stack cooked pancakes. Spray pan again, if necessary. Makes 12 pancakes.

To serve, spoon 2 tablespoons filling in a strip along one side of each pancake. Lift filled edge and roll onto pancake to enclose filling completely. Place two pancakes on each serving plate and garnish with raspberries.

Serves 6

Cinnamon Cheese Filling

12 ounces nonfat cottage chees
1 tablespoon ground cinnamon
1 teaspoon ground nutmeg
1 tablespoon fructose or sugar
1/2 cup golden raisins

Combine all ingredients. Refrigerate for 1-1/2 hours to let flavors blend.

Makes about 2 cups

pying the rest. Frying and sautéing generally were taboo; instead, foods got steamed, grilled, roasted, or poached. Flavor came from herbs and spices, not salt. Honey replaced sugar.

Despite the daily goal of 1,000 calories at most spas, the menu was made appealing and the foods presented beautifully. Breakfast concentrated on fruits, high-fiber cereals (with skim milk), and whole-grain bread or muffins. Soup and salad were served for lunch; dinner might be a baked fish fillet or a slice of lean beef, plus vegetables and a steamed grain such as wild rice—and there was sherbet or a baked apple for dessert.

FAUX FOODS

The creation of *faux*, or fake, foods wasn't new. Vegetarians, Kosher dairy restaurants, and Catholics observing Lenten food rules—all had improvised steak and cutlet analogues out of grains, beans, and seasonings from time immemorial. Margarine had passed as butter since the 1870s. Saccharin dated back to 1879.

At the turn of the century, the vegetarian and Seventh-day Adventist Dr. John Harvey Kellogg (whose brother became the cereal magnate) had experimented with nut "meats" made from peanuts and gluten. Another church member transformed soybean into a semblance of bacon bits; he called them "smoein." A later generation of Americans proudly sent Tang orange drink to the moon with the astronauts in 1965.

However, the manufacturing and use of *faux* foods took off during the 1980s as never before, partly fueled by cooks' concerns about cholesterol, partly because analogues saved money.

Tofu graduated from the bland soybean cakes familiar in Asian stir-fried dishes to a basic ingredient in ice cream. The mozzarella cheese on store-bought pizza often was an ersatz product created from milk protein and vegetable oil.

The salty, rubbery imitation lobster and imitation crab legs served in delicatessen salads were *surimi*—colored, flavored, and molded fish paste the Japanese pressed, usually, from Alaskan pollock.

The supermarket contested with the health food store in its eagerness to display the latest technological wonders. And Worthington Foods, Inc., in Worthington, Ohio, was ready to grab the golden ring. Founded in 1939 by Seventh-day Adventist Dr. George T. Harding III, the company followed Kellogg's lead to transform ground peanuts, salt, flavorings and colorings into a dark "meat" called Proast and a light "meat" called Numette A little later wheat gluten and mushroom broth yielded Choplets.

During the Second World War, meat rationing gave Worthington's products a broader appeal, and pushed sales in 1945 to $100,000. As the audience grew, new foods were added—Meatless Wieners, for example—but the major breakthrough in *faux* meats came in the late 1960s with the ability to spin soybean fibers into high-protein meat analogues that simulated texture as well as flavor and color.

The number of vegetarians in the United States tripled from about 2 million in 1960 to more than 6 million in 1989. At the same time, Worthington's sales skyrocketed from approximately $6 million to more than $65 million. By then the firm was making more than 200 fresh, canned, and frozen products under four brand names: Worthington, Morningstar Farms, La Loma, and Natural Touch. In addition to Stakelets, Breakfast Links, and Dixie Dogs, they sold a roasted grain beverage as a caffeine-free replacement for coffee (Kaffree Roma) and had a selection of Tofu Toppers to compete with flavored sour-cream mixtures.

Worthington also makes Scramblers—one of several egg substitutes, which actually are 99 percent egg whites. That remaining 1 percent does wondrous things to color and flavor, so the product can take the place of whole eggs for breakfast and baking.

COOKING SCHOOLS

"Everyone" attended a cooking school in the late 1970s or early 1980s—unless, of course, they were too busy running one of their own. In 1978, Francois Dionot, director of L'Academie de Cuisine, and Donald Miller organized the Association of Cooking Schools. By 1984, some 1,200 schools were members.

But as the decade ended, the number of hobbyists plummeted and most small schools closed. Many large schools had always had training programs for chefs. Now they turned their energies toward producing professional programs with state accreditation. In 1990, with Anne Willan of La Varenne as president, the organization became the International Association of Culinary Professionals.

Instead of going to cooking schools, hobbyists could buy the VCR cassettes that many celebrated cooks worked on in the 1980s. These video demonstrations were accompanied by printed recipes, sparing the students any need to take notes. Because the demonstration was on tape, students could stop and start it as often as needed until got they got the technique down pat.

The C.I.A.

Initials can be deceiving. There's nothing secretive about the Culinary Institute of America, which has no special links to Washington. In fact, it is the most publicized U.S. school for professional chefs.

The C.I.A. grew out of the New Haven Restaurant Institute, founded in 1946 in New Haven, Connecticut, to increase the number of fine chefs available to American restaurants. Attorney Frances Roth became its first director, and Katharine Angell, wife of a former Yale University president, was the first chair of the board of directors. The teaching staff of three—chef, baker, and dietician—conducted a sixteen-week program.

As the school grew in size and prestige, it changed both its name and headquarters—finally purchasing a seminary with a seventy-five-acre campus in Hyde Park, New York. It opened there in September 1972. By the end of the 1980s, the staff represented twenty countries and numbered 100 chefs and instructors, including David St. John-Grubb shown here demonstrating culinary techniques. The school offered two 21-month degree-granting programs (Associate in Occupational Studies) to almost 2,000 full-time students.

HOUSE CALLS With video cassettes introduced during the 1980s, cooks could watch the stars of the culinary world demonstrate how to make dishes. In the privacy of their homes, they could look at a cassette again and again, stopping it and restarting it repeatedly. Here, the demonstrators are master cooks and writers Pierre Franey and Craig Claiborne.

Although *The Pleasures of Cooking* magazine attained a circulation of 100,000, publication stopped with the July-August 1987 issue. *The International Review of Food and Wine* was bought by the American Express Publishing Corporation and resumed publication as *Food and Wine* in the summer of 1980. It reported a circulation of about 850,000, making lots of advertisers as well as readers happy. *Bon Appétit* circulation went to over 1.3 million and *Gourmet* had a circulation of over 800,000.

COOKBOOKS

The computerized recipes that had been predicted for decades did not appear. Books did. By the carload. *Publishers Weekly* reported that 1,137 books on food and wine were published in 1985—compared to 49 in 1960.

Time magazine called Jeff Smith of Seattle the "most visible gourmet" of the 1980s. In his television shows and books, he styled himself the Frugal Gourmet, and ironically—in a period of prosperity—found the title very popular.

The prize for "fastest gourmet" was undoubtedly won by Barbara Kafka, whose 1987 *Microwave Gourmet* was the

THE FRUGAL GOURMET Trying to dispel the notion that all "fine" food is expensive, Jeff Smith styled himself the Frugal Gourmet. A Methodist minister from Seattle, he proved an irrepressible as well as an informed cook. Here, he shows off a Turkish coffee set. During the 1980s, millions watched his television programs on PBS stations nationwide. His four cheery cookbooks—THE FRUGAL GOURMET, THE FRUGAL GOURMET COOKS WITH WINE, THE FRUGAL GOURMET COOKS AMERICAN, and THE FRUGAL GOURMET COOKS THREE ANCIENT CUISINES—had hardcover sales totaling 3.4 million.

most comprehensive (and imaginative) book on the subject. For conventional ovens honors might need to be shared: both Carol Cutler and the *New York Times* team of Pierre Franey and Bryan Miller published books called *Cuisine Rapide*; hers was a paperback version of the 1976 *Six-Minute Gourmet* and the Franey-Miller volume was based on "60-minute Gourmet" articles written for the *New York Times*. A newspaper colleague of theirs, food writer Marian Burros, put together the quickest of conventional cooking strategies and recipes in her 1988 *20-Minute Menus*.

No statistic from *Publishers Weekly* included all of the uncounted hundreds of community or charity fund-raising cookbooks. The prototypes for these were published in 1861 by ladies working for the so-called Sanitary Commissions, groups organized primarily to make bandages for Union troops. To raise money for their work, the ladies compiled books of their own recipes, which sold well, particularly if they contained "secret family receipts." Women in Confederate states liked the idea, and emulated it.

The Food Writer of Record

Craig Claiborne was born in Sunflower, Mississippi, and remained enthusiastic about Southern cooking—no matter how sophisticated and cosmopolitan he became. Claiborne was finishing his undergraduate work at the University of Missouri School of Journalism when Pearl Harbor was bombed. After graduation, he enlisted in the Navy, and served in North Africa, then England and Europe. On his return to the United States, Claiborne worked in advertising and publicity in Chicago, but went back into the Navy during the Korean War. By the time he finished his tour of duty, he had decided to study cooking and went to the Professional School of the Swiss Hotel Keepers Association in Lausanne, Switzerland. A job at GOURMET magazine in New York City was the stepping stone to his appointment in August 1957, as food editor of the NEW YORK TIMES. Besides providing recipes, food news, and interviews with amateur and professional cooks, Claiborne wrote weekly restaurant reviews. His food reportage took him on trips around the world. In addition to his newspaper work, Claiborne wrote more than a dozen books—beginning with the classic THE NEW YORK TIMES COOK BOOK, which has been reprinted repeatedly. By the end of the 1980s, Claiborne had given up his role as food editor of the TIMES, although he still contributed articles.

First Lady of French Fare

From her 1963 debut as "The French Chef" on Boston's WGBH public television station, Julia Child has entertained and educated millions of American cooks—and become the most universally loved of all food authorities. Her sensible, informal presentation earned her show a Peabody Award in 1965 and an Emmy in 1966. Since those days, she has appeared in three subsequent television series, while also writing half a dozen cookbooks and—during the early 1980s—a monthly feature for PARADE magazine. Born in Pasadena, Child graduated from Smith College; during World War II she worked in Asia for the OSS (now CIA). After the war, Child lived in Paris where she first studied, then taught cooking.

Over the decades, an almost unimaginable variety of good causes have been supported by books, most of which followed the early format: recipes grouped by food type (soup, meats, desserts, and such) and identified by the names of their contributors. Sometimes pages were simply duplicated on copying machines and stapled together. Most were professionally printed and held together by plastic-comb or wire binding.

As Americans grew more fascinated by regional culinary customs, community cookbooks became recognized as an important source of information. What better way to find out about the day-to-day lifestyle, family celebrations, and social events in Tupelo, Mississippi, for example, than to read a cookbook put together by a local garden club or church organization? Community cookbooks had always been desirable travel souvenirs. Now cooks collected such books with renewed enthusiasm.

During the 1980s, Anne Seranne tested and edited recipes from Junior League cookbooks, then compiled them in collections by region—Eastern, Southern, and so on. And Ann Harvey of Oxmoor House, Inc. headed a staff that assembled, tested, and edited recipes from community cookbooks of all kinds for *America's Best Recipes*, an annual series started in 1988.

A PLUMP, TIRELESS SALESMAN Nearly forty years since his inception on an artist's drawing board, the Pillsbury Doughboy still works hard promoting prepared dough for breads, rolls, cookies, and pies. The chef's TOQUE he wears is still cocked at an angle, as it was when he was created by the Leo Burnett Co. advertising agency in 1952.

NEW WAYS TO PAY FOR GROCERIES Special equipment made it possible for some shoppers of the late 1980s to access their bank accounts at the supermarket checkout line. This made it possible for them to pay their bills with electronic funds transfers, eliminating the need to write and verify checks.

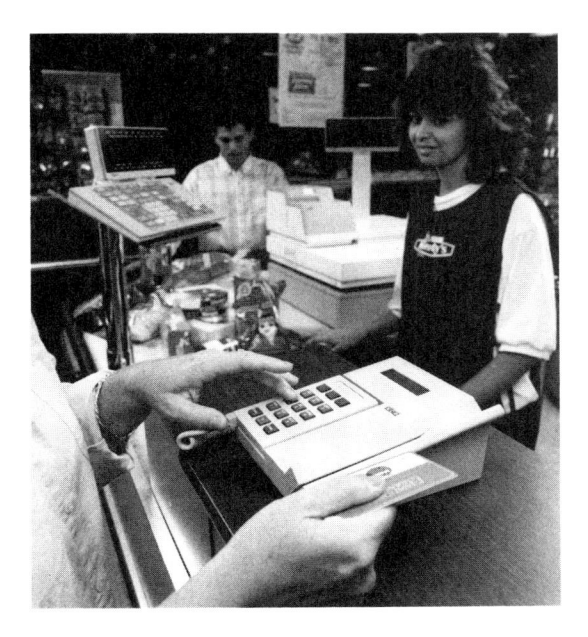

KITCHEN CULTURE

SUPERMARKETS

Shopping from home by computer—that world of the future—was still years away. But at the supermarket checkout, food was placed on a conveyor belt and a laser beam read the coded price symbol, then fed the data into a computer that toted up the bill in a fraction of a second and produced a receipt listing foods by name and cost, indicating refunds, and so on. At the same time, the purchase was entered into the store's inventory.

The average supermarket of the late 1980s was about 43,000 square feet, although a goodly number were as large as 60,000 feet square. The items stocked rose to as many as 35,000 to 40,000 in 1989. About 60 percent of the roughly 20,000 food labels in supermarkets displayed information about calorie, vitamin, and mineral content, although not in standardized form.

Americans bought 82 percent of all their bakery goods and 69 percent of their fresh seafood at supermarkets, according to a Food Marketing Institute survey of 1987. More surprising, they also bought 67 percent of their paper products there and went to the supermarket to use the cash machine and Federal Express drop-off box, and to buy flowers and houseplants, or motor oil for the car.

The typical supermarket was part of a chain, controlled by an unreachable "headquarters" that dictated merchandise, display, prices, and employee and consumer policies. Year by year it got harder for the customer to "always be right" in such circumstances.

During the 1980s, supermarkets were deluged with new products and new sizes or flavors of old ones; nine out of ten of these

PRESSURE IN A SKILLET Back in the 1940s, all pressure cookers looked like saucepans or kettles, and held huge amounts of food. Such cookers still are made, but this new-style "pressure frypan" measures only 3 inches deep and 9 1/2 inches across. It works every bit as fast as its predecessors: beef stew for six takes twenty minutes, risotto a mere seven minutes. Made of heavy-gauge stainless steel, the frypan has a solid disk of aluminum in the base to distribute heat evenly. Inside, the bottom is textured to suit fatless browning and prevent sticking.

INSTANT HEAT The sleek black cooktops that Amana introduced in 1988 were the first American-made quartz halogen products. This smooth cooktop has two quartz elements (vacuum-sealed quartz glass tubes filled with halogen glass) that produce heat and light virtually the second they are turned on, so food is heated more rapidly than with earlier smoothtop cooking systems. There are two electric resistance elements as well—one 6-inch and one that can be used as either a 5 1/2-inch or an 8-inch burner with the turn of a knob.

RANGETOP GLASSWARE A transparent glass-ceramic with a golden tint became Visions cookware, introduced by Corning in 1983. Depending on the cook's fancy (and recipe), the pots and skillets could be used in a conventional or microwave oven, under a broiler, or over a burner on top of the stove. Like Pyroceram, the opaque glass-ceramic, this cookware could go directly from the heat to freezer or refrigerator.

failed. Campbell Soup Co., for example, introduced over 500 new items in three years—including Fresh Chef chilled salads, which failed, and the successful Le Menu frozen dinners.

Even in gigantic markets, shelf space had a limit. Furthermore, unpacking cases and putting goods on shelves proved costly. To control the numbers of introductions, grocers began to impose charges of different kinds on old as well as new items. Putting a product onto a shelf might require paying a slotting allowance. If the product failed to sell, there might be a flop fee. When a market put up a special display, the food manufacturer paid. And at some stage all these fees got tacked onto the cost to the customer.

KITCHEN APPLIANCES

Once they discovered the fun of playing with electric kitchen appliances, Americans couldn't get enough of them. Adding to an already abundant number of options, manufacturers in the 1980s produced ever more elaborate toasters, coffee grinders and breakfast coffeemakers, small espresso machines, ice cream makers, even pasta

Wondrous Worksavers

AUTOMATIC was the buzzword of the 1980s—and a surprising array of kitchenware fit the category. The espresso-cappuccino pump machine (left) not only brews both kinds of coffee, but also grinds the beans for them, ensuring unsurpassed freshness. The pasta maker (center) can create eleven different shapes in about ten minutes; the bread baker (right) produces a 1-pound loaf in as little as two hours and forty minutes. All the cook need do with either the pasta or bread machine is put in the ingredients. (Photographs courtesy The Chef's Catalog)

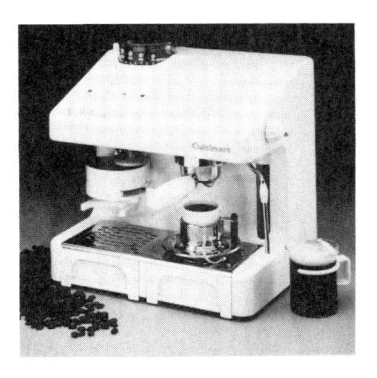

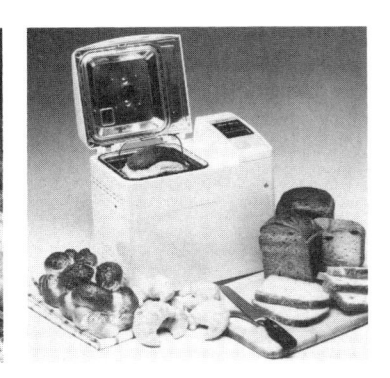

KITCHEN CULTURE

Everything-Proof Counters

Plastic laminate countertops delighted cooks of the 1960s with vivid colors and textures ranging from slick to slate. But the plastic sheathing was thin, and burns or cuts spoiled its beauty. In the 1980s, manufacturers solved the wear problem with solid plastic countertops that could be sanded if accidentally marred—without losing their lovely hues or appealing surfaces.

equipment that the cook need only feed with ingredients in order to get fettuccine or lasagne or other pasta shapes. The topper must have been the bread machines: put in raw ingredients and a few hours later take out a loaf of baked bread.

The Cuisinart reigned as supreme food processor until 1985, when Sunbeam brought out the OSKAR, or Outstanding Superior Kitchen All-Rounder. Half the size of other food processors, it chopped and minced with the best of them—and cost only $60. In the first year, Sunbeam sold 750,000, which was as many as they could produce.

Most big-city customers found these devices in kitchenware stores, which proliferated as the decade went on. Small-town America finally was able to buy the same goods through the catalogs of an ever-increasing number of mail-order firms.

MICROWAVES

By 1980 the appliance everyone wanted was a microwave oven. At the beginning of the decade fewer than 10 percent of American homes owned them. In 1989 more than 75 percent had microwave ovens, and foodmakers were scurrying to produce microwave-compatible foods: packages designed specifically to go from cabinet or freezer directly into the microwave oven.

By the decade's end, just about half of all American households had dishwashers. A third of them had freezers. Refrigerators were in 99.8 percent, and two-thirds of those refrigerators were frost-free. Electric stoves and ovens outnumbered gas models about three to two.

Not everyone looked on the appliance explosion with approval. Historian Ruth Schwartz Cowan observed in *More Work for Mother*, published in 1983, that American housewives worked fifty hours a week at home in 1980—about as many

THE EIGHTIES: HEALTH AND WEALTH

Cooking with Éclat

In the 1980s designers brought back the all-white kitchen they had banished thirty years before. Appliances and cabinets, even floors and countertops, were white again; new materials and coatings gave practicality to the renaissance. For cooks preferring more traditional styles, wooden cabinets and ceramic tiles were in fashion. Cabinets in both kinds of designs boasted an amazing array of special features: pull-out cutting boards and pantry baskets, revolving shelves, and storage doors. (Photographs courtesy Kraftmaid Cabinetry)

hours as they had in 1910. Rather than reducing time spent, the appliances usually introduced new standards and tastes that created new time-consuming tasks and, as often as not, new needs for money. Thus, women went to work to pay for the appliances, so they had even less free time than before.

TAKEOUT

A quasi-joke of the 1980s was that dinks thought the four food groups were canned, frozen, catered, and takeout. Behind the joke was the serious fact that more and more Americans—married or single, with or without kids—had less and less time for cooking.

Takeout food was a $43 billion business. Sometimes dinner came from a tablecloth-type restaurant and cost $25 or more. Far commoner was the low-priced, fast-food dinner bought at a drive-through window. For the couch potato—that addict who could not tear himself or herself away from the television set—many food services and restaurants took telephone orders and delivered meals to the door. Though not as profitable as takeout food, the phone-delivery business in 1989 reached about $5.6 billion.

Additionally, after decades in which

First Lady of Southern Cooking
Edna Lewis, who popularized Southern food in three best-selling cookbooks, is shown below discussing culinary matters with fellow chefs Felipe Rojas-Lombardi, left, and Mark Miller. Lewis began to cook while she was growing up on a Virginia farm. Her first professional job was in Manhattan at the Cafe Nicholson in 1948. From there she went to the Fearington House in Chapel Hill, North Carolina, and later the Middleton Place in Charleston. She finally returned to Manhattan at Aschkenasy's U.S. Steakhouse, but then—in her early 70s—went to Gage & Tollner's landmark Brooklyn restaurant after Peter Aschkenasy bought it in 1988. There she enlivened the menu with crab soup, seafood gumbo, beef brisket—and splendid desserts like lemon meringue pie and chocolate souffle. A believer in natural foods, Lewis shopped at farmers' markets for organically grown produce; her pie was made with unsprayed lemons. In addition to her kitchen career, Lewis has raised a family of adopted Masai and Ethiopian children. She lectures on African culture at the American Museum of Natural History in Manhattan. (AP/Wide World Photo)

Cajun Cooking Star

Growing up in the heart of the bayous, Paul Prudhomme learned the secrets of Cajun cooking early. At eighteen he went to New Orleans and from there traveled around the country teaching himself about other kinds of food by serving as a cook in diners and truckstops. When he returned to New Orleans, Prudhomme went to work for the Brennan family, finally becoming corporate chef and overseeing Commander's Palace and all of their other restaurants. After five years with the Brennan's, Prudhomme opened a neighborhood lunchroom in July 1979 with his wife Kaye; he got up at 4 a.m. to prep the kitchen at K-Paul's, then turned it over to his wife while he went to his job at Brennan's. Eventually the lunchroom stayed open for dinner and Prudhomme left Brennan's. In time, his success made it possible for him to concentrate on dinners only. By 1985, when Prudhomme branched out with a restaurant in New York City, he had a repertory of 2,000 dishes: blackened redfish was his most famous creation, but he also served blackened prime ribs, gumbo, stuffed eggplant and mirliton squash (called pirogues after flat-bottomed bayou boats), and the spicy fried crayfish tails known as "Cajun popcorn." (AP/Wide World Photo)

---

catering services closed almost as fast as they opened, so-called social caterers—those providing foods for weddings, anniversaries, birthdays, and other special occasions—caught on. Catering developed into a major money-maker earning more than $2 billion nationwide in 1989. When cooking schools had shut down, their proprietors often turned to catering. Although some lost money, others became local success stories.

THE CELEBRITY CHEF

For centuries, a chef was an anonymous kitchen servant, probably uneducated, certainly a man. Women could become culinary professionals, but they were called cooks.

By the 1970s, Bocuse, Guerard and other *nouvelle cuisine* chefs became international celebrities. So did New American chefs like Alice Waters. By the 1980s, kitchen work was invested with glamour. The newly-hired American chef was likely to have a college degree and/or a diploma from a professional culinary school. He—or, with increasing frequency, she—demanded a higher salary than most restaurants had ever paid chefs before. With the salary came more attention and respect. The chef became the restaurant's major attraction. His or her name could draw critics and diners alike. Many chose to assemble their presentations in open kitchens where diners could see them at work.

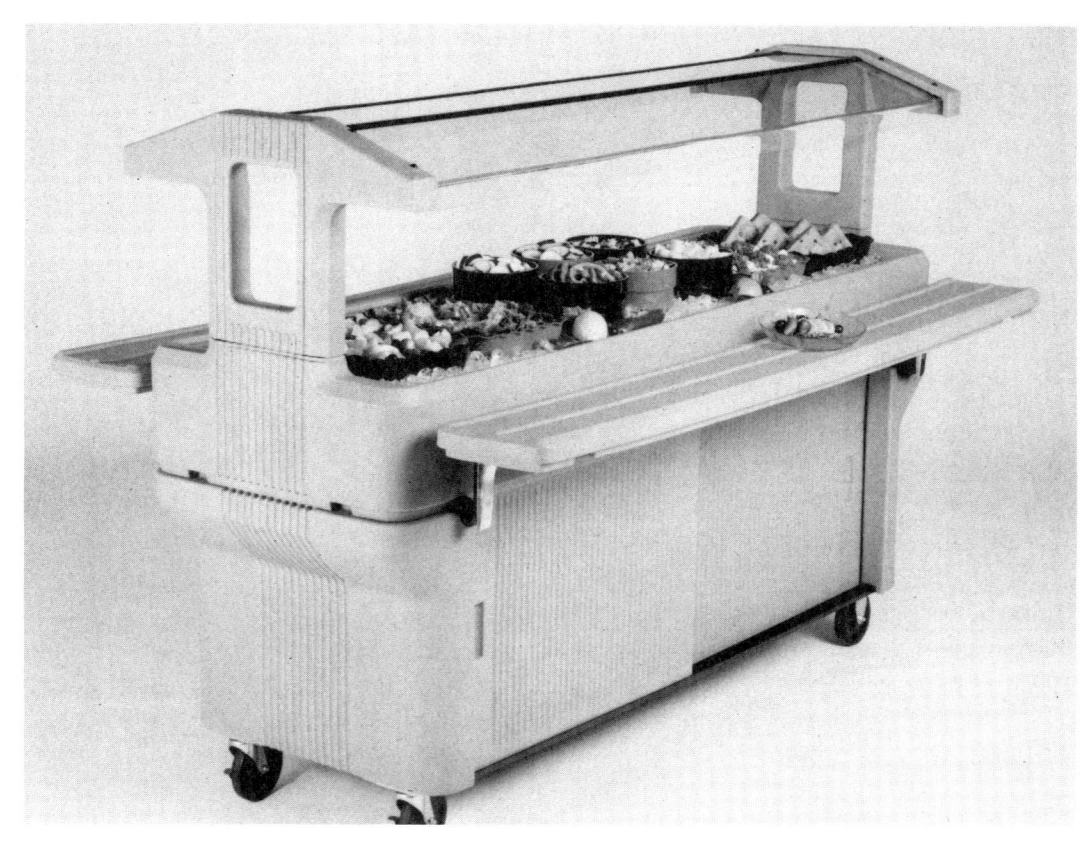

SALADS ON WHEELS By the 1980s, the salad bar became a standard feature in most restaurants—including those of schools, hospitals, even cruise ships. To make it easy for restaurants to add a bar, manufacturers created portable units like this one that could be wheeled to wherever it was needed. Bars were refrigerated and insulated to keep the containers cold and the salad ingredients fresh. The "sneeze guard" above the food was made of see-through polyethylene plastic, which blocked the germs but not the view. (Photograph courtesy Continental Carlisle, Inc.)

Women who took over kitchens of "serious restaurants" in the 1980s included such star chefs as Susan Spicer at Maison de Ville in New Orleans, Anne Rosenzweig at Manhattan's Arcadia, and Joyce Goldstein at Square One in San Francisco. Lydia Shire worked in both Boston and Los Angeles restaurants.

Among the dozens of outstanding men were Jeremiah Tower of Stars in San Francisco; Wolfgang Puck at Los Angeles's Spago; Michael Foley of Printer's Row in Chicago; Patrick O'Connell at The Inn in Little Washington, Virginia; Stephen Pyles at the Routh Street Cafe in Dallas; Larry Forgione at An American Place in Manhattan.

ELEGANT DINING

In 1989 Americans spent $114 billion eating at the tables and counters in restaurants, lunchrooms, fast-food eateries, commercial cafeterias, bars, and taverns. An additional $2 billion went to ice cream and frozen-custard stands. Big business indeed, and growing.

Upscale, serious restaurants got only a

small percentage of those billions, but their influence on American cooking was great nonetheless. They set the pace locally and, through food critics, dictated what cuisines and dishes would be stylish and which wines or bottled waters in fashion in other establishments across the United States. When magazines photographed such restaurants and published recipes for their food, the chefs became as famous nationwide as rock stars.

During the 1980s, restaurants were "theater" and eating out was in. Never had restaurants been so stylish—even though dinner for two might cost $200 (or more) in big cities. If an establishment was new, diners wanted to be among the first in their social group to visit it, especially if it had been favorably reviewed. Even the creation of "smoking" and "non-smoking" sections in the last years of the decade failed to dampen diners' enthusiasm.

Decor meant more than food, unless, of course, the chef was a celebrity. For some diners, good food or good service, even a good location, didn't matter much: to see and be seen were reasons enough to choose a particular place for lunch or dinner. A few carried this pattern further and needed to be seated in a particular part of the restaurant, even at a special table. At the "21" Club in Manhattan, for example, a table anywhere except in the front room was "Siberia."

When times were good, the freespending yuppies and dinks found new restaurants opening—as food writer Molly O'Neill put it—like popcorn in a hot pan. When starting a restaurant, the motto was borrow and spend, leaving many places heavily in debt. If the rent rose or operating costs climbed, the restaurant went broke—often to open again under a different name and with new ownership. Another truism of the 1980s was that the only way to make money on a restaurant was to sell out as soon as it became popular.

French food, clearly *nouvelle* in direction, was served at the finest restaurants. As new cuisines came into fashion—Southwestern, Cajun, Southeast Asian—they inspired new thinking among even the most conservative chefs.

American concern with health led to smaller servings, more vegetarian dishes, more salads. Restaurants—even steak and ale dinnerhouses—joined the fish parade. Trendy Spago featured catfish.

In the mid 1980s, many diners stopped ordering regular lunch or dinner entrees and chose instead a collection of *hors d'oeuvre* or *antipasto* so they could "graze"—nibble on a variety of foods. The servings were sometimes likened to *tapas*, the small containers of assorted raw and cooked appetizers presented with drinks in Spanish bars. A French chef also might offer an assortment of tidbits as a *menu dégustation*; rather than producing two or three full portions, the chef would serve half a dozen or more tiny "tastings" to better show off his or her talents.

The fashion in traditional American foods inspired by the Bicentennial contributed to new popularity for game—venison, grouse, pheasant—although most of the birds came from Scotland and the venison from New Zealand. The restaurant reviewer Tim Zagat observed that only thirteen New York City restaurants had served game in 1985, but 133 had it in 1989.

As the decade wound down, it took the economy along with it. The 1986 tax reform allowed firms to deduct only 80 per-

LOW-TEMPERATURE COOKING During World War II, Quartermaster Corps experiments showed that cooking foods at low temperatures retained nutrients, reduced shrinkage, and conserved energy. During the 1980s restaurants took advantage of these savings with special ovens like the two stacked units here. Each oven surrounded food with a "halo" of radiant heat so it could be safely baked at 250° and safely held at 150° for up to twenty-four hours—using one-third the electricity required by a conventional oven for simply cooking it. (Photograph courtesy Alto-Shaam Inc.)

cent of the cost of business meals; many employers reduced expense accounts to the dismay of local restaurateurs.

Many fancy restaurants closed. Others began to lower prices in search of new customers. They simplified their menus and called themselves cafés or grills. Some entrepreneurs opened ersatz diners, complete with jukeboxes, gum-snapping waitresses, and "real down-home American cooking."

WHO PREPARED RESTAURANT FOOD?

Chefs at the finest, often costliest, restaurants insisted on the freshest, most perfect ingredients. Some still followed the age-old tradition of visiting wholesale food markets early in the morning to pick out produce, meats, and seafood for themselves. Even if they didn't do the shopping, the first-rate chefs took great pride in their own cooking, and checked meticulously the work of their staffs. To prepare in advance for a rush of diners at noon or night, they made up an array of appropriate stocks and sauces. Meats were roasted and pastries baked ahead of time. But much of the menu was made to order for each diner.

So-called white tablecloth restaurants with moderate prices had, for decades, purchased such ingredients as potatoes that were already peeled and cut into julienne or shelled hard-boiled eggs. Now, they often counted on institutional producers to cook finished dishes for them. If the beef Stroganoff in a Connecticut restaurant reminded a diner of the Stroganoff in a Nevada restaurant, it may have been because they came from the same kitchen. Ditto the serving of moo shu pork or grilled chicken breast.

As restaurant business increased, extra dining space often came at the expense of the kitchen, which could no longer accommodate much equipment. At the same time, shortages of skilled cooks and rising labor costs led to hiring staffs with less and less skill—workers who were prone to wasteful mistakes. Yet the restaurant needed to serve food of uniform quality in portions of predictable size if it was to keep its patrons.

For all these reasons, restaurants became increasingly dependent on institutional producers who could reduce kitchen chores to defrosting, reheating, deep-frying, and assembling finished dishes—jobs that required little training.

In the 1970s and 1980s local and regional purveyors furnished all manner of sliced or chopped foods, often pre-measured for portion control, ready to be tossed in a salad or stir-fried in a wok. Commissaries sold fully-prepared portion-controlled baked or stewed foods such as lasagne or chili that needed only to be rethermalized (reheated) for serving. Sometimes an institutional producer or processor would cook to a chef's own recipe so that his or her specialty could be kept on the menu.

BREWING WHILE CUSTOMERS WATCH The Santa Cruz Brewing Company—like many other 1980s brewpubs—put a window between the pub and the brewery to display its gleaming vats and kettles. Customers often could see the equipment in use and witness the marvels of turning malt, hops, sweetener, yeast, and water into a steinful of beer or ale.

Single-serving entrees, prepared in pouches by a vacuum cooking process and then quick chilled, began to catch on in America as they already had in Europe. The process was frequently referred to by its French name *sous vide* (meaning, under vacuum). The pouches could be safely stored in the refrigerator or freezer—unlike the home cook's "boil-in-bag" foods that came frozen and needed to be kept that way. Depending on the entree and the chef's equipment, pouches could be rethermalized individually or in batches in hot water; or food could be removed from its pouch and heated in a conventional or microwave oven.

BREW PUBS

The newest kind of burger-and-salad eatery, individually owned in most cases, was the brew-pub, a restaurant with a brewery on its premises. The pioneer was Bert Grant who opened Yakima Brewing and Malting in Yakima, Washington, in 1982. For a few years, the brew-pubs were a West Coast phenomenon, as the microbreweries had been. But by the end of the decade, 135 pubs were serving up their robustly flavored beers across the country in the thirty states where they were legal. Besides brewing rich, malty beers, the pubs turned out ale, lager, stout, porter, and barley wine (extra strong ale).

Designed for discriminating beer lovers, the pubs priced their wares high enough to discourage the beer-guzzling college crowd. Sizes ranged from intimate 75-seat rooms to huge 400-seat operations such as the Goose Island Brewing Company in Chicago and the Gordon Biersch Brew Company in San Jose. The Fort Mitchell,

Kentucky, brew-pub held nightly floor shows. The Mission Theater & Pub in Portland, Oregon, included a cinema.

FAST FOOD

Pizza was the dinner preferred by one out of five fast-food customers, according to the National Restaurant Association. To win even more business during the 1980s, Pizza Hut promoted the personal pan pizza—a 6-inch pizza with cheese, sausage, or peperoni topping cooked in a black skillet (aluminum although it looked like iron). At lunchtime during the week, they guaranteed the pizza would be ready within five minutes, or be free.

Among delivered foods, pizza was unmatched. An American hero straight out of Horatio Alger, orphan Tom Monaghan wheeled his way to fame and the *Fortune* 500 with Domino's Pizza. Founded in 1960, the stores sold just pizza and cola drinks, but brought them to the customer within thirty minutes—or, when they first opened, the customers got a pizza for free. In 1989 Domino's reported sales of $2.5 billion at 5,185 units.

The croissant—pronounced every imaginable way—added another kind of

PIZZA IN A HURRY With approximately 5,200 outlets nationwide in 1989, Domino's used more than 132 million pounds of cheese on the 250 million pizzas they delivered to their customers—in 30 minutes or less. No wonder pizza was considered as American as apple pie. In addition to its U.S. operations, Domino's had outlets in Australia, Canada, Colombia, Costa Rica, Germany, Guam, Guatemala, Honduras, Hong Kong, Japan, Mexico, the Netherlands, Panama, Puerto Rico, Spain, and the United Kingdom.

SALADS REPLACE BURGERS Although McDonald's got its start with hamburgers, at the end of the 1980s they responded to the health conscious American by putting salads on their menus. The hamburgers stayed at the head of the list, of course: McDonald's cooked up about 10 percent of all beef produced in the U.S. (Photograph courtesy McDonald's Corporation)

"bun" to the fast-food trade. Chinese food franchises such as Quick Wok and Eggroll Express added another cuisine. Oversized tortillas no Mexican would recognize turned up as ruffled "salad bowls" holding chili-flavored beef and beans along with tomatoes, peppers, and lots of lettuce.

The salad bar proved such a success for fast-food chains that many looked for ways to expand the concept. Some added tacos and their traditional accompaniments to the salad fixings. Some put in bars with assorted hot and cold soups and breads. Other chains set up dessert bars with selections of pastry, puddings, and cakes. A favorite bar was the one with sherbets and ice creams of different flavors plus sweet sauces and candy sprinkles so customers could make their own sundaes.

Rotisserie-cooked corn on the cob appeared. Cole slaw entered the picture. No matter what options customers were given, though, French fries seemed as inseparable from hamburgers as mashed potatoes were from fried chicken. To capitalize on the American fondness for potatoes, fast-food eateries of the 1980s featured them baked, opened, and gussied up with slatherings of sour cream and bacon bits or broccoli and melted Cheddar cheese.

Despite such indulgences, public concern about healthy diets had its effect on fast food. When McDonald's Chicken McNuggets debuted in 1983, they were said to contain ground chicken skin as well as chicken meat; McNuggets were fried in vegetable oil—and six of them had twice as much fat as a Big Mac, the ingredients of which television advertising immortalized as "two all-beef patties, special sauce, lettuce, cheese, pickles, onions on a sesame seed bun."

By removing all skin, McDonald's got the count on six McNuggets down to 16.3 grams fat compared to 9.5 grams for a regular burger and 32.4 grams for the Mac. (The mere fact that a hamburger chain would have laboratories check the fat content in its products underscores how great popular worries over nutrition appeared to be in the 1980—and how far restaurants and manufacturers went to soothe them.) In 1987, McDonald's added mixed-green salad, and, in 1991, a McLean Burger to their menus.

Epilogue

Mason jars and stewing hens, like the neighborhood grocers who sold them, are as out of style as cars with running boards and rumble seats. Science, technology—and entrepreneurs—have reshaped the food industry. Education, travel, enthusiasm, and a spirit of adventure have in turn created a new kind of cook.

Today most food is mass-produced, and sold in enormous supermarkets, where much of it arrives ready to cook or, more modern yet, to "heat and eat." Many fresh fruits and vegetables, for example, travel cross country from huge agribusinesses that clean, chill, and wrap them while still in the fields where they grew; beef is slaughtered, sectioned, and put into boxes for easy handling by plants near fields where the cattle has been fattened.

An estimated 30 percent of America's crops are canned to preserve them for future use and nearly 20 percent are frozen. Manufacturers busily stock shelves with mixes for lasagne as well as cake, and thus produce aisles full of completely-cooked foods that need little more than microwaving to prepare them for the table.

Cooks who want organically grown or chemical-free products find them at health food stores or farmers' markets. In metropolitan areas, specialized stores purvey myriad coffees, cheeses, sausages, or greengroceries. Ethnic markets provide exotic fresh fruits and vegetables as well as packaged products from overseas.

In the kitchen, the microwave oven obviously is a newcomer. However, the rest of the major equipment was originated or developed within the past five decades, too: the stove with a self-cleaning oven, the counter cooktop and wall oven, frost-free refrigerator, home freezer, dishwasher, garbage disposer, trash compacter. As if this weren't enough technological wonderment for one room to hold, industry turns out electric can openers and coffee makers; food mixers, blenders and processors; devices for easy creation of pasta, ice cream, even bread.

When the contemporary cook puts all this food and equipment together, opportunities seem unlimited. Where the goal of the 1940s often was simply to satisfy people's hunger, the new vision is to present diners with some treat that's particularly flavorful and nutritious—and good to look at, too. Something that does the cook proud.

The forces driving this modern approach are many: More money. More education. More knowledge about how foods affect human health. More inspiration from meals eaten away from home at breakfast and dinner as well as lunch. More ethnic restaurants and food products. More travel within the United States and to foreign countries. Less time—and therefore more planning—for the increasing numbers of women who worked outside their homes. More couples who cook together as a hobby. Single-parent families where children help prepare food.

To help sort out which influences have been most far-reaching, I asked important American food writers for their opinions.

Here's what they had to say:

Irena Chalmers
(author and publisher of food books and cookbooks)

What factors have been responsible for the changes in the way we eat? We have lost our innocence. We are frightened. And confused. We are eating today as though we are out-patients suffering (or about to suffer) from a disease that no one yet understands. We are deathly afraid of eating the wrong thing. But do not know what is that one right thing that will guarantee us life everlasting and keep us regular at the same time!

Our concerns have arisen as a result of dozens of factors that have simultaneously reached a confluence. Big business is increasingly getting into the act of take-out and so-called "fresh" alternatives to home cooked meals.

The scientists have joined forces with the commercial cooks and together they have devised ways to attractively package and sell the idea that 'tis a far, far better thing to have food zapped in a minute than to toil for hours preparing it ourselves. They are, of course, quite right.

Nevertheless, the folks who still enjoy nurturing those they love will always find multitudes of friends flocking to their door.

Julia Child
(author of seven cookbooks, television cooking-class teacher EXTRAORDINAIRE)

More than any other factor in the last fifty years, in my opinion, preoccupation with nutrition is profoundly influencing the American diet. This is useful and necessary, and all the current information for healthful, happy eating is readily available; however too many of us are being so intimidated through media hype, fear, and misinformation that a restaurant meal or the family dinner table has become a trap and a denial rather than a delight.

Carol Cutler
(author of eight cookbooks, syndicated newspaper columnist, restaurant critic)

The jet airplane, I believe, opened America's culinary horizon. Approximations, and worse, of foreign cuisines were tolerated—until we tasted the real thing. Once the market appeared, specialty stores and authentic restaurants responded quickly. Today the American pot is truly blended.

Barbara Kafka
(author and editor of cookbooks and food books, magazine and newspaper contributor)

The greatest influences for change on the American diet have been the rapid transportation that permits us to have foods out of season from all over the country, the urbanization of American life, the entry of vast numbers of women into the work force, and a vast amount of travel coupled with massive printed information on all kinds of food. Increased affluence, of course, certainly cannot be underrated as a factor.

George Lang
(New York restaurateur, restaurant consultant, cookbook author, magazine columnist)

It was a machine that had the broadest influence on the way we eat and drink, but it wasn't the television, the microwave or even the Cuisinart. It was the airplane, which for a relatively low cost—affordable to almost everybody in our society—for the first time offered first-hand, authentic experiences of the cuisines of the world. Everything else that followed since the first Pan American around-the-world trip was not only logical but inevitable.

Phyllis Richman
(The WASHINGTON POST food editor)

I think the major influence on our shopping/cooking/eating habits has been heart disease. In our frenzy to avoid it, we have introduced cholesterol into every food conversation, we've tarnished the reputation of our formerly revered beef, eggs, and butter while we have grown to idolize corn, oats, and soybeans, and we have learned to worship the salad.

Elizabeth Schneider
(author of food books and cookbooks, magazine contributor)

Over the last fifteen years the number of items available in supermarket produce aisles has quadrupled—and more. The main reasons for this boom are, in short: health consciousness (fruits and vegetables comprising a food group comparatively high in fiber, vitamins, and minerals, and low in calories); our new immigrants—primarily of Latin American and Asian origin—who have introduced their culinary heritage to this country; an increase in restaurants and take-out shops, places where exotic cuisines and ingredients first appear; improved methods of harvesting, handling, and shipping produce.

In addition, the wealth of fruit and vegetable varieties now evident in the marketplace may be due, in part, to a rebirth of regional American cuisine, which stresses the importance of locally cultivated specialties, and to the proliferation of farmers' markets.

What comes next, I hope, will be a grand scale reversion to organic farming techniques, which will result in safer, more flavorful crops to further develop our use of fruits and vegetables, grains and legumes—our earthly goods.

Carolyn Stallworth
(cookbook author, cooking instructor, magazine contributor)

I think that two factors are most important: refrigeration (including freezing) and transport. We may slight frozen foods now, but they were hot stuff (though cold) when they appeared. Frozen foods (vegetables especially) are certainly nearer the real thing than canned ones.

Transportation signified in two ways—first, the move to the suburbs, and the change to a large weekly shopping in the car, rather than daily shopping or tradesmen bringing milk, groceries, etc. to the home. Secondly, the growers and shippers could speed perishables to stores in refrigerated trucks over a post-war highway system. The consumer got an increasingly wide variety of everything to choose from, and that trend is continuing.

Television has some effect, but I don't know exactly what—the majority of food ads seem to be for cereals, followed by those for fast food and soda pop. Apparently many people put eye appeal over taste, and speed (microwave) over everything. I do know that a lot of people can't cook. And a lot can't taste.

Louis Szathmary
(Chicago restaurateur, cookbook author and editor, food and restaurant consultant)

The changes in American food habits during the last fifty years are only skin deep. Yes, skin deep only, but don't forget that skin is the largest human organ. It is by weight one-third of the body, and covers it from tip to toe. So a "skin deep" change on such a surface can be much greater than a deeper change would be on an organ with a smaller surface.

I tend to believe firmly in the changes when I read the newest food reports, but when I wait in line at a McDonald's for a Big Mac during my travels, or when I order a sinfully rich dessert after a lean fish and salad dinner, I start to wonder: did we really change that much?

Jeremiah Tower
(San Francisco restaurateur, cookbook author, food and wine consultant)

I think the most important change in American food in terms of emotional satisfaction and quality of life, was the victory achieved as a re-awakened interest in European, or even world, food (*Time-Life Foods of the World*), achieved through travel books and television, a victory over the insane FDA-U.S. Home Economist frenzy of denial and fake scientific achievement after World War II, that occurred in the Sixties and Seventies.

Clark Wolf
(restaurant and wine consultant)

Success and wealth, especially the new kind, breed the desire for sophistication. Superpowers want and need the proof *and* the pudding.

Since WWII America has come through its culinary adolescence with a few exciting as well as some amusingly embarrassing moments, and now begins to enjoy a real gastronomic maturity as we careen headlong towards the next century.

Clearly many factors have played a part in shaping America's cuisine. If the experts don't agree completely on which of these is most important, they all share an enthusiasm for good food. None more, though, than the nineteenth Century English author and art critic, John Ruskin, who set these high standards:

"What does cookery mean? ... It means knowledge of all herbs, and fruits, and balms, and spices, and of all that is healing and sweet in groves, and savory in meat. It means carefulness and inventiveness, watchfulness, willingness, and readiness of appliances. It means the economy of your great-grandmother, and the science of modern chemistry, and French art and Arabian hospitality. It means, in fine, that you are to see imperatively that everyone has something nice to eat."

Bibliography

GENERAL READING

My aim in writing this book was to entertain as well as inform. The copious statistics are my way of underscoring facts—for example, to say that Americans drank a lot of bottled water in 1989 doesn't have the impact of saying they drank two billion (2,000,000,000) gallons of bottled water. The numbers come from many sources. Where possible, I have used official government figures such as those in the *Statistical Abstracts* cited below. For statistics that the government had not compiled, I went to manufacturers, retailers, food processors, trade association literature, trade journals, and articles in newspapers and general-interest magazines.

Bailey, Ronald H. *The Home Front: U.S.A., World War II.* Alexandria, Va.: Time-Life Books, 1977.

Beard, James. *Delights and Prejudices.* New York: Atheneum, 1964.

Beard, James; Glaser, Milton; Wolf, Burton; Kafka, Barbara Poses; Witty, Helen S.; and Associates of the Good Cooking School; eds. *The Cooks' Catalogue.* New York: Harper & Row, 1975.

Belasco, Warren J. *Appetite for Change.* New York: Pantheon Books, 1989.

Brands, Trademarks and Good Will, The Story of the Quaker Oats Company. New York: McGraw-Hill Book Company, 1967.

Bridge, Fred, and Tibbetts, Jean F. *The Well-Tooled Kitchen*. New York: William Morrow and Company, Inc., 1990.

Brown, Dale. *American Cooking/Foods of the World.* New York: Time-Life Books, 1968.

Campbell, Hannah. *Why Did They Name It?* New York: Fleet Publishing Corporation, 1964.

Chalmers, Irena with Milton Glaser and Friends. *Great American Food Almanac*. New York: Harper & Row, Publishers, 1986.

Charvat, Frank J. *Fifty Years of Supermarketing*. New York: Macmillan & Co., 1961.

Claiborne, Craig. *Craig Claiborne's A Feast Made for Laughter*. Garden City, N.Y.: Doubleday & Company, Inc., 1982.

Committee on Food Consumption Patterns, Food and Nutrition Board, National Research Council. *Assessing Food Consumption Patterns*. Washington, D.C.: National Academy Press, 1981.

Elfun Historical Society. *A Walk Through The Park, The History of GE Appliances and Appliance Park*. Louisville, Kentucky, 1987.

Ensrud, Barbara. *American Vineyards*. New York: Stewart, Tabori & Chang, 1988.

Frederick, Christine. *Selling Mrs. Consumer*. New York: The Business Bourse, 1929.

Gallup, George H. *The Gallup Poll: Public Opinion, 1935-1971*. New York: Random House, 1972.

Gallup, George H. *The Gallup Poll: Public Opinion, 1972-1977*. Wilmington: Scholarly Resources, 1978.

Gibbons, Euell. *Stalking the Wild Asparagus*. New York: David McKay, 1962.

Hess, John L., and Hess, Karen. *The Taste of America*. Columbia: The University of South Carolina Press, 1989.

Hines, Duncan. *Adventures in Good Eating*. Bowling Green, Ky.: Adventures in Good Eating Inc., 1942, 1944.

Hooker, Richard J. *Food and Drink in America: A History*. Indianapolis/New York: The Bobbs-Merrill Company, Inc., 1981.

Household Food Consumption Survey. Washington, D.C.: United States Agricultural Research Service, 1965-1966.

Jacobson, Michael F. *Eaters Digest: The Consumer's Factbook of Food Additives*. Garden City, N.Y.: Doubleday & Company, 1972.

Jones, Evan. *American Food: The Gastronomic Story*. New York: Vintage Books, 1981.

Jones, Evan. *Epicurean Delight: The Life and Times of James Beard*. New York: Alfred A. Knopf, 1990.

Kaiser, Charles. *1968 in America: Music, Politics, Chaos, Counterculture, and The Shaping of A Generation*. New York: Weidenfeld & Nicolson, New York, 1988.

Katz, Sylvia. *Plastics: common objects, classic designs*. New York: Harry N. Abrams, Inc., 1984.

Lang, Jenifer Hardy. *Larousse Gastronomique: The New American Edition*. New York: Crown Publishers, 1988.

Langdon, Philip. *Orange Roofs, Golden Arches*. New York: Alfred A. Knopf, New York, 1986.

Levenstein, Harvey. *Revolution at the Table.* New York: Oxford University Press, 1988.

Lifshey, Earl. *The Housewares Story.* Chicago: National Housewares Manufacturers Association, 1973.

Lingeman, Richard R. *Don't You Know There's a War On?/The American Home Front 1941-1945.* New York: G.P. Putnam's Sons, 1970.

Liquor Marketing Handbook. New York: Jobson Publishing, 1990.

Lynes, Russell. *The Domesticated Americans.* New York: Harper & Row, New York, 1963.

Mariani, John F. *The Dictionary of American Food & Drink.* New Haven and New York: Ticknor & Fields, 1983.

Mayer, Jean, Ph.D., and Goldberg, Jean P., Sc.D. *Dr. Jean Mayer's Diet & Nutrition Guide.* New York: Pharos Books, 1990.

Margolius, Sidney. *Health Food Facts and Fakes.* New York: Walker, 1973.

Paarlberg, Don. *Farm and Food Policy: Issues of the 1980s.* Wash-American Enterprise Institute for Public Policy Research, 1980.

Riepma, S.F. *The Story of Margarine.* Washington, D.C.: Public Affairs Press, 1970.

Root, Waverley. *Food.* New York: Simon and Schuster, 1980.

Root, Waverley, and de Rochement, Richard. *Eating in America.* New York: William Morrow and Company, Inc., 1976.

Ross, William, and Romanus, Charles F. *Quartermaster Corps Operations in the War Against Germany.* Office of Chief of Military History; United States Government Printing Office, 1965.

Samtur, Susan J., and Tuleja, Tad. *Cashing In at the Checkout.* New York: Stonesong Press, 1979.

Selitzer, Ralph. *The Dairy Industry in America.* New York: Dairy and Ice Cream Field and Books for Industry, 1976.

Stare, Fredrick J.; Olsen, Robert E., M.D.; Whelan, Elizabeth M.,Sc.D. *Balanced Nutrition: Beyond the Cholesterol Scare.* Holbrook, Mass.: Bob Adams, Inc. Publishers, 1987.

Statistical Abstract of the United States. United States Department of Commerce, Bureau of Census, 1940, 1950, 1960, 1970, and 1988 editions.

Stauffer, Alvin P. *Quartermaster Corps Operations in the War Against Japan.* Office of Chief of Military History; United States Government Printing Office, 1956.

Stern, Jane, and Stern, Michael. *Sixties People.* New York: Alfred A. Knopf, 1990.

Strasser, Susan. *Never Done: A History of American Housework.* New York: Pantheon Books, 1982.

Survey of Buying Power Data 1990. New York: Bill Publishers, 1991.

Suyvenberg, J.H. *Margarine: An Economic, Social and Scientific History, 1869-1969.* Liverpool: Liverpool University Press, 1969.

Tannahill, Reay. *Food in History.* New York: Crown Publishers, 1988.

Time Capsules: 1940, 1941, 1942, 1943, 1944, 1945. New York: Time-Life Books, 1968.

Trading Stamps: Past, Present and Future. Red Bank, N.J.: Association of Retail Marketing Services, 1981.

Trager, James. *The Enriched, Fortified, Concentrated, Country-Fresh, Lip-Smacking, Finger-Licking, International, Unexpurgated Foodbook* New York: Grossman Publishers, 1970.

Visser, Margaret. *Much Depends on Dinner.* New York: Collier Books, MacMillan Company, 1988.

Whelan, Dr. Elizabeth M., Sc.D., and Stare, Fredrick J., M.D. *Panic in the Pantry.* New York: Atheneum; 1977.

Wilson, José. *The Eastern Heartland/Foods of the World.* New York: Time-Life Books, 1971.

The World Almanac and Book of Facts 1991, Edited by Mark S. Hoffman. New York: Pharos Books, 1991.

COOKBOOKS

The American Heritage Cookbook and Illustrated History of American Eating & Dining. Edited by the Editors of American Heritage. New York: American Heritage Publishing Co., Inc., 1964.

Beck, Simone; Bertholde, Louisette; and Child, Julia. *Mastering the Art of French Cooking.* New York: Alfred A. Knopf, 1961.

Better Homes & Gardens Heritage Cook Book. Edited by the Editors of Better Homes & Gardens. Des Moines: Meredith Publishing Company, 1976.

Bocuse, Paul. *Paul Bocuse's French Cooking.* Translated by Colette Rossant; edited by Lorraine Davis. New York: Pantheon Books, 1977.

Burros, Marian. *20 Minute Menus.* New York: Simon and Schuster, 1989.

Cannon, Poppy. *The Can-Opener Cookbook*. New York: Thomas Y. Crowell, 1951.

Cannon, Poppy. *The New New Can-Opener Cookbook*. New York: Thomas Y. Crowell, 1968.

Dahnke, Marye, *The Cheese Cook Book.* Chicago: Kraft Cheese Company, 1942.

Davis, Adelle. *Let's Cook It Right.* New York: Harcourt, Brace & World, Inc., 1954.

Guérard, Michel. *Michel Guérard's Cuisine Minceur.* Translated by Narcisse Chamerlain with Fanny Brennan. New York: William Morrow and Company, Inc., 1986.

Guérard, Michel. *Michel Guérard's Cuisine for Home Cooks.* Translated and Annotated by Judith Hill and Tina Ujlaki. New York: William Morrow and Company, Inc., 1976.

Hibben, Sheila. *American Regional Cooking.* Boston: Little, Brown and Company, 1946.

Junior League of Pasadena. *California Heritage Continues.* Garden City, N.Y.: Doubleday & Company, Inc., 1987.

Kafka, Barbara. *The Microwave Gourmet*. New York: William Morrow and Company, Inc., 1987.

Levy, Faye. *Vegetable Creations*. New York: E.P. Dutton, 1987.

Paddleford, Clementine. *How America Eats*. New York: Charles Scribner's & Sons, 1960.

Peck, Paula. *The Art of Fine Baking*. New York: Simon and Schuster, 1961.

Pépin, Jacques. *La Technique*. New York: Quadrangle Books, 1976.

Roberson, John, and Roberson, Marie. *Complete Small Appliance Cookbook*. New York: A.A.Wyn Publishers, 1953.

Root, Waverely. *The Food of France*. New York: Simon and Schuster, 1958.

Szekely, Deborah. *Vegetarian Spa Cuisine*. Rancho La Puerta, 1990.

Stegner, Mabel. *Electric Blender Recipes*. New York: M. Barrows and Company, Inc., 1952.

Stern, Jane, and Stern, Michael. *Square Meals*. New York: Alfred A. Knopf, 1985.

Tower, Jeremiah. *Jeremiah Tower's New American Classics*. New York: Harper & Row, 1986.

Waters, Alice. *The Chez Panisse Menu Cookbook*. New York: Random House, 1982.

Newspapers and Magazines

Newspapers and magazines were invaluable for tracking down information and checking facts. Among the newspapers I relied on were the *Chicago Tribune*, the *Los Angeles Times*, the *New York Times*, the *St. Louis Post Dispatch*, and *USA Today*.

The general circulation magazines I found helpful were *American Cookery*, *American Heritage*, *Bon Appétit*, *Esquire*, *Food & Wine*, *The Journal of Gastronomy*, *Gourmet*, *Harper's Bazaar*, *Harrowsmith/Country Life*, *Ladies Home Journal*, *Newsweek*, *Petits Propos Culinaire* and *Time*. The trade journals I used most often were *Beverage Industry*, *Food News*, *Progressive Grocer*, *Restaurants and Institutions* and *Supermarket News*.

Index

(Note: Page numbers of illustrations are in italics)

Aerobics, 85, *132*
Airplane food, *28*
Alcoholic beverages, 6, 47-48, 50, 77, 110-12
   See also Beer; Wine
Aluminum wrap, 52
Amaranth, 153
Appliances, 26-27, 56-58, *56*, *57*, *88*, 89-91, 117, 119-20, *166*, 166-67, *168*, 169
Arby's, 94
Army food, 13, 15, 16
Artichoke spread, 99 (recipe)
Arugula, 107
   and radicchio with warm mushroom dressing, 106 (recipe)
Aspic ring, tomato, 30 (recipe)
Automat, *32*

Bagna cauda, 122 (recipe)
Bake-off Pillsbury, *2*, 42
Banana split, *62*
Barbecue, *36*, 43-44, *44*, *70*, *74*, 138
Barbecue sauce, 44

Baskin-Robbins, *127*, 127-28
Baum, Joseph H., *116*, 126
Beard, James, 21, 51-53, *52*, 81, 118, *121*, 123
Beef, 76
   chile con carne, 13 (recipe)
   creamed chipped, 16
   grades, 108-9, 144
   hamburger steaks with goat cheese, 144 (recipe)
   Stroganoff, 18 (recipe)
   tamale pie , 20 (recipe)
   Wellington, 71 (recipe)
   See also Steak
Beer, 50, 110
   brew pubs, *174*, 174-75
   microbreweries, 148-49
Betty Crocker, 12, 35, 53, *133*
Beverages. *See specific types*
Big Boy barbecue, 44
Birdseye, Clarence, 23
Blue cheese, 51
   dressing , 146 (recipe)
Bocuse, Paul, *103*, 103-04, 105, 170
Boiardi, Paul, 31
Bon Appetit, 124, 161
Bread(s)
   brown n' serve, 23

   honey graham, 112 (recipe)
   machine, *166*, 167
   refrigerated dough, 43, 75
   wartime, *10*, 12, 13
   whole grain, 114
Brew pubs, *174*, 175-76
Bridge, Fred, 86, *86*
Brody, Jane E., 114-15, *115*
Buffalo chicken wings, 146 (recipe)
Buffalo gourds, 153
Buffalo meat, 5
Bundt cake, *42*
Burger Chef, 65
Burger King, 65, 94-95, 128
Burros, Marian, 162
Butter, 51, 107
   buerre blanc, 103
   stretcher, 12 (recipe)

Caesar salad, 61 (recipe)
Cafeterias, 31-32
Cajun food, 132, 142, 170
Cakes
   Bundt, *42*
   chiffon, 19
   chocolate torte, 156 (recipe)
   mixes, 42-43, *55*
   one-bowl, 12

Strawberry shortcake, 74
tomato soup, 41 (recipe)
California cooking, 104, 105, 132, 139
Canned food, 41, *117*
Canning, *4*, 4-5
Cannon, Poppy, 40, 41-42
Can opener, 40, 42
Caplan, Frieda and Karen, 76, *140*
Capon, 147
Carney, Frank and Dan, 35
Carson, Rachel, 82, *82*
Casseroles, 42
tuna and noodle, 13 (recipe)
Catfish, 76, 151
with mustard-dill sauce, 150 (recipe)
Celestial Seasonings, 114
Cereal, 115, 157
candy from, *18*
granola, 113 (recipe), 114
Chafing dish, *85*
Chalmers, Irena, 180
Charcoal briquets, 44, *45*
Char-Glo Broilers, 44
Cheese, *11*, 51, 100, *142*, 142-43, 159
fondue, 49 (recipe), 49-50
and sausage pizza, 137 (recipe)
yogurt with parsley, 155 (recipe)
See also Blue Cheese; Goat Cheese
Chef Boy-Ar-Dee, 31
Chen, Joyce, 77
Cherry pie, 3 (recipe)
Chicken, *1*, 43-44, *68*, *69*, 76, *109*, 109-10, 147
breasts Veronique, 73 (recipe)
Divan, 62 (recipe)
fajitas with fresh tomatoes, 134 (recipe)
Kiev, 99 (recipe)
salad, tomato stuffed, 41 (recipe)
Tetrazzini, 46 (recipe)
yakitori, 125 (recipe)
Chicken livers, rumaki, 50 (recipe)

Chicken wings (Buffalo), 146 (recipe)
Chiffon cake, 19
Chiffon pie, lemon, 43 (recipe)
Child, Julia, 77, 87, 120, 123, *163*, 180-81
Chile con carne, 2, 13 (recipe)
China Institute, 52, 122
Chinese food, 52, *98*, 121-22
Chocolate chip cookies, 4 (recipe)
Chocolate torte, 156 (recipe)
Chu, Grace, 52, 81
Church's Fried Chicken, 65
Claiborne, Craig, 72, 85, *121*, *163*
Clancy, John, 126
Cocktail parties, 48-50, 100-101
Coeur à la Crème, 78 (recipe)
Coffee, 9, 77, 159
Coffee houses, 62, 64
Coffee makers, 120, *166*
Consumerism, 115-16, 153-54
Convenience food, 2-3, 18-19, 40, 41, 106-7, *136*
Cookbooks, 21-22, 40, 41-42, 52-53, 74, 78-79, 81, 122-24, 161-64
Cookies, chocolate chip, 4 (recipe)
Cooking, home, 1, 3-5, 18-22, 10-44, 72-75, 98-101, 135-59
Cooking schools, 51-52, 81-82, 121-22, 159-60
Cooking shows, 19, 20-21, 77-78, *80*, *162*, *163*
Cooking videos, 160, *161*
Cook's Catalogue, The, 116, 118
Cooktops, 87, 89, *165*
Cookware, 27, *56*, 56-57, *58*, 58-59, 85, 86, 87-89, *166*
Cooper, Kenneth, H., 85
Copper bowls, *116*
Coquilles St. Jacques, 46 (recipe)
Corning cookware, *58*, 58-59, *166*
Corn pups, *40*
Cottage cheese, 12, *17*, 51
Countertops, *167*
Coupons, manufacturer, *119*, 121
Couscous with vegetables, baked, 106 (recipe)
Crab Louis, 20, (recipe)
Credit cards, 61-62, 125

Crème fraiche, 105
Crudites, 100-101, *107*, 122
Cuisinart, 117, 119-20, 167
Cuisine minceur, 104-5, 157
Culinary Institute of America (C.I.A.), *160*
Cullen, Michael, 24-25
Curry
apricot glaze, 108 (recipe)
lamb, 79 (recipe)
Cutler, Carol, 181
Cyclamates, 83
Damigella, Tom, 60
Davis, Adelle, 114
Diat, Louis, 79
Dickson, Paul, 13
Diets, 84, 86
Diner's Club, 61
Dining cars, *63*
Dinnerhouse restaurants, 93, 126
Dips, 49
Bagna cauda, 122 (recipe)
Dishwashers, *26*, 58, 89, 167
Dishwashing detergent, 53, 58
Domino's Pizza, *175*
Doughnut, 13
Drive-ins, 33, 64
Duck, 147
breasts with raspberries, 146 (recipe)
Dunkin' Donuts, 65

"Elsie Presents," 21
Entertaining, 19-20, 47-50, *48*, 73, 100-101, 139

Farms
fish, 76-77, 150-151, *151*
in 1980s, 151-54, *152*
organic, 82, 114, 157
wartime, 7, 7-8
Fast food, 65, 93-95, 128, 175-77
Fats
dietary, 144, 154-55
wartime saving of, *10*, 11
Faux food, 159
Fettuccine Alfredo, 80 (recipe)
Fish
blackened, 132
consumption, 150
farming, 76-77, 150-51, *151*
See also specific types

Fisher, M.F.K., *124*
Fitness, 85, 86-87, 131, *132*
Flour, 11, 133
Fondue, cheese, 49 (recipe), 49-50
Food additives, 82-83, 115-16
Food and Wine, 161
Food cooperatives, 82, 120
Food labeling, 115
Food magazines, 124-25
Food processors, *117*, 119-20, 167
Food wrap, 53, *54*, *118*
Ford, Henry, *45*
Ford charcoal briquets, *45*
Foreign food, 20, 92, 121, 126, 132, 134
Franey, Pierre, 162
Freezers, 23, 42, 57-58, 167
French cooking, 102-5, 126
French dressing, 21 (recipe)
Frieda's Finest, 76, 140
Frozen food, *22*, 22-23, *40*, 76, *83*, 166
Fruit, *17*, *74*, 75-76, 107, 141
and pasta salad, walnut, 154 (recipe)

Garbage disposers, 26, 58, 89
Gardens, victory, 12, 14
Gault, Henri, 102, 103
Gazpacho, 75
Gibbons, Euell, 81-82, *81*
Gino's, 65
Goat cheese, 143
baked, salad with, 134 (recipe)
hamburger steak with, 144 (recipe)
Golden Door spa, *84*, 85-86
Goose, 147
Gourmet, *21*, 22, 53, 78, 119-20, 161
Gourmet clubs, 73
Graham, Sylvester, 113
Granola, 113 (recipe), 114
Grapes Juanita, 106 (recipe)
Grasshopper pie, 49 (recipe)
Gravlax with mustard sauce, 100 (recipe)
Greene, Gael, 104, 126
Gregoire, Marc, 87
Guacamole, 73 (recipe)

Guerard, Michel, 104-5, 157, 170

Hamburger stands, 32-33
Hamburger steaks with goat cheese, 144 (recipe)
Hardee's, 94
Hardie, Thomas G., 87-88
Harding, George T. III, 159
Harvey, Ann, 164
Hauser, Gayelord, 113
Health food stores, 113-14, 155-56
Heavenly hash salad, 47 (recipe)
Herbal tea, 76, 107, 142
Hibachi, 44
Hines, Duncan, *37*
Hohensee, Adolphus, 113
Home delivery, 3, 22
Honey, 113
Horlick Corporation, 26-27
Horn & Hardart, 32
Horsemeat, *10*

Iceboxes, 1, 2
Ice cream, 13, 115, 156-57, 159
banana split, *62*
dipping stores, *127*, 127-28
International Review of Food & Wine, 124, *125*, 161

Jack in the Box, 65
Jarvis, D.C., 113
Jeffries, Bob, 77
Jelly, red pepper, 50 (recipe)
Jewell, Jesse, 110
Jicama remoulade, 135 (recipe)
Johnson, Howard, 127
Johnson, Sherwood, 65

Kabobs, *70*, *74*
Kaffee klatch, 39
Kafka, Barbara, 118, 161-62
Kellogg, John Harvey, 113, 114, 159
Kellogg, Will, 113
Kentucky Fried Chicken, 65, *94*, 128
Kerr, Graham, 77-78, *79*
Ketchup, *8*
King Kullen, *24*, 24-25
Kitchens, 1-2, 25-27, 38-39, *39*, *57*, *87*, 116, 118, *167*, *168*

See also Appliances
Kirchenware. *See* Cookware
Kroc, Ray, 64

Lamb
curry, 80 (recipe)
grilled butterflied, 108 (recipe)
Lang, George, 181
Lasagne, *90*
La Varenne, 122, 160
Lemon chiffon pie, 43 (recipe)
Lettuce, wilted, 14 (recipe)
Lewis, Edna, *169*
Lippert, Albert, 84
Lobster Newburg, 27 (recipe)
Lockers, freezer, *22*, 23
Lucas, Dione, *19*, 21, 52
Lunch counters, *31*, 64, 68
Lunchrooms, 31

MacAusland, Earle R., 21, 22
McDonald, Richard and Maurice, 33, 64
McDonald's, *64*, 65, 93-94, 95, 128, *176*, 176-77
McNamara, Frank, 60-61
Marama bean, 153
Margarine, 12, 51, 83, 107
Martini, 48
Master, Melvyn, 139
Maytag, Fritz, 148-49, *149*
Meat(s)
and consumerism, 115-16
consumption, 19, 76, 107-8, 109, 144, 146
lockers, 23
wartime, *5*, *10*
See also specific type
Meatpacking industry, 145
Melamine, 27
Melmac, 28, *59*
Meringue tarts, *70*
Mesclun salad, 138 (recipe)
Mesquite barbecue, 138
Microbreweries, 148-49
Microwave food products, *136*
Microwave ovens, 89-90, *89*, 167, 169
Milk, 3, 22, 50-51, 77, 112-13, 148
Millau, Christian, 102, 103
Miller, Bryan, 162
Mister Donut, 65

Mixes, 42-43, *55*
Molds, gelatin, *48*
Monosodium glutamate (MSG), 83
Mushroom(s), 76, 141
   salad dressing, warm, 106

Nader, Ralph, 115
Natural food, 82, 114,15, 155-56
New American cooking, 132, 134, 138
Nidetch, Jean, 84
Nitrates/nitrites, 115-116
Noodle and tuna casserole, 13 (recipe)
Nouvelle cuisine, 102-4, 132, 139, 140, 170
Nutrition, 5, *6*, 7, 82-83, 113-15, 131, 154-57

Omelets, 90
Onion(s), 76
   and orange salad, 75 (recipe)
   sandwiches, 53 (recipe)
Orange(s), 107
   and onion salad, 75 (recipe)
   souffle, 102 (recipe)
Organic produce, 82, 114, 157
OSKAR, 167

Paddleford, Clementine, 53
Pancakes, Persian with cinnamon cheese filling, 158 (recipe)
Pasta, 143-44, *144*
   fettuccine Alfredo, 79 (recipe)
   lasagna, *90*
   machine, *101*, 144, *166*, 166-67
   noodle and tuna casserole, 13 (recipe)
   primavera, 139 (recipe)
   and walnut fruit salad, 154 (recipe)
Pauling, Linus, 114
Peas, sugar snap, 107
Peck, Paula, 74
Perdue, Frank, 110
Perrier water, 147
Pesto sauce, 122 (recipe)
Pie(s)
   cherry, 3 (recipe)
   grasshopper, 49 (recipe)
   lemon chiffon, 43 (recipe)
   tamale, 20 (recipe)
Pie-baking contest, *3*
Piggly Wiggly, 24, 92
Pillsbury bake-off, *2*, 42
Pillsbury Doughboy, 75, *164*
Pizza, 31, *53*, 65, *137*, 175
   sausage and cheese, 137 (recipe)
Pizza Hut, 35, 65, 175
Plastics, 27-28, 59-60
Plastic wrap, 53, *54*, *118*
Pleasures of Cooking, 124-25, 161
Point, Fernand, 102-3
Polyethylene, 28
Poplawski, Stephen J., 26, 27
Pork, 109, 152
   spareribs with curry-apricot glaze, 198 (recipe)
   tamale pie, 20 (recipe)
   See also Sausage
Post, Charles W., 113
Potato
   and carrot gratin, 135 (recipe)
   salad, French, 102 (recipe)
Poultry. *See specific type*
Pressure cookers, 27, *165*
Progressive dinners, 47
Prudhomme, Paul, 126, 132, *170*
Pyroceram cooktop, *88*, 89

Quiche Lorraine, 72 (recipe)
Quinoa, 153

Radicchio, 197
   and arugula with warm mushroom dressing, 106 (recipe)
Rancho La Puerta, 86
Ratatouille, 75 (recipe)
Rationing, *8*, *9*, 8-10, 159
Red pepper jelly, 50 (recipe)
Refrigerated dough, 43, 75
Refrigerators, 2, 22, *26*, 42, 57, 89, 167
Remoulade, jicama, 135 (recipe)
Restaurants(s), 28-33, *29*, 37, 60-62, 64-65, 91-95, 116, 125-29, 170-77
Restaurant Associates, 60
Revere Ware, 27
Richman, Phyllis, 181

Roberson, John and Marie, 57
Rock cornish game hens, roast, 47 (recipe)
Roseleip, Gordon W., 83
Rumaki, 50 (recipe)

Saccharin, 115
Salad(s), 107
   with baked goat cheese, 134 (recipe)
   Caesar, 61 (recipe)
   chicken, tomato stuffed, 41 (recipe)
   fruit and cottage cheese, *17*
   heavenly hash, 47 (recipe)
   mesclun, 138 (recipe)
   molded gelatin, *48*
   Nicoise, 78 (recipe)
   orange and onion, 75 (recipe)
   potato, French, 102 (recipe)
   radicchio and arugula, 106 (recipe)
   tomato tulips, *29*
   Waldorf, *81*
   walnut fruit and pasta, 154 (recipe)
   wilted lettuce, 14 (recipe)
Salad bars, 129, *171*, 176
Salad dressing
   blue cheese, 146 (recipe)
   French, 21 (recipe)
   mushroom, warm, 106 (recipe)
Salmon
   Gravlax with mustard sauce, 100 (recipe)
   mousse, 71 (recipe)
Salton Hotray, 90
Samtur, Susan J., 119, 121
Sanders, Harlan, *94*
Sandwich(es)
   bags, *118*
   grilled cheese, 51, 64
   onion, 53 (recipe)
Sangria, 76 (recipe)
Saran wrap, 53 *54*
Saunders, Clarence, 24
Sausage
   and cheese pizza, 137 (recipe)
Scallops
   coquilles St. Jacques, 46 (recipe)
   seviche, 100 (recipe)

Schneider, Elizabeth, 181
Scramblers, 159
Seranne, Anne, 164
Seviche, 100 (recipe)
Shakey's, 65
Shellfish
   farming, 151
   faux, 159
   See also specific types
Shopping cart, 24
Smith, Jeff, 161, *162*
Soda fountains, *33*, 62
Soda jerks, *33*
Soft drinks, 112, 148
Sontheimer, Carl, *117*, 119, 124
Sorenson, Jacki, 85
Souffle
   orange, 102 (recipe)
   sponge roll with nut filling, 143 (recipe)
Soul food, 77
Soup
   canned, 42, *117*
   gazpacho, 75
   mix, 49
   vichyssoise, 61 (recipe)
   See also Tomato soup
Southern food, 77, 169
Spa(s), 86-157-58
Spaghetti
   Chef Boy-Ar-Dee, 31
   Spaghettio Os, 76
Spam, 15
   baked like ham, 15 (recipe)
Spareribs with curry-apricot glaze, 108
Spices, 142
Stallworth, Carolyn, 182
Stanish, Rudy, *91*
Steak
   Diane, 56 (recipe)
   planked, *74*
   au poivre, 122 (recipe)
Steakhouses, 93
Steam Beer, 148-49
Stephen, George, 35, 36
Stookey, Donald, 58
Stoves, 2, *25*, 26, 58, *87*, *88*, 89-90, *165*, 167, *173*
Strawberry shortcake, *74*
Styron, 28
Sugar, 8-9, 11, 154

Supermarkets, 3, 23,25, *24*, *54*, 54-56, 91-92, 120-21, 159, *164*, 165-66
Surimi, 159
Szathmary, Louis, 182
Szekely, Edmond Bordeaux, 86

Tabbouleh, 155 (recipe)
Takeout food, 169-70
Tamale pie, 20 (recipe)
Tang, 76, 159
Tarwi, 153
Tea, herbal, 114
Tearooms, 29
Teflon cookware, 87-88
Television
   cooking on, 19, 20-21, 77-78, 80, *162*, *163*
   eating in front of, *39*, 39-40, 136
Tex-Mex food, 132
Thai food, 132
Theme parties, 47
Time-Life Books, *Foods of the World* series, 79
Toaster oven, 91
Tofu, 159
Toll House cookies, 4 (recipe)
Tomato(es), 101, 141
   aspic ring, 30 (recipe)
   green, oven-fried, 156 (recipe)
   stuffed with chicken salad, 41 (recipe)
   tulips, *29*
Tomato soup
   canned, *117*
   cake, 41 (recipe)
   golden dried, 141 (recipe)
"To the Queen's Taste," 19, 21
Tower, Jeremiah, *104*, 105, 182
Trading stamps, *54*, 55, 121
Trash compactor, 89
Tuna
   and noodle casserole, 13 (recipe)
   vitello tonnato, 123 (recipe)
Tupper, Earl, 59
Tupperware, 59-60
   parties, *60*
Turkey, 109
   croquettes, 30, (recipe)
   oven bags, *99*

TV dinner, *40*

Veal, vitello tonnato, 123 (recipe)
Vegetables, 75-76, 100-101, *107*, 140-41
Verdon, Rene, *67*
Vichyssoise, 61 (recipe)
Victory gardens, 12, 14
Vietnamese food, 132
Vinegar, 138, 142
Visser, Margaret, 153
Vitamin C, 114
Vodka, 110, 112

Wakefield, Ruth, 4
Waldorf salad, *81*
Warehouse stores, 92
Waring Blendor, 26-27
Water, bottled, 110, 147
Waters, Alice, 104, *105*, 126, 170
Waxman, Jonathan, 139-40
Weber barbecue, 35, *36*
Weight Watchers, *84*, 84-85
Wendy's, 128
White Castle, 32-33
White House chef, *67*
Wild food, 80, 82
Willan, Ann, 122, 160
Williams, Charles E., 86-87, *87*
Williams-Sonoma, 86-87
Willoughby, Lively, 43
Wilted lettuce, 14 (recipe)
Wine, 50, 73, 77, 148
   American, 110, 111
   sangria, 76 (recipe)
Wine cooler, 148
Wise, Brownie, 60
Wolf, Clark, 182-83
Women's roles, 6, 7, 18, 71-72, 98, 167, 169
World War II, 5-15
Worth, Helen, 52, 81
Worthington Foods, 159

Yakitori, 125 (recipe)
Yogurt, 20, 114
   cheese with parsley, 155 (recipe)

DATE DUE

ILL: 726528		
UWC: 2/25/98		
Due 3/26/98		
ILL 768514		
OST Osterhout		
Due 10/12/01		

k purchases
itional use.
ent,

Demco, Inc. 38-293